Revised

..........Growing From Salvation into a Mature Disciple

Russ Crites
& Rick Hill

Published by CPC Dallas, Texas.

Printed in the United States of America

Library of Congress Control Number: 2023911601

Journey Into Discipleship / Floyd Russell Crites, Jr. & Rick Hill

ISBN: 979-8-9869377-3-1

NOTE: Please note that some Scriptures have **bold letters** so that you can quickly identify key words or phrases that the authors are attempting to share.

Also, please consider looking at the Scriptures in context. Read several verses around each verse listed to get a fuller meaning.

Special Thanks

The following people have read and given me some detailed feedback regarding this work. Tim, Phillip and Lori, Patsy, Tammy, and Linda. I want to give you a special thanks for your assistance.

I also want to thank Derek, my son, for giving me valuable input for the Prayer and Fasting chapters of this work.

There were others that reviewed the work and gave me valuable feedback that helped improve the content of this work. Thank each of you for your feedback.

History and Thanks

Over forty years ago Rick Hill and I wrote the Journey Into Discipleship manual. This is a major revision of that work. Some text that was duplicated was removed. Much of the text has been altered or updated. The section that was a Gifts Test was removed, and it was turned into a much larger book of its own titled, Spiritual Gifts and Ministry by Russ. It is much more detailed in scope and has much more information about the different gifts and how they connect to ministry and evangelism. In several places this revision of Journey Into Discipleship has additional information has been added for clarification and to make the segment more meaningful. The new version is also divided into parts and specific chapters. An attempt was made to organize the work so that it flows much better than the original version.

For those of you that didn't see the original version, you wouldn't know the history of where it came from and why. Back in the late 1970's, when Rick and I and several others were traveling with Al Pickering and the Mobile Evangelistic Force (MEF), it became evident that many churches needed a practical way to teach new converts and current members more about what being a Christian meant. Journey Into Discipleship was the solution that Rick and I came up with, and it was thankfully received by many. We were blessed to be able to teach from the content when we were at various locations as we traveled. Using Abilene, Texas as a home base, we traveled with the Mobile Evangelistic Force or MEF. Along with Al Pickering, who led the evangelistic effort, we traveled across the United States speaking, teaching, evangelizing and touching people's lives. Dozens of others were involved who gave summers and weekends to this great effort.

Al preached and taught Sharpening the Sword, which is a Bible study technique that teaches you to underline your Bible with different colors as you study. A new version of Sharpening the Sword has recently been made available through Al's Ultimate Life Now website. In addition to the Sharpening the Sword Revision, Al has written several other very helpful books. For more information about Dr. Pickering, Sharpening the Sword, his other books and workshops please go to: **www.ultimatelifenow.com.**

Russ has two websites that describe his work and the books and workbooks he has written or co-authored. His professional website is **www.critescounseling.com**. His professional author page is Amazon.com/author/russcrites His website that promotes his Biblical works is **www.cpcchristianministry.com**.

Being somewhat nostalgic, I want to thank all those who were part of MEF; the Singing Group, the Drama group, those that knocked on doors, those that talked to people and to everyone else for what you did to make MEF a success. A special thanks has to go out to Al Pickering who was the driving force behind MEF. Whether it be his teaching Sharpening the Sword or preaching, he impacted people everywhere we went. It was a great part of my life and will never be forgotten. If it weren't for all of you, we would not have touched nearly as many lives for Christ.

Thank you all and God bless you always!

F. Russell Crites, Jr.

Journey Into Discipleship

Journey Into Discipleship is volume two in a series of books to help people grow up in Christ. Keep in mind that this work was intended to be used for those who have already become a Christian and who now want to know more about the God-Man relationship and what you can do to avoid sin. It also addresses how you can ultimately become a more mature spiritual person and hopefully become a disciple-maker. Volume One of this series addresses grace and how you become a Christian. It is titled, Grace and Salvation (Crites, 2022). It covers all the aspects of grace and does a deep dive into the salvation process and how you can communicate it to others. It includes information from historical documents that show you how people became Christians in the early church and much more. Those examples should be our model for becoming a Christian today. A list of the other books in this series can be found in the appendices.

There is one underlying purpose for this book. Its inspiration comes from Matthew 28:18-20 when Jesus gave his great commission.

And Jesus came and said to them,
"All authority in heaven and on earth has been given to me.
Go therefore and make disciples of all nations, baptizing them in the name of the Father and of the Son and of the Holy Spirit, teaching them to observe all that I have commanded you. And behold, I am with you always,
to the end of the age."

This work focuses on the statement in Jesus' great commission that says, 'teaching them to observe all that I have commanded you.' So, to become a Christ follower a person must become a disciple, be baptized and learn what Jesus taught from the writers of the Bible. How much of it should you know? Even more important, how much of it should you understand and make part of your life? In Galatians 2:20 Paul wrote, "I have been crucified with Christ. It is no longer I who live, but Christ who lives in me. And the life I now live in the flesh I live by faith in the Son of God, who loved me and gave himself for me." In other words, we should want to put self away and seek to put on Christ in all things. To do this you must know the written Word. In addition, God also wants you to teach others to observe, do, become like Christ. To do this you must know God's will, which is identified in the written Word. If you don't know what His Word communicates, what doctrine and lifestyle the Word teaches, you can't internalize, observe, do, follow or become like Jesus the Christ. If you don't understand the Word, it will be hard to deal with the trials you face. How can God help you? What can you do to better prepare yourself? If you don't understand the Word you will not have the knowledge you need to fight back against spiritual forces of darkness that constantly seek to distance you from Christ and all that is good. Sometimes these evil spiritual forces are so subtle that you may not even perceive that they are attacking you. In addition, understand the Word helps you know what your place is in God's Kingdom and what He wants from you as you participate within His body, the church. It is through the written Word and assistance from the Holy Spirit that you can mature spiritually. God expects growth. God wants you to mature so that you can have a greater understanding of good and evil. The Hebrew writer stated, "But solid food is for the mature, for those who have their powers of discernment trained by constant practice to distinguish good from evil" (Hebrews 5:14). Last, if you don't understand the written Word it makes it more difficult for you to go out and fulfill the first part of Jesus' commission. Yes, it has been given to you also. All Christians should be seeking to go out in their God given way to make disciples and teach them to observe the written Word of God. That's what this work is about. The goal is to help you understand all of the above so that you can be a knowledgeable Christian who is more than capable of growing spiritually and who can help others become part of God's Kingdom.

We have to admit that this is not a 'normal' Discipleship book. The focus is building your Christianity from the very beginning and then helping you grow and mature into a disciple who can truly help others. Several important topics are addressed that can help lead you towards greater spiritual maturity and also provide you with knowledge that will help you deal with darkness in your daily life.

Part One addresses the need we all have to understand and know God. As you develop a better understanding of God, it should give you a greater desire to follow His will so that you can live a Godly life.

Part Two addresses how we make a greater connection to God. It also discusses the importance of faith. There are levels to faith and it is up to you to learn how to grow into a deeper faith. The Godliest Disciples we know have grown over the years to have deep faith in their relationship with God.

Part Three specifically addresses spiritual growth which is vital in discipleship. All those who become Christians should want to grow spiritually. Sanctification or holiness as it applies to both internal and external change is addressed in detail. We will also look at specific stages of spiritual growth and what God's expects from you.

Part Four addresses information about the Holy Spirit, who he is, what His indwelling means and how he helps with spiritual growth. We also discuss how the Holy Spirit works and whether or not he is involved with providential working in your life.

Part Five looks at four key elements to a balanced Christian life: 1) prayer, 2) knowing God's Word, 3) outreach, evangelism and gifts, and 4) fellowship. Without proper balance your spiritual growth can be minimized.

Part Six looks at applied discipleship. The ability to be a disciple is not always immediately apparent when someone becomes a Christian. Sometimes it is important for that person to understand some of the basic doctrines and principles about how to live a Christian life and start applying them. How to become a more effective disciple and options to assist with developing a personal method for Discipleship is also discussed.

When you have finished working through this book you will have taken a fresh look at your Christianity, the God-Man relationship involved, the problems you face as a Christian, the helps you have available to get you through inevitable conflict and the security you have for eternal life. There is a workbook that supplements what you are learning in this book and will be available when the revision is complete. It's called, Journey Into Discipleship Workbook. This workbook has been used in Bible classes, workshops and for individual growth.

As you take your Journey into Discipleship you will be challenged to think through some of your current beliefs. You will also have an opportunity to develop a greater awareness of what you believe and why. This work will provide information about the importance and practicality of some very key issues in your belief system.

We feel that the relationship factor is one of the most basic, yet significantly important concepts in our Christianity. This applies to your own personal development with God, your relationship with others and also to how you will share God with others.

In addition, we urge you to keep in mind that Christ sought for his disciples to have internal commitment that would produce external actions, or better communicated, a reflection of Jesus. It is through relationship with Him that true internal commitment and change becomes a reality.

One last thing. If you know about the Bible Study system called Sharpening the Sword, you will understand the reasoning for suggesting that you underline specific Scriptures with certain colors. Throughout this work there will be times where you can underline. If you want to do this, you can. If you don't, it's not necessary. It's up to you.

We want you to know that several Scriptures may be addressed in multiple chapters for different reasons or simply because it makes an important point that we should all be aware of.

Now, are you ready? Let's begin your Journey into Discipleship!

Table of Contents

History and Thanks
Journey Into Discipleship

Part One: Getting to Know God 19

Chapter One: Knowing About God 21

- Aspects of God
- God is Omnipotent
- God is Omniscient
- God is Omnipresent
- God is Eternal
- God is Sovereign
- God is Immutable

Chapter Two: Knowing God's Will 39

- The Holy Spirit and Knowing God's Will
- Pursue God's Will
- Read the Instruction Book
- Focus on God's Will
- Intentionally Apply God's Will
- Internalize God's Will and Make it Automatic
- Generalize God's Will in Your Life
- Daily Determine God's Will

Chapter Three: Understanding God's Will 55

- The Foundation of God's Will
- Renewing of Your Mind
- Offer Your Body as a Living Sacrifice
- Do Not Be Conformed to the Pattern of this World
- Being Transformed

Part Two: Now That I'm a Christian 63

Chapter Four: Connecting with God 65

- Spiritual Birth
- The Greatest Relationship of All
- Grace and the Heart Relationship
- Faith: The Foundation
- Saving Faith
- Four Elements of Saving Faith
- Don't Fall off the Wall
- Fact or Feeling
- Overcoming Negative Spiritual Dissonance

Chapter Five: Growing Your Faith 83

- Stages of Faith like Abraham
- The God Can Stage of Faith
- The God Will Stage of Faith
- The God Does Stage of Faith
- Promises: The Benefits of Faith
- Cause and Effect Relationship

Part Three: Spiritual Growth 91

Chapter Six: Brokenness and Christianity 93

- Symptoms of Not Being Broken
- Brokenness and Eden
- Brokenness and Spiritual Maturity
- The Holy Spirit and Brokenness

Chapter Seven: Sanctification, Holiness and Inner Change 103

- Sanctification is a Process
- Desiring the Holy or Sanctified Life
- Heart Relationship
- Developing a Right Heart
- The Importance of the Heart or Mind
- The Holy Spirit Helps You

Chapter Eight: Sanctification and External Change 119

- Holiness is also a Behavioral Process
- Striving to Be Holy
- The Importance of Self-Control
- External Evidence of an Internal Change
- The External Side of Bearing Fruit

Chapter Nine: Keys to Spiritual Growth 135

- Before Thought is What's Most Important
- Thought and Spiritual Growth
- Capturing Unwanted Thoughts
- Words and Spiritual Growth
- Actions and Spiritual Growth
- Self-Judgment and Self-Control
- Christian Confession and Spiritual Growth

Chapter Ten: Stages of Spiritual Growth 153

- Who is your Discipler
- Stages of Spiritual Growth
- Baby Stage of Spiritual Development
- Child Stage of Spiritual Development
- Youth Stage of Spiritual Development
- Adult Stage of Spiritual Development

Chapter Eleven: Does God Judge a Christian by His Work 167

- Covenant Concept
- Perversion of the Work Ethic
- God's Judgment and the Work Ethic
- Who is Paul Speaking to
- Right Behavior or Deeds
- Getting Judgment for Your Sinful Nature

Part Four: The Holy Spirit 175

Chapter Twelve: The Holy Spirit 177

- The Time of the Holy Spirit
- The Holy Spirit's Initial Work
- The Holy Spirit and the Bible
- The Holy Spirit is Promised
- The Holy Spirit Is a Distinct Individual
- The Holy Spirit is Male
- The Holy Spirit has Godly Attributes
- Providential Working and the Non-Christian
- Warning About Blasphemy
- Key Facts About the Holy Spirit

Chapter Thirteen: Indwelling and Work of the Holy Spirit 193

- The Holy Spirit Regenerates and Sanctifies
- The Holy Spirit is a Gift
- The Indwelling of the Holy Spirit
- The Holy Spirit's Role in the Christian Life

Chapter Fourteen: The Holy Spirit and Spiritual Growth 201

- Being Filled with the Holy Spirit
- The Holy Spirits Role in Spiritual Growth
- Getting Help from the Holy Spirit
- Being Tempted vs Being Tested
- The Holy Spirit, Testing and Spiritual Growth

Chapter Fifteen: Works of the Spirit 211

- Miraculous Works or Not
- Specific Works of the Holy Spirit
- Providential Working of the Holy Spirit
- Holy Spirt, Prayer and Providential Working
- Working Behind the Scenes
- Providential Working and Spiritual Forces

Part Five: Balanced Christianity and Discipleship 223

Chapter Sixteen: Motivation and Balance is Key to Spiritual Growth 225

- The Underlying Motivation for Balance
- The Purpose of Your Motivational Gift
- Key Takeaways Regarding Our Gift
- Motivational Gifts
- The Proper Balance

Chapter Seventeen: Prayer 233

- The Purpose of Prayer
- The Conditions of Prayer
- Pray as the Master Would
- Your Prayer Life
- Different Kinds of Prayer
- Answered Prayer
- Some Keys to Prayer

Chapter Eighteen: Prayer and Fasting 247

- Old Testament and Fasting
- New Testament and Fasting
- The Purpose of Fasting
- Physical Effects and Benefits of Fasting
- Spiritual Benefits of Prayer and Fasting

Chapter Nineteen: Meditation 255

- Old and New Testament View of Meditation
- Physical and Mental Benefits of Meditation
- What We Think is Important
- The Spiritual Side of Meditation
- Optimist and Health
- The Positive Side of What We Think About
- The Spiritual Side of Meditation
- What God Wants From Us
- Prayerful or Meditative Application

Chapter Twenty: Knowing God's Word 273

- Reasons to Study the Word
- A Proper Perspective of the Word
- Application of the Word
- Enjoying the Word

Chapter Twenty-One: Outreach, Evangelism and Gifts 283

- Evangelism and Disciple Making
- Evangelism of Jesus Christ
- Evangelism of the Early Church
- Three Basic Stages to Evangelism
- Methods of Evangelism
- Developing Your Testimony
- The Gospel Message and Doctrine

Chapter Twenty-Two: Fellowship and One Anothering 301

- Benefits of Fellowship
- Fellowship and Spiritual Health
- Christian Relationships
- Fellowshipping with One Another

Chapter Twenty-Three: Fellowship and Worship 309

- Fellowship in the Worship Experience
- The Worship Experience
- The Holy Church Building

Chapter Twenty-Four: Confession and Forgiveness in Relationships 315

- Confession and Christian Relationships
- The Godlike Trait of Forgiveness
- Forgiving Others
- Forgiving Self

Chapter Twenty-Five: Fellowship, the World and Spiritual Warfare 329

- Fellowship and Your Gift
- Fellowship with the World
- Fellowship and Spiritual Warfare

Chapter Twenty-Six: Judging, Reproving, Rebuking and Helping Fellow Christians **337**

- To Judge or Not to Judge
- Righteous Judgment
- Reproving or Rebuking One Another
- Disfellowshipping
- Help for the Unwilling
- Return of the Fallen

Part Six: Discipleship **351**

Chapter Twenty-Seven: Discipleship Made Practical **353**

- Discipleship
- New Testament Disciples
- Characteristics of a Mature Disciple

Chapter Twenty-Eight: Applied Discipleship **365**

- The Problem with Disciple Making
- Applied Discipleship
- Essential Elements in Applied Discipleship
- The Best Way to Identify Possible Converts
- Spiritual Multiplication
- The Process of Discipleship
- Relational Activities
- The Discipleship Family
- How a Discipleship Family Can Help
- Integration of New Members
- Keeping the Converted…Converted
- Become a Discipler
- Response Ministry

Appendices **383**

Determining God's Will Worksheet
Personal Sin and Scripture Worksheet
Conversion Examples
Character Checklist for New Testament Disciples
Characteristics Not Acceptable for New Testament Disciples

Book Series on Christianity
Suggested Readings and Resources

Part One: Getting to Know God

The first chapter is meant to help you get to know more about God. The reality of God is staggering when you look closely at who He is and what He can do. We will look at all of His major aspects which include His Omnipotence, Omniscience, Omnipresence, Eternal Life, Sovereignty and His Immutability. The second chapter explains the necessity of knowing God's will. If you don't know His will, it becomes more difficult to live the life He wants you to live. The last chapter will help you see how you can better understand and follow God's will.

- Knowing About God
- Knowing God's Will
- Understanding God's Will

Knowing About God

Chapter One

The most basic and important relationship that exists today is the relationship that exists between God and man. No matter who you are or what you believe, you can't escape the fact that you must in some way relate to God. As a Christian, you have entered into a father-child relationship with your loving God. It is this relationship that ultimately makes your life worth living or dying for that matter. When you come into this proper relationship with God you are now living a meaningful life with hope for eternity. For such a relationship to grow and develop you must continue the process of getting to know God better and better as your relationship continues. God's wisdom, stemming forth out of His love for man (1 John 3:16) calls for you to know Him well and have a personal relationship with Jesus Christ, His only Son and your mediator (Hebrews 4:15). It is therefore essential for abundant living (John 10:10) that you, 1) know about God, and 2) know God on a personal level. We, the created, can never have a true understanding of ourselves until we comprehend 1) who our God is, 2) how we should relate to Him, and 3) how He responds to us. We will cover the following in this chapter:

- Aspects of God
- God is Omnipotent
- God is Omniscient
- God is Omnipresent
- God is Eternal

- God is Sovereign
- God is Immutable

Aspects of God

It is essential for man to know about God if he is to truly worship Him in spirit and truth. For instance, we must first know someone before we can have a relationship with him. So, it is with God. How much do you really know about God? Are your concepts accurate? As you begin your Journey Into Discipleship your first step is to get to know some things about your God. As we have stated, to really know Him you must first know about Him. God has given us a clear picture of Himself in the Scriptures.

God is Omnipotent

One of the first things we might note about our God is that He is omnipotent. This simply means that His power is unlimited. Where things are impossible with man, they are ever possible with God (Luke 18:27). In Hebrews 6:18, we are told that God's only limitation is His inability to go against His own nature. Other than that, there is nothing impossible with God.

Let's take a different look at what God's Omnipotence should mean to us today. Keep in mind that God Created our world. That was a very, very small part of His creation. However, He also created everything around it. Our sun, which is a star, is in the Milky Way Galaxy. Let's take that one step further. How many stars are in the Milky Way. Astronomers estimate there are about 100 thousand million stars in the Milky Way alone and there are often many planets around each star. The closest star to us, Proxima Centauri, is 4.24 light-years away. A light-year is 9.44 trillion km, or 5.88 trillion miles. The Andromeda Galaxy is 2.2 million light-years away, with a single light-year being almost 10 trillion kilometers (6 trillion miles). God made all of that during creation.

If that doesn't suggest how large space is around us then this next statement should awestrike you. The Hubble Deep Field telescope did an extremely long exposure of a relatively empty part of the sky. It provided evidence that there are about 125 billion (1.25×1011) galaxies in the observable universe. To create a world is beyond explanation. To create a Galaxy is even more unbelievable. To consider that there are 125 billion galaxies, that they have found, in this universe is mind boggling. Yet our

Omnipotent all-powerful God created it all. Let's look at the creation story. It is totally amazing if you really dig deep into it. Genesis 1:1-2 speaks volumes about what God is capable of accomplishing. Let's look and see what it says.

"In the beginning God created the heavens and the earth.
Now the earth was formless and empty,
darkness was over the surface of the deep,
and the Spirit of God [Holy Spirit] was hovering over the waters."

Let's take a closer look at what God did on each day.

Day One

Genesis 1:1-2 The Making of Matter, Space, Light and Dark. What's amazing to us is that He started with nothing. "People can fashion or make things, but only God can "create" (Bara). He created (bara) ex hihilo (out of nothing) everything that currently exists" (Morris, 2013). To make it clear, God created the heavens which could also be defined as space and matter, but it was without form. It was empty. Imagine, if you can, a bunch of matter that had no real form. That concept in and of itself it hard to visualize, yet that is what happened on the first day. Out of nothing God decided to create our world (planet earth as we know it), all that would be around it and the matter and space needed to accomplish His plan. There was no form yet. Earth didn't exist. There was no universe, no galaxies, no stars, planets or earth. Everything was still without form, but God wasn't finished.

Then in verse three He said, "Let there be light." God had created matter and space, now he created light. Keep in mind that there is no sun yet, nor were there any stars. He took another step and separated the light from the dark. In Genesis 1:5, "God called the light 'day,' and the darkness he called 'night.' And there was evening, and there was morning—the first day.

So, God created matter and space on the first day and ultimately formed the earth and called the light day and darkness night. Keep in mind that there was no star yet, there were no other planets, there was no galaxy, nor was there a universe. God wasn't finished. However, we find it comforting and interesting that God formed our earth first above all things. At least it appears that is what He did.

Day Two

Genesis 1:6-8: The making of the firmament and the dividing of the waters. Dr. Henry Morris wrote a commentary on Genesis that is very revealing. He discussed the firmament in detail. Morris believed that when God separated the water that He had created, he left some on earth and sent some to the other side of the firmament. So, what is the firmament? The firmament was a place surrounding the earth. Basically, it was thin stretched-out space. Morris believed that there were two bodies of water that were separated by this firmament or thin space. "Separated by this firmament, or atmosphere, the two bodies of water henceforth were ready for their essential functions in sustaining future life on earth" (Morris, 1976). This body of water above the firmament was most likely water vapor that could be both seen through and would allow the light of the sun and stars to shine through. The water that was still on the earth would provide all creation with what was needed to live. Have you ever tried to move water from one place to the next and cause it to stay in one place? Unless you encapsulate it, the task is impossible. Yet with our God He did exactly that. Not only did He create water, but He left some on earth and sent some that would be above the firmament in the atmosphere above planet earth. That is an amazing feat in and of itself. Yet it was just one of many things that God did that prove He is Omnipotent.

Day Three

Genesis 1:9-10 Let the waters be gathered together into one place and the dry land appears. The earth is starting to take shape. Keep in mind that there is still no sun or stars. God is working on planet earth as we know it. After the waters were separated, the water on planet earth moved as dry land began to appear. Lakes and oceans became distinct as land appeared.

When He was finished separating the water and dry land appeared He still had more work to do. In Genesis 1:11-13 we are told that once earth or dry land appeared, God called for grass, herbs and trees of all kinds to grow; and they did. So ended the third day.

Day Four

Genesis 1:14-19 God made two great lights: the sun and the moon. Finally, we get the sun that we all know well and the moon that we look at each night. We want you to really think about what we are going to share next. What has happened up to now is extraordinary, but what God did next is even more extraordinary, mind-bending and near unbelief. On that same day he also made all of the other stars. Verse 17 "God set them in the vault of the sky to give light on the earth," This certainly appears to be where God creates the stars, the galaxies, and the Universe. In Psalm 147:4 we are told that, "He determines the number of the stars; he gives to all of them their names."

When you consider all He did and when He did it, it certainly suggests that planet earth was at the center of His creation. He created all the stars and the space they would be in. How many stars do you think are in our Galaxy? There are over **one hundred thousand million stars in the Milky Way.** Guess what? It is a relatively small galaxy. Now, guess how many galaxies scientists have found so far? There are **one hundred twenty-five billion galaxies in the observable universe.** So, what is one hundred thousand million (Stars) times one hundred twenty-five billion (Galaxies). We are assuming that there is a name for that number, but we don't think that one person on planet earth could count it out in a lifetime no matter how fast he or she counted. Keep in mind that is only the Galaxies that scientists have found up to this point in time. Are there more galaxies that we simply cannot see? Yes, there are! Who created all of that and how long did it take? Not only that, but God named each and every star He created (Psalm 147:4). The Bible says God created all of it in one day. How powerful is our God. We should be in awe of Him.

Day Five

Genesis 1:20-23 God created living creatures in the water, and birds that flew in the air. How many creatures did He create in the sea? We may never know. However, science estimates that there are over 228,000 known species in the ocean. They also suspect that there may be as many as 2 million more that they have not yet identified. How many birds did he create? Currently science has identified close to 11,000 species of birds and there are still many that have not yet been identified. Each sea creature was unique, different. Each one of them had a purpose. Science is still trying to figure out how many species there actually are in our world.

Day Six

Genesis 1:24-25 God created everything that would walk on the land; cattle, creeping things, beasts of the earth. Just keep in mind that that is also a lot of creatures. We suspect that there are more than we could count in a day or possibly a week. And then something even more amazing happened.

Genesis 1:26-27 God created man; male and female He created them. Man was His greatest achievement in many ways. Man would eventually become responsible for the world he was given. He would take care of his world and his world would take care of him. As a side bar, do you think God is happy about how mankind is taking care of His creation today?

Day Seven: God Rested

After all that work, God rested. He sat back and looked at His creation. He must have smiled as He looked at His Son and said, "This is the beginning and there is still much for both of us to do." In my mind I can see the Holy Spirit nodding His head. He too knew that creation was just the beginning. He too had much work to do. I wonder what kind of conversation the three of them had at this momentous point in time.

So, why did we review creation? The simple answer is that we all need to realize the unbelievable awesome and mighty power of God. He really did all of the above and He gave this earth to us to live on and to take care of. He gave us food to eat and water to drink. Most of all he gave us an opportunity to live with Him. We want you to consider one piece of information that we shared above one more time. If you are to accept the Genesis account, which we hope you do, God created our earth before He created our star and the other stars and worlds. It certainly appears that earth was central to His creation project. We are ever amazed at the Omnipotence of God. It's something that we will never be able to completely comprehend. He can create a world or a universe, yet He is concerned about every individual who has, is and will live on it. We feel so small, but so thankful. Let's look at some other the Scriptures that describe God and His power.

Scriptures

As an option, you can color the Scriptures below that address God's power. Using Sharpening the Sword coloring system you would underline all the following Scriptures in orange.

Scripture	Summary
Genesis 1:1	In the beginning, **God created the heavens and the earth.**
Psalms 139:13-14	For **you formed my inward parts; you knitted me together in my mother's womb.** I praise you, for I am fearfully and wonderfully made. Wonderful are your works; my soul knows it very well.
Psalm 147:4	**He determines the number of the stars; he gives to all of them their names.**
Jeremiah 10:12	It is he **who made the earth by his power**, who established the world by his wisdom, and by his understanding stretched out the heavens.
Jeremiah 32: 17	"Ah, Sovereign Lord, you **have made the heavens and the earth** by your great power and outstretched arm. Nothing is too hard for you."
1 Corinthians 6:14	And **God raised the Lord** and will also raise us up by his power.
Ephesians 3:20	Now to him who is **able to do far more abundantly than all that we ask or think,** according to the power at work within us,
Hebrews 1:1-4	Long ago, at many times and in many ways, God spoke to our fathers by the prophets, but in these last days he has spoken to us by his Son, whom he appointed the heir of all things, through whom **also he created the world.** He is the radiance of the glory of God and the exact imprint of his nature, and he upholds the universe by the word of his power. After making purification for sins, he sat down at the right hand of the Majesty on high, having become as much superior to angels as the name he has inherited is more excellent than theirs.
1 Peter 1:5	who **by God's power are being guarded through faith for a salvation** ready to be revealed in the last time.
STS: These Scriptures may be underlined in orange.	

God is Omniscient

It's hard to realize that a being exists that knows everything; absolutely everything. However, it is good to know that even though our God knows everything, including everything about us and what we think and do. Even so, He still loves us and wants us as His children. But what does that look like to us? Let's see if we can get a grasp on this part of God. In Psalm 139:1-4 David wrote,

"O Lord, you have searched me and known me!
You know when I sit down and when I rise up;
you discern my thoughts from afar.
You search out my path and my lying down
and are acquainted with all my ways.
Even before a word is on my tongue,
behold, O Lord, you know it altogether."

God knows us better than we do. He knows our thoughts. He knows what we will say before we say or even think it. But there is more. He sees everything. In Proverbs 15:3 we are told,

"The **eyes of the Lord are in every place**,
keeping watch on the evil
and the good."

In 1 Chronicles 28:9 we are told that God knows what is in our heart. Not only that, but he also understands every plan and thought that we have.

"And you, Solomon my son, know the God of your father
and serve him with a whole heart and with a willing mind,
for the Lord searches all hearts and understands
every plan and thought. If you seek him,
he will be found by you, but if you forsake him,
he will cast you off forever."

Let's consider the planets, stars, galaxies, our universe and possibly other universes that may be out there. Does He know where each one of those planets, stars and galaxies are located? Can He name the billions of celestial bodies that we can see and even those that our eyes and even telescopes cannot yet see? Yes, He can. He could also easily point them out and tell us the names He has given them. He knows them. He created them. To even try to consider that God knows where every planet, star and galaxy is located and be able to name them is beyond our ability to comprehend. In Psalm 147:4 it says,

"He determines the number of the stars;
he gives to all of them their names."

He Created them. He knows where each star is located and he has named each of them. That is amazing. Yet, God can and has done just that and so much more. Let's look at some additional Scriptures that tell us about what God knows.

Scriptures

As an option, you can color several Scriptures that address God's power. Using Sharpening the Sword coloring system you may underline all the following Scriptures in orange.

Scripture	Summary
Psalm 102:25	**Of old you laid the foundation of the earth, and the heavens are the work of your hands.**
Psalm 139:1-4	"O Lord, you have searched me and known me! You know when I sit down and when I rise up; **you discern my thoughts from afar.** You search out my path and my lying down and **are acquainted with all my ways.** Even before a word is on my tongue, behold, O Lord, you know it altogether."
Psalm 139:7-9	**Where shall I go from your Spirit? Or where shall I flee from your presence? If I ascend to heaven, you are there! If I make my bed in Sheol, you are there!** If I take the wings of the morning and dwell in the uttermost parts of the sea,
Psalm 147:5	Great is our Lord, and abundant in power; **his understanding is beyond measure.**
Proverbs 15:3	The **eyes of the Lord are in every place**, keeping watch on the evil and the good.
Matthew 6:7-8	And when you pray, do not heap up empty phrases as the Gentiles do, for they think that they will be heard for their many words. Do not be like them, for your **Father knows what you need before you ask him.**
Luke 16:15	And he said to them, "You are those who justify yourselves before men, but **God knows your hearts.** For what is exalted among men is an abomination in the sight of God.

Colossians 1:16	**For by him all things were created, in heaven and on earth, visible and invisible, whether thrones or dominions or rulers or authorities—all things were created through him and for him.**
STS: These Scriptures may be underlined in orange.	

God is Omnipresent

God can actually be here with us at this very instant, yet at the same time He is on the other side of the earth, on Mars and in a sense stands on every star we can see at night. Even such a statement as this is limiting for God is everywhere all the time. The concepts of space, distance and boundaries have no meaning when we speak of God's omnipresence. He can be in the presence of man (Adam, Eve, Moses and others), while at the very same time he is present in heaven, or on the furthest star. In Isaiah 57:15 we are told,

For thus says the One who is high and lifted up,
who inhabits eternity, whose name is Holy:
"I dwell in the high and holy place,
and also with him who is of a contrite and lowly spirit,
to revive the spirit of the lowly,
and to revive the heart
of the contrite."

In Psalm 33:13-14 it says,

"The Lord looks down from heaven;
he sees all the children of man;
from where he sits enthroned
he looks out on all the inhabitants
of the earth,"

So, God can see all and understand what He is seeing. That's amazing. The following Scriptures also tell us of God's omnipresence.

Scriptures

As an option, you can color several Scriptures that address how God is everywhere. Using Sharpening the Sword coloring system you can underline all the following Scriptures in orange.

Scripture	Summary
1 Kings 8:27	"But will God indeed dwell on the earth? **Behold, heaven and the highest heaven cannot contain you;** how much less this house that I have built!
Psalm 33:13-14	**The Lord looks down from heaven; he sees all the children of man;** from where he sits enthroned he looks out on all the inhabitants of the earth,
Psalm 139:8-10	If I ascend to **heaven, you are there! If I make my bed in Sheol, you are there!** If I take the wings of the morning and dwell in the uttermost parts of the sea, even there your hand shall lead me, and your right hand shall hold me.
Isaiah 57:15	For thus says the One who is high and lifted up, who inhabits eternity, whose name is Holy: **"I dwell in the high and holy place, and also with him who is of a contrite and lowly spirit,** to revive the spirit of the lowly, and to revive the heart of the contrite.
Jeremiah 23:23-24	"Am I a God at hand, declares the Lord, and not a God far away? Can a man hide himself in secret places so that I cannot see him? Declares the Lord. **Do I not fill heaven and earth?** Declares the Lord.
Matthew 18:20	**For where two or three are gathered in my name, there am I among them."**
Romans 8:9	You, however, are not in the flesh but in the Spirit, if in fact the **Spirit of God dwells in you.** Anyone who does not have the Spirit of Christ does not belong to him.
Galatians 2:20	I have been crucified with Christ. It is no longer I who live, **but Christ who lives in me**. And the life I now live in the flesh I live by faith in the Son of God, who loved me and gave himself for me.
Ephesians 4:6	one God and Father of all, **who is over all and through all and in all.**
STS: These Scriptures may be underlined in orange.	

God is Eternal

God had no beginning nor will He have an end. God is eternal. The Bible describes God as being 'from everlasting to everlasting.' When you read Genesis 1:1 what do you think the writer was saying? "In the beginning God created the heavens and the earth." That verse had nothing to do about God or His beginnings. It had to do with what God was going to create. God was, is and always will be. He has no beginning or end. Before He created earth and the billions of stars that He called into existence, He existed. In other words, he existed even before time began as we know it. From eternity to eternity, God was and is forever. The Scriptures below tell us of God's eternal nature.

Scriptures

As an option, you can color several Scriptures that address God's eternal nature. Using Sharpening the Sword coloring system you may underline all the following Scriptures in orange.

Scripture	Summary
Deuteronomy 33:27a	The **eternal God** is your dwelling place, and underneath are the everlasting arms.
Psalm 90:2-4	Before the mountains were brought forth, or ever you had formed the earth and the world, **from everlasting to everlasting you are God.** You return man to dust and say, "Return, O children of man!" For a thousand years in your sight are but as yesterday when it is past, or as a watch in the night.
Psalm 102:25-27	Of old you laid the foundation of the earth, and the heavens are the work of your hands. They will perish, **but you will remain;** they will all wear out like a garment. You will change them like a robe, and they will pass away, **but you are the same, and your years have no end.**
Isaiah 9:6	For to us a child is born, to us a son is given; and the government shall be upon his shoulder, and his name shall be called Wonderful Counselor, Mighty God, **Everlasting Father,** Prince of Peace.
Colossians 1:17	And **he is before all things**, and in him all things hold together.
1 Timothy 1:17	To the King of the ages, **immortal,** invisible, the only God, be honor and glory forever and ever. Amen.
Revelation 1:4	John to the seven churches that are in Asia: Grace to you and peace **from him who is and who was and who is to come,** and from the seven spirits who are before his throne,
Revelation 4:8b-10a	"Holy, holy, holy, is the Lord God Almighty, who was and is and is to come!" And whenever the

	living creatures give glory and honor and thanks to him who is seated on the throne, who **lives forever and ever**, the twenty-four elders fall down before him who is seated on the throne and **worship him who lives forever and ever.**
STS: These Scriptures may be underlined in orange.	

God is Sovereign

Look up the word "sovereign" in the dictionary. If you do, you will find many words and phrases that attempt to communicate what the Sovereignty of God means. Some of these words you will find are superior, greatest, supreme in power and authority, ruler, and independent of all others. God's Sovereignty refers to the fact that He is above all, overall and is supreme in every sense of the word. Simply stated, God was, is and always will have complete and total control over everything that exists or has yet to exist. There is no one who is as great or majestic as God. No one has, or ever will have, the control over creation, life, death and eternity as God does. As ultimate ruler and creator He does as He wills. God has the right and the power to do anything He decides to do. Many historians believe that Job was written by Moses. It probably was not written by Job since it acknowledges his death in Job 42:17. Let's look at Job 42:2. Listen to what the writer says about God.

"I know that **you can do all things**,
and that no purpose of yours can be thwarted."

This has to do with God's power and His right to use it. Moses would certainly be one of those who understood God's power and might. He experienced it many times and actually spoke with God.

Most Biblical historians believe that Jeremiah authored the Book of Jeremiah, the Books of Kings and the Book of Lamentations. He wrote these books with the assistance of Baruch ben Neriah who was his scribe and disciple. Let's look at what Jeremiah had to say about God. In Jeremiah 32:17 he stated,

"Ah, Sovereign Lord, **you have made the heavens and the earth** by your great power and outstretched arm.
Nothing is too hard for you."

God is, was and always will be the ultimate source of power and He has the authority to use it as He wills. We should be constantly thankful that He wants only the best for us and has a place prepared for us so that we too can live with him forever and ever. The following Scriptures tell us more about how God is sovereign, above all, in control and ultimate ruler of all creation..

Scriptures

As an option, you can color several Scriptures that address God as the supreme ruler. Using Sharpening the Sword coloring system you may underline all the following Scriptures in orange.

Scripture	Summary
Job 42:2	I know that **you can do all things,** and that no purpose of yours can be thwarted.
Job 42:17	I know that **you can do all things,** and that no purpose of yours can be thwarted.
1 Chronicles 16:25	For great is the Lord, and greatly to be praised, and he is to be **feared above all gods.**
1 Chronicles 29:11	Yours, O Lord, is the greatness and the power and the glory and the victory and the majesty, for all that is in the heavens and in the earth is yours. Yours is the kingdom, O Lord, and **you are exalted as head above all.**
Daniel 4:35	all the inhabitants of the earth are accounted as nothing, and **he does according to his will among the host of heaven and among the inhabitants of the earth; and none can stay his hand** or say to him, "What have you done?"
Jeremiah 32:17	Ah, **Sovereign Lord**, you have made the heavens and the earth by your great power and outstretched arm. Nothing is too hard for you.
Amos 4:7	I also **withheld the rain** from you when there were yet three months to the harvest; I would **send rain on one city**, and **send no rain on another city**; **one field would have rain, and the field on which it did not rain would wither;**
1 Timothy 6:15	which he will display at the proper time—he who is the blessed and only **Sovereign**, the King of kings and Lord of lords,

Revelations 6:10	They cried out with a loud voice, "**O Sovereign Lord,** holy and true, how long before you will judge and avenge our blood on those who dwell on the earth?"
STS: These Scriptures may be underlined in orange.	

God is Immutable

The most common phrase that defines immutability in the dictionary is unchanging over time or unable to be changed. The words fixed and set are also often seen. God is who He is and will always be that. As humans we both desire and seek stability in life. It's nice to know that our God offers us the stability we all want and need through Him. He truly is unchanging. He is perfect and infinite in every way, so there is no need for change. He is all that He needs to be. Even though the book is short, Malachi is very powerful and to the point about God and what He wants for His people. It's interesting that in the Hebrew Malachi's name means 'My Messenger'. Malachi's message from God was that even though His people had failed over and over, He would never abandon them. He never gave up on them. He promised to redeem a remnant of His people and send a Messiah that would fulfill His promises and He did what He said He was going to do. In Malachi 3:6 God's message was given.

"For **I the Lord do not change**; therefore you,
O children of Jacob, are not consumed.

Moses also wrote the Old Testament Book called Numbers. In that book Moses communicates God's immutability. In Numbers 23:19 he states,

"God is not man, that he should lie,
or a son of man, that he should change his mind.
Has he said, and will he not do it?
Or has he spoken, and will he not fulfill it?"

New Testament writers also shared information about the immutability of God. In James 1:17 we are told,

"Every good gift and every perfect gift is from above,
coming down from the Father of lights, with whom **there is no variation or shadow due to change."**

It's important to keep in mind that when the Holy Spirit came, one of the things that He was to do was to bring to remembrance all that Jesus had shared with them. We know that He spoke of the Holy Spirit on multiple occasions. James knew and remembered what he had learned from Jesus, so when he spoke the words in James 1:17 he was speaking for God and the Holy Spirit.

Scriptures

The following Scriptures tell us about the immutability of God. Using Sharpening the Sword coloring system you may underline all the following Scriptures in orange.

Scripture	Summary
Isaiah 14:24	The Lord of hosts has sworn: "**As I have planned, so shall it be, and as I have purposed, so shall it stand,**
Numbers 23:19	God is not man, that he should lie, or a son of man, **that he should change his mind.** Has he said, and will he not do it? Or has he spoken, and will he not fulfill it?
Malachi 3:6	**For I the Lord do not change**; therefore you, O children of Jacob, are not consumed.
Hebrews 1:12b	**But you are the same, and** your years will have no end."
James 1:17	Every good gift and every perfect gift is from above, coming down from the Father of lights, with **whom there is no variation or shadow due to change.**
STS: These Scriptures may be underlined in orange.	

To sum up the attributes of God, it is obvious that He is amazing. To even try to understand the greatness and vastness of His ability and more is beyond our limited abilities. Yet, He loved us enough to want us to be His children. Have you ever been away from someone you loved desperately for a period of time? It may have been your mother, your father, a sister or brother, husband or wife, or even a friend. When you saw them did you run to them because you missed them so much? Most of us have. How much more should we want to run to God the Father and do all we can to be the person He wants us to be so that we can live with Him in His home that has been prepared for all of His children. We should want to do all that we can to be close to God. We should want to become what He wants us to become so that we can be more like what He wants us to be. It should be one of our greatest priorities in life.

The question is, 'Are you running toward this all powerful, amazing God or not?' God wants you to know how to run to Him. He wants you to develop a closer relationship the way He intends for you to develop it. He wants you to avoid your sinful nature and become more spiritually mature. He wants you to let others know how important He is in your life. He wants you to help others find Him. That's called Disciple Making.

This work helps you see what you need to understand so that you can overcome sin, be better prepared to protect yourself from the evil one and ultimately teach others to become disciples of Christ so that they too will run to God.

Personal Reflection

List three things that you learned or that were reinforced that will help you know and appreciate God on a more personal level.

1.

2.

3.

Knowing God's Will

Chapter Two

If you don't read the instructions, it's hard to know how to build something the right way. That simple statement is extremely true and certainly applies when it comes to Christianity. You must know what God expects of you if you are to become what He wants and if you are to know how to fulfill His will. Throughout this book there is information about what God wants from you and for you. However, in this specific chapter we are going to focus on what God's will is for you as a Christian. There are several general steps or stages to learning, internalizing and following God's will in your life so that it can become a natural part of you. Keep in mind that you may have new insights or greater understanding of God's will as you grow spiritually. As a result, it is important to constantly be in a state of learning as you work through each of these steps to understand God's will over and over. In this chapter we will cover:

- The Holy Spirit and Knowing God's Will
- Pursue God's Will
- Read the Instruction Book
- Focus on God's Will
- Intentionally Apply God's Will
- Internalize God's Will and Make it Automatic
- Generalize God's Will in Your Life
- Daily Determine God's Will

The Holy Spirit and Knowing God's Will

When you became a Christian an amazing thing happened to you. God gave you the Holy Spirit to dwell inside of you. A divine life was literally placed within you. It was meant to take the place of your human nature. "The very seed of the life of Christ sown in us by the Spirit of God can germinate in the ground of our being to mature into magnificent fruitage if we permit it to happen" (Keller, 1979). As a Christian you have probably heard that you are to die to self (Galatians 2:20). What does that Scripture mean and what does it have to do with knowing God's will? The point is twofold.

First, and most important, you should want God's nature to take the place of your nature. Your lifetime goal is to be spiritually mature or in other words become Godly in all that you think, do and say. That goal is manifest as you seek to put away your carnal, fleshly nature and allow the Holy Spirit to reshape your very nature. That task is not always easy, so it takes time to let go of your self-wants, needs and desires. It takes time to allow the very nature of God to germinate and eventually become your nature. It's the Holy Spirit's job, so to speak, to help you accomplish this.

This leads us to the second important element that requires your help. One of the fruit or characteristics of the Holy Spirit that God wants you to internalize and exhibit is self-control. God wants you to make right choices using self-control. He wants you to get better at discerning right from wrong, godly versus ungodly, as you study and apply His Word. It takes time, effort and practice to be able to distinguish good from evil. However, that is your responsibility. In Hebrews 5:14 the author states,

> But solid food is for the mature, for those **who have their powers of discernment trained by constant practice to distinguish good from evil.**

You must control your input, your thoughts, your word and your actions. Does it help if you 'listen' to the urging or nudges of the Holy Spirit as he seeks to guide you? Absolutely, it does. That's how he helps. However, God also calls for all Christians to exhibit the fruit of the Spirit called self-control in all they do. As you grow and mature spiritually it should become easier to distinguish good from evil and make right choices just as the verse above suggests. It is a process and it is your responsibility as a Christian to train your powers of discernment if you are to live the life God wants you to.

With this in mind, most new Christians start off as spiritual babies who need support and training. They struggle with knowing good from evil, right from wrong, spiritual from unspiritual. Deeper concepts are more difficult to understand, internalize and generalize into their lives. They resist the Holy spirit because of their childish ways. That's why God started with simple easy to understand commands that all of us can understand. It also allows new Christians to better recognize what He wants and doesn't want from and for them.

So, you should daily pursue God's will by learning, attempting to be self-controlled and seeking to allow his Spirit to change you from the inside out. Let's see what the Bible says.

Pursue God's Will

You must want to pursue God's will in your life. You must be in the process of seeking to understand what God's will is for you. Pursuing God's will simply means that you desire to know more about what God's will is for you. We have to assume that you have done some of this or you would not be a Christian. Regardless, this is something that you don't ever stop doing. You should make it a daily habit to pursue God's will as you live each day of your life. The Scriptures have much to say about pursing God's will. It can help you understand what God's plan is for you and everyone else. If you don't know what God's will is, it is very hard to pursue it. Here are a few examples of what pursuing God's will means so that you can see for yourself what God wants you to pursue.

You must be in process of seeking to understand what God's will is for you. Pursuing God's will simply means that you desire to know more about what God's will is for you.

Pursuing God's Will Scriptural Study	
God's Will for You	
1 Timothy 2:3–4	**God's will is for all people to be saved.**
John 6:38–40	**God's will is** that everyone who looks to the Son and believes in him shall have eternal life.
Ephesians 5:15–20	Do not be foolish but understand what the Lord's will is. **You have to learn what His will is for you. You must pursue it.**
Romans 12:1-2	Do not be conformed to this world, but be transformed by the renewal of your mind, **that by testing you may discern what is the will of God**, what is good and acceptable and perfect.
1 Thessalonians 4:3–5	It is **God's will that you should be sanctified; you should live a holy life.** He wants each of you to **learn how to control your own body in a way that is holy and honorable,**
Matthew 6:33	**Focus on pursuing Jesus** and learn what it means to live as a citizen in God's kingdom.
Matthew 6:9	By **praying for God's will to be done**, we're asking for any obstacles (including our own weakness) to be diminished.
Hebrews 13:20–21	He wants you to be equipped with everything **good for doing his will.**
1 Thessalonians 5:16–18	**God's will is** for you to rejoice always, pray continually, give thanks in all circumstances.
1 Peter 2:15	For **it is God's will that by doing good** you should silence the ignorant talk of foolish people.
Hebrews 10:35–36	When you have persevered and **done the will of God**, you will receive what he has promised.
Mark 3:33–35	Jesus says, Whoever **does God's will** is my brother and sister and mother.
STS: These Scriptures may be underlined in orange.	

Read the Instruction Book

So, God wants you to pursue His will. He wants you to understand how you must change and become more like Him. It's interesting to note that God communicates what He wants from all of us in both objective and subjective ways. It's also interesting that as humans we have a tendency to initially focus on objective do's and don'ts. They are clearer and easier to understand. With this in mind, what are some of the basics that God wants us to know? Specifically, what is the first thing you must do if you are to understand what God wants from and for you? Simply stated you must learn what God communicates in His book, the Bible. You must read it, really read it for information.

Specific Commands or Do's and Don'ts

The first type of command is very specific and clear. They are obvious do's and don'ts that God wants us to follow. Such commands should be easy to understand, even though they may be hard to follow at times. This is often what new Christians focus on and that's alright. Why is that alright? Before a new Christian can truly understand the deeper principles of God's word they must have a strong understanding of the basic beliefs. These beliefs are the do's and don'ts that are so clear in the Scriptures. Once a person has a good understanding of basic Biblical beliefs, they are more prepared to delve deeper into the principles that leads to a deeper Godly life (Hebrews 5:12-14). The Hebrew writer refers to basic teachings as milk of the word and encourages all of us to begin to study, learn and apply deeper, meatier principles.

God has had specific expectations from man since He created the Garden of Eden and placed Adam and Eve in it. He told them what they could eat and what they were not supposed to eat. He gave them specific guidelines to live by. That continued throughout the Old Testament and into the New Testament. There are several behaviors that He wants to see and several that He doesn't want to see in your life. In some ways these do's and don'ts are the easiest pieces of information for most of us to understand. Most of us are good at lists. Give us a list and we can check things off as we do them. It's important to know what God expects us to act like and what He doesn't want us to act like. That's why He starts off with specific easy to understand commands that are hard to misunderstand. Keep in mind that one of the fruit of the spirit is self-control. It is obvious when you read the Scriptures that self-control is something we choose to do and God wants us to utilize it in our choices (2 Peter 1:5-7; Titus 2:11-12; Galatians 5:22-23). We will discuss self- control or self-discipline in much greater detail in a later chapter. Be aware that having self-control or self-discipline simply means you have choices to make. God wants you to make the right choice regarding your behavior. Since self-control is actually one of the Holy Spirit's characteristics, He too will seek to nudge you and help you make right choices. Here are some Scriptures that suggest several of God's Do and Do Not commands that you should learn to follow.

Do's

- Do good to them that hate you (Matthew 5:44; Luke 6:27).
- Do to others what you expect of them (Matthew 7:12; Luke 6:31).
- Do violence to no man (Luke 3:14).
- Do good (Luke 6:35; Romans 13:3).
- Do this (put God first) and live (Luke 10:28).
- Do all to God's glory (1 Corinthians 10:31; Colossians 3:17,23).
- Do all things without murmuring and disputing (Philippians 2:14).
- Do those things, which were seen and heard in me (Philippians 4:9).
- Do your own business (1 Thessalonians 4:11).
- Do the work of an evangelist (2 Timothy 4:5).

Do Nots

- Do not practice righteousness before people to be seen by them (Matthew 6:1).
- Do not sound a trumpet before you when giving alms (Matthew 6:2).
- Do not do works of Pharisees (Matthew 23:3-33).
- Do not love in word only (1John 3:18).
- Do not give heed to fables (1 Timothy 1:4).
- Do not give heed to genealogies (1 Timothy 1:4).
- Do not err (James 1:16) .
- Do not commit adultery (James 2:11).
- Do not kill (James 2:11).
- Do not fashion yourself according to former lusts (1 Peter 1:14).

Look back at these do's and don'ts and think about the ones that you may struggle with. If you are following all of them well, then that's fantastic. However, if you struggle with any of them you now have an opportunity to grow by denying self, more effectively utilizing self-control and becoming more like God or Jesus. Each command that you follow the way God intends, causes you to die to self a little more and as a result you grow spiritually. That's what God wants. He knows you can't live a perfect life. He just wants you to work toward being the best you can be by dying to self and becoming more like him (Galatians 2:20).

Obviously, these are not all of the do's and don'ts that you can find in the Bible. There are scores of them and they all teach a lesson that can lead you to a more spiritual life. That's why reading the Bible is so important. You need to learn what God expects of you.

Principles of the Word

The second type of command deals with principles and they can be a bit more complicated. In that Hebrew passage shown a few pages back we are told what God expects of us. God wants us to understand and internalize Biblical principles that can easily be generalized to multiple situations (Hebrews 5:14). For instance, God wants us to love others. Who are others? Is it everyone? Even our enemy? What does He mean by love? God's aim is a new mind, a new way of thinking, not just new information. His aim is that we be transformed and live a holy or sanctified life, that is revealed in His Word (John 8:32; 17:17).

God's aim is a new mind, a new way of being, not just new information. His aim is that we be transformed and live a holy or sanctified life, that is freed by the truth of His revealed Word. (John 8:32; 17:17).

The word "meat" in 1 Corinthians is from the Greek word "Broma". Its Strong's number is G1033. It means the deeper, more complete teachings of God's Word. God wants you to internalize and become the deeper principles that the Bible teaches. You will find that when you begin to focus on these teachings it will open doors for you in regard to how you live your Christian life. Here are a few meatier Biblical teachings that you can grow inside of you as you maintain self-control and as you seek to allow the Holy Spirit to work and have more control in your life. Take a moment and write down an application for each principle shown on the worksheet below. Being able to consider options as to how to show each of those important spiritual principles in your life is important.

Principles that Help You Grow as a Christian **Worksheet**	
Meat of the Word	Personal Applications
Love	
Joy	
Peace	
Patience	
Kindness	
Goodness	
Faithfulness	
Gentleness	
Self-control	
Holiness	
Righteousness	
Justice	
Mercy	
Humility	

We believe that we should listen to and follow all of the Word of God, both the milk and the meat. We hope that you too will want the Scriptures to reveal themselves to you as you study. Keep in mind that through constant prayer and systematic study you should ultimately be feasting on the "meat" of God's Word and the Holy Spirit will be shining in all you think, say and do.

Focus on God's Will

As you learn God's commands, you must also seek to make them part of your life. You need to put them in your mind and think about them as you face life's struggles. Some people think if you know God's will you are focusing on it. That's not necessarily true. Demons know about God, Jesus and yes what the Bible teaches, but they don't follow God's will in action nor in inner transformation. They certainly do not ponder, think about, or focus on what God wants. They have another agenda and that's to hurt you spiritually.

So, what do we mean by focus? That is one of the most important questions you can ask, and the answer is extremely important. Remember when you wanted something so much. You looked forward to having it. You couldn't wait. And then you received it. What did you do? You finally received that Barbie doll you had wanted for some time, that Guitar you had your eye on, or that (fill in the blank) you had wanted for months. You couldn't wait to get it in your hands and use it, play with it, etc. You wanted to spend time with it. You were excited to learn more about it. Because of what God, Jesus and the Holy Spirit has done for you, you should feel that way about Christianity. In Colossians 3:16 we are told to,

"**Let the word of Christ dwell in you richly,**
teaching and admonishing one another in all wisdom,
singing psalms and hymns and spiritual songs,
with thankfulness in your hearts to God."

We can't just acknowledge God's will in our lives. We can't just read the Bible for information. We need to desire to understand it. We need to let it dwell in us richly. We need to set aside time to figure out what Scriptures truly mean to us in our daily walk. You should want to learn more about the Bible and what God wants you to be like.

Here is the point. The more you focus on God's Word and the more you make it part of your daily life, the greater it will actually become part of you. Bottom line is that if you want to know God's will, you must read the Scriptures. There are commands, as we documented earlier in this chapter, and if you focus on them it will gradually lead you to a more mature spiritual life.

Intentionally Apply God's Will

After you start focusing on God's will; really making it a priority in your life, you need to take the next step. You need to consider how knowledge of God's will for you could be applied in your everyday life and in all situations. In other words, you need to learn how to apply what you have learned to new situations that may or may not be specifically addressed in the Bible. The Bible does not tell us what to do in every situation. If it did, the Bible would be a very lengthy book to read and study. We certainly couldn't carry it around in book form.

Internalize God's Will and Make it Automatic

What kind of change does Jesus expect of us if we are to follow him? Jesus' expectations are shared by multiple writers in the New Testament. In Matthew 23:26-28 Jesus stated,

> "Blind Pharisee! **First clean the inside of the cup and dish, and then the outside also will be clean.**
> "Woe to you, teachers of the law and Pharisees,
> you hypocrites! You are like whitewashed tombs,
> which look beautiful on the outside
> but on the inside are full of the bones of the dead
> and everything unclean.
> In the same way, on the outside you appear to people
> as righteous but on the inside
> you are full of hypocrisy and wickedness.

So, Jesus wants you to be clean on the inside. He wants you to be righteous on the inside, not just act pure and holy on the outside. Exhibiting pure and holy behavior should be evident, but it should be a result of internal change.

Let's look and see what Paul has to say about this. First of all, he stated that the Scriptures are truly inspired and that they can lead the Christian to be equipped for every good work (2 Timothy 3:16–17). What does equipped mean in this verse? In Hebrews 13:20-21 the writer gives us more information about what equipped means. We are not just called to just exhibit specific behaviors, we are also to allow God or the Holy Spirit to work in us or equip us to do what He wants us to do. Understanding what these two writers are truly saying helps us see the how God wants us to exhibit Godly behaviors.

"Now may the God of peace who brought again from the dead
our Lord Jesus, the great shepherd of the sheep,
by the blood of the eternal covenant, **equip you with everything
good that you may do his will**, working in us
that which is pleasing in his sight, through Jesus Christ,
to whom be glory forever and ever. Amen."

So, equipping has to do with you internalizing all that is good so that He can work in you to do His will or what is pleasing to Him. That can only occur when you die to self (Galatians 2:20). Milligan wrote several biblical works including a Commentary on Hebrews. MacLaren's Expositions also has an interesting take on this Scripture. Here is what they had to say about Hebrews 3:21 and what equipping means for all of you and everyone else.

Milligan Commentary on Hebrews
"The work rendered make perfect (katartizo) means properly to make quite read, to put in order, to make complete. Here, it means so to adjust, strengthen, and rectify the power of the soul, as to thoroughly fit and prepare it for God's service" (Milligan, 1989).
MacLaren's Expositions
The Spirit of God which cleanses men's hearts cleanses them on condition, first, of their faith; second, of their submission; and third, of their use of His gift..... If God dwells in us and works in us, let us yield ourselves to the workings and open our hearts to the Guest, and say, 'Into every corner, O Lord, I would that Thou wouldst go, to restore and complete.' This practical obedience to God's will is the perfection of human conduct..... But no good thing reaches its supremist goodness unless it is an act of conscious obedience to God's will.

The King James version interpreted this Scripture as, "Make you perfect in every good work" instead of "Equip you with everything good." In the Greek the meaning is the same.

So, the most important change is the change that occurs on the inside. When you know that your internal change is essential, it is easy to understand why you must focus on what God wants and grow as you read the Bible. So, how do you let go and let God work inside of you? To answer this, we want to ask a question.

Why does the Bible tell us over and over to think about Godly things? In Philippians 4:8 it says,

> "Finally, brothers, whatever is true, whatever is honorable, whatever is just, whatever is pure, whatever is lovely, whatever is commendable, if there is any excellence, if there is anything worthy of praise, think about these things."

> *God knew exactly why He wanted you study His word, and to internalize and 'think on holy, pure, good things'. It's because what we internalize and think about is what defines what we become. God wants us to become holy just as He is holy.*

Research has shown that what a person reads, listens to, and what he watches can determine his very nature. What he internalizes ultimately leads him to think in ways that are consistent with what he has read, heard or seen. That in turn leads him to speak based on what he has internalized and that in turn ultimately leads him to the very action he will take in any given situation without any thought on his part. There doesn't even need to be a decision. It becomes automatic. What you internalize, you become. God knew exactly why He wanted you study his Word, internalize it and 'think on holy, pure, good things'. It's because what you internalize and think about is what defines what you become. It also allows the nudges of the Holy Spirit to have a greater impact on your choices. God wants you to become holy just as He is holy. He wants you to internalize the attributes of Christ and meditate on those attributes so much that they become your very nature. He wants you to immerse yourself in the written Word of God. It should saturate your very being. He wants your automatic responses in what you think, say and do to be Godly. To jump ahead a bit, this is part of what is meant when we say you need to be broken. Self needs to die, and you need to internalize the nature of Christ so thoroughly that in every situation you automatically respond in thought, words and deeds just as Christ would. None of us are perfect and yes, we will make mistakes. But when we get to the point where we have truly internalized the attributes of Christ we will have a greater chance to automatically respond in a Godly way. You should seek to make your tree (mind) good and the fruit will be good (Matthew 12:33).

There is a very practical and truthful warning. Jesus said,

"You brood of vipers! How can you speak good,
when you are evil? For out of the abundance of the heart
the mouth speaks."

Jesus knows. God knows. The Godly person, out of his true Godly self, brings forth good, and the evil person, out of his evil nature, brings forth ungodly behavior.

Generalize God's Will in Your Life

The next important element of internalizing God's will in your life is that it should be generalized. That simply means that God's will should be evident in all parts of your life or in all situations. You must lean to generalize the application of the Scriptures to new situations in your daily life. Another way of saying this is that you allow God, Christ and the Holy Spirit to work and act in you to exhibit their good pleasure in every situation, not just when It makes you look good for some reason. Obviously, if as Christians we don't know what the Word says, it becomes difficult, if not impossible, to be like Christ and it stunts the Holy Spirits ability to work within us in any situation.

Daily Determine God's Will

Learning to follow God's will is a lifelong process. No matter how spiritually mature you become you will always need to search out how you can become more like Jesus your master. The rest of this work describes what you can do to put yourself in God's hands. He has shown us what we must do to build a greater faith. He shows us how to identify and fight our sinful nature. He shows us what His nature looks like so that we can put on and look like his Son Jesus. He shows us how to use the spiritual aids we have available to us to, 1) help us not let the world damage us spiritually, 2) help us overcome our fleshly nature, and 3) to help us fight spiritual forces of evil. He also shows us what we must do to help others become part of this Kingdom. That's called Discipleship.

With all of the knowledge that you had and what you have learned how will you decide if something you want to do is truly God's will? Lot's people struggle with this and keep trying to find an easy solution to determining what God would want them to do in a variety of situations. Our goal is not to tell you to use any particular method of accomplishing this. However, we have identified a method that has helped us. Is it fool proof? Probably not. Will what we have to share give you an option for thinking through each situation. We think it can help. So, let's look at the Determining God's Will chart below. You can use this any time you have a decision to make.

<table>
<tr><th colspan="3">Determining God's Will</th></tr>
<tr><td colspan="3">Instructions:
1. Write down your question in the space below.
2. Ask yourself the following questions as they pertain to the situation or decision you are trying to make.</td></tr>
<tr><td colspan="3">Question or decision:</td></tr>
<tr><th>Scriptures</th><th>Questions</th><th>Response</th></tr>
<tr><td>""All things are lawful for me," but not all things are helpful.
1 Corinthians 6:12a</td><td>Will it help you socially, mentally, spiritually or physically.</td><td>___Yes
___No</td></tr>
<tr><td>"All things are lawful for me," but I will not be dominated by anything."
1 Corinthians 6:12b</td><td>Will this bring me under its power in some way?</td><td>___Yes
___No</td></tr>
<tr><td>Therefore, if what I eat causes my brother to fall into sin, I will never eat meat again, so that will not cause him to fall.
1 Corinthians 8:13</td><td>Will this hurt others?</td><td>___Yes
___No</td></tr>
<tr><td>God created men for His Glory.
Isaiah 43:7</td><td>Will this Glorify GOD?

Could I do this in a way that would bring more glory to GOD?

Could I do something different that would Glorify GOD more?</td><td>___Yes
___No

___Yes
___No

___Yes
___No</td></tr>
<tr><td colspan="3">Optional Solution:</td></tr>
<tr><td colspan="3">See Appendices. Journey Into Discipleship Revised (Crites and Hill, 2023)</td></tr>
</table>

The rest of this work will help you see what you need to do to accomplish all that we have discussed above. As you learn to follow God's will, you will become one who truly is a Discipler of God. Your goal and Jesus' command is that you go and teach others to become Disciples. The good news is that there are many ways to accomplish this. Toward the end of this book we will discuss several God inspired ways to fulfill Jesus' great commission (Matthew 28:18-20).

As a Christian or Disciple of Christ you must be willing to seek out God's will in your life. The following Scriptures address how God wants you to seek out His will for you.

Seek Out God Will In Your Life	
Jeremiah 29:13	Diligently
Psalms 119:48	Reverently
Luke 8:15	Honestly
Luke 11:15	Obediently
Psalms 119:60; John 13:17	By immediate obedience
Psalms 119:15, 23, 48, 78, 97, 99, 148	Meditatively
Psalms 119:18	Prayerfully
Ephesians 3:4-5	Expecting Understanding
James 1:5; Psalms 25:4-5	Expecting God's Help
STS: These Scriptures may be underlined in yellow.	

Bottom line is that you must study the word. You must know where Scriptures are located so they can help you with sin. You must know where Scriptures are located that define Biblical doctrine. You must also dig deeper as you study God's Word so that you can understand the deeper meanings of God's word and what it means in your life. This can only be accomplished when you spend time with the Word. Keep in mind that the more you study the Bible, the more it becomes part of you. When it becomes more and more a part of you the Holy Spirit can nudge and subtly speak to you in more powerful ways to help you with sin. He might help you recall a Scripture that helps you deal with a specific issue. He might help you see what is right or wrong in a certain situation. Regardless, He will help you spiritually mature.

The more you know and understand the Bible, the more Help the Holy Spirit can offer you.

Just keep in mind that the more you know and understand the Bible, the more Help the Holy Spirit can offer you.

Personal Reflection

List three things that you learned or that were reinforced that will help you know God's Will for your life.

1.

2.

3.

Understanding God's Will

Chapter Three

As you begin to learn about God's will, you should want to truly understand it. The very beginning of understanding His will is for you to learn how you become one of His children and then live the Christian life. In book one of the series, Grace and Salvation, both Grace and how you become a Christian are reviewed in great detail. The absolute best way to learn about Grace and salvation is to simply read His Word. You must know and understand what God wants for you and from you. With that in mind, what is the will of God?

The will of God is what He has outlined in His Word so that you can, 1) learn how to become one of his children, 2) learn how to deal with your fleshly or carnal nature so that you can grow and mature spiritually, 3) learn how to better resist the wiles, schemes and attacks by spiritual forces of darkness, and 4) learn how to live the best possible life given the distractions and often times damage that the world sends your way. Why does He want you to learn these important lessons? The answer is simple. First, He wants you and everyone else to live with Him in the place He has prepared for you. He doesn't want anyone to end up in hell. Second, if you do become a child of God, He has given you a blueprint as to how you can accomplish His will in your life so that you can live the best possible life given your life situations. What is that blueprint? It's the Bible. It teaches you all that you need to know, but you must seek to follow His will by reading His Word and following what is shared in the pages of the Bible, especially the New Testament. We will cover the following in this chapter:

- The Foundation of God's Will
- Renewing of Your Mind
- Offer Your Body as a Living Sacrifice
- Do Not Be Conformed the Pattern of this World
- Being Transformed

The Foundation of God's Will

The foundation or the beginning point of a new Life in Christ is summed up in a Scripture written by Paul. These verses communicate the inner sense of self and actions that will set every Christian apart from the world in which he lives. Romans 12:1-2 are a call for you to internalize a new Godly nature and have a new way of thinking and behaving. Let's look to see what he said,

"Therefore, I urge you, brothers and sisters, in view of God's
mercy, **to offer your bodies as a living sacrifice,**
holy and pleasing to God—this is your true and proper worship.
Do not conform to the pattern of this world,
but be transformed by the renewing of your mind.
Then you will be able to test and approve what God's will is
—his good, pleasing and perfect will.
For by the grace given me I say to every one of you:
Do not think of yourself more highly than you ought,
but rather think of yourself with sober judgment,
in accordance with the faith God has distributed to each of you."

Let's break this Scripture down and look at it more closely. We will look at it in a slightly different order that may help all of us better understand what Paul is telling us that we must do.

Renewing of Your Mind

First, let's look at "the renewing of your mind." What does that mean? It means that you must constantly seek to internalize new, spiritually based information. Simply put, if you want to understand and follow God's will, you must first put to death your personal will and become obedient to all that Christ asks of you. It's not always an easy task, but every Christian should attempt to do what Paul has written in this text. If you take this stance your foundation will be strong. When you read the words of the Bible you will see how God's will can and will work in your life. If you read the first book in this series titled, Grace and Salvation (Crites, 2022) you will recall that repentance was discussed and how it plays a role in the change that should have occurred when you decided to become a Christian. Let's review what repentance means and how it relates to what Paul is saying in Romans. "Mounce (2006) defines repentance or 'metanoia' as "a radical, moral turn of the whole person from sin and to God." He says it is a radical turn. What does radical mean? The dictionary defines radical as, a "change or action, relating to or affecting the fundamental nature of something; far-reaching or thorough." That means that repentance calls for a 'radical change within you', if you are to become one of God's children. "We believe that means you must seek to internalize, think, speak and act as Jesus would and not listen to your fleshy nature that calls you to sin" (Crites, 2022). So, your repentance, that is necessary for you to become a Christian, calls for you to radically turn away from internalizing anything ungodly, thinking in ungodly ways and behaving in sinful ways. That is exactly what Paul is talking about when he says, 'renew your mind'. You renew your mind when you put off your old fleshly mind set and put on a Godly mindset. But it's not just the mind set or the renewal of your mind that is essential. It must also be seen in your actions. Let's take a closer look at actions or behavioral change.

Offer Your Body as a Living Sacrifice

In Romans 12:1 Paul says, "I appeal to you therefore, brothers, by the mercies of God, to present your bodies as a living sacrifice, holy and acceptable to God, which is your spiritual worship." Let's take a closer look at this.

What Does this scripture mean? Your body is also holy and it should be treated as such. Your sacrifice is for you to live the best life you can live for God. You should be a living sacrifice. What do you sacrifice? Death is actually involved in this living sacrifice. The death that is spoken of here is that you die to your fleshly or ungodly nature. When you are raised into a new life through Jesus Christ you must put off your old self and put on a new self. That includes both your body and your mind. Paul explains this in Galatians 2:20.

"I have been crucified with Christ.
It is no longer I who live, but Christ who lives in me.
And the life I now live in the flesh I live by faith in the Son of God,
who loved me and gave himself for me."

So, you are to put on Jesus the Christ in what you internalize, what you think, what you say and by what you do. At the end of this chapter, we will discuss a method by which you can better know the will of God. You will be able to better determine if your decisions are more in line with God's will or your own. This tool will help you as you seek to see if you are truly dying to self and letting Jesus live within you.

Do Not Conform to the Pattern of This World

Why is this important? There are several reasons why God does not want you to conform to the pattern of this world. If you conform to this world, you are choosing darkness over God. If you choose this world you have ignored the choice that you made to repent of your sinful old life and to radically turn to God. If you choose the world, you have dismissed God. You have put something else in His place. Just keep in mind that without God there is no salvation, even if you have followed God's word and have become a saved believer. If you conform to the world, you have chosen to not belong to God. If you conform to this world you are allowing the forces of evil to tempt you to be ungodly. They often do this in very deceptive ways at times. This will be discussed in much greater detail later in this work. What are some examples of being conformed to this world. This is addressed in several Scriptures. Here are a few:

Conformed to the World or Not	
As obedient children, do not be conformed to the **passions of your former ignorance,**	1 Peter 1:14
In which you once walked, **following the course of this world, following the prince of the power of the air,** the spirit that is now at work in the sons of disobedience—	Ephesians 2:2
And to **put on the new self**, created after the likeness of God in true righteousness and holiness.	Ephesians 4:24
Do not love the world or the things in the world. If anyone loves the world, the love of the Father is not in him.	1 John 2:15

Set your minds on things that are above, not on things that are on earth.	Colossians 3:2
Therefore, if anyone is in Christ**, he is a new creation. The old has passed away**; behold, the new has come.	2 Corinthians 5:17
You adulterous people! **Do you not know that friendship with the world is enmity with God**? Therefore, whoever wishes to be a friend of the world makes himself an enemy of God.	James 4:4

Being Transformed

How do you change your outward actions or behavior? As shown above, Paul tells you that you must renew your mind. What you internalize and as a result think, is key in verse three. Your thinking is a result of the inner change you have experienced because of what you are internalizing. You are called upon to set your old carnal mind to the side and focus on having a mind like Christ.

If you change or renew your mind, how should that transform your behavior or actions? Keep in mind that the renewing of your mind is foundational to your transformation. *Being transformed is what happens after you have renewed your mind.* As you accomplish this you should begin to exhibit Christlike behavior.

Being transformed is what happens after you have renewed your mind.

Transformation Benefits

What happens as you accomplish this? You will be able to test and approve what God's will is—His good, pleasing and perfect will. We believe that your transformation and your change in behavior is an ongoing process as you mature spiritually. In Hebrews 5:11-15 it clearly talks about how we should be growing spiritually so that we can better understand God's will in our lives. That suggests a growth process. The writer specifically tells us in the fourteenth verse that, "...**solid food is for the mature, for those who have their powers of discernment trained by constant practice to distinguish good from evil."** So, as you grow spiritually or in other words as you transform your mind, it will become easier for you to know what is right or wrong, good or bad, spiritual or non-spiritual. See the chapter on Spiritual Growth.

So, how can you better know what God's will is in your life? There are several important steps you must take if you listen to Paul.

1. You must offer your whole body to God for it is your Spiritual Worship. Not just your mind, but your body also.
2. You must not allow yourself to conform to the patterns, beliefs, actions of this world. The world is filled with darkness.
3. You must transform from darkness to light and goodness by renewing your mind. Yes, it has to do with what you put in your mind and what you focus on.

In Romans 12:3 we are given an important message. Paul says,

"For by the grace given me I say to every one of you:
Do not think of yourself more highly than you ought,
but rather think of yourself with sober judgment,"

When you become a Christian you should begin the process of thinking less about yourself and more about others, especially God. Christianity is not a selfish religion. It is based on love for each other and God. When Jesus was asked what the greatest commandment was in Matthew 22:37-39 He said,

"You shall love the Lord your God with all your heart
and with all your soul and with all your mind.
This is the great and first commandment. And a second is like it:
You shall love your neighbor as yourself.

As previously stated, if you do these things then the will of God will be much more evident to you. Following the truths found in this Scripture is the beginning point for being a person of goodness and light vs darkness and evil. If you attempt to act like a Christian without having the right heart, you are doing what the Pharisees were doing in Jesus' day. In Matthew 23:26 Jesus stated,

"You blind Pharisee! First clean the inside of the cup and the plate,
that the outside also may be clean."

Let's look on the next page and see how the Pulpit Commentary explains this.

Pulpit Commentary
"The external purity should proceed from and be a token of the internal. So, in the case of the moral agent, the ceremonial purity is a mockery and hypocrisy unless it be accompanied by holiness of the heart. That the outside of them may be (γένηται, may become) clean also. However fair to see, the man is not pure unless his soul is clean; he cannot be called pure while the higher part of his being is soiled and foul with sin. An inward saintliness cannot be hidden; it shines forth in the countenance; it is known by speech and action; it sheds sunshine wherever it goes. 'Keep thy heart with all diligence; for out of it are the issues of life' (Proverbs 4:23)."

Other commentaries have similar explanations. So, it appears that Jesus himself communicated that to abide by and accept the New Covenant, the New Law of God, it could not just be a change of external behavior. It had to start with a change of heart, mind or your internal self. This now brings us back to Romans 12:2 where Paul tells us that you must be transformed by the renewing of your mind and that by testing you may discern what is the will of God, what is good and acceptable and perfect.

The word testing is important. Why? It's because it's through testing that you have a better understanding of specific Biblical teachings. Let's look at another important Scripture that explains why testing is so important to the person who truly has and is continuing to renew his mind so that he can be more Christ like. In Hebrews 5:14 we are told that you must be learning and growing by internalizing God's will in your life. As you grow or spiritually mature your powers of discernment regarding good versus evil, light versus dark, are enhanced as you practice your Christ like mind set. The greater your understanding of God's will, the more mature you can become. The more mature you become the easier it is to understand and follow God's will in your life. As a Christian, you should be in a constant state of transforming your mind into a Christlikeness.

Personal Reflection

List three things that you learned or that were reinforced that will help you understand and apply God's Will in your life.

1.

2.

3.

Part Two: Now That I'm a Christian

Now that you have become a Christian and have understood the greatness of God and what His will is for you, it's time to build a stronger connection to God, grow your faith and mature spiritually. Part two addresses how you can do exactly that.

- Connecting with God
- Growing Your Faith

Connecting with God

Chapter Four

People often believe that by just knowing about God, they actually have a connection with him. They believe that they have a father-child relationship with Him. This is not necessarily true. Knowing God involves much more than just an intellectual knowledge or mental assent to the fact that He is real. Such knowledge is important, but without a real one-on-one relationship, no one will ever truly know Him. Most of us can say we know about the president of the United States. We see him on T.V., hear about him on the radio and read about him on a variety of devices, in the paper and in magazines. We all have some knowledge about him, but most of us really don't personally know Him. The same thing applies to Jesus and His Father. If you are a Christian, you have already started your faith journey. However, your faith should and will grow as you connect with God in a deeper more meaningful way. We will cover the following in this chapter:

- Spiritual Birth
- The Greatest Relationship of All
- Grace and the Heart Relationship
- Faith: The Foundation
- Saving Faith
- Four Elements to a Saving Faith
- Don't Fall Off the Wall
- Feeling in the Faith Experience
- Overcoming Negative Spiritual Dissonance

Spiritual Birth

The new Christian must develop a deeper understanding of God and what it means to be His child. Lemon stated that, "One of the greatest changes a man makes in the new birth is taking him from the visible to the invisible. A Christian ceases trusting himself to trust another. He shifts the reins of life from himself to God. If a Christian has not done that, he has not been truly converted. Spiritual birth is a process. It takes me from me and gives me to God (Lemon, 1981)." That's what happens when you make Jesus Lord of your life. That is your confession when you are saved, and it cannot just be words.

With the above in mind, we acknowledge that everyone does not come to God spiritually mature, but there must be a change of direction. When a person becomes a child of God there is a good chance he may be a baby in his Christian beliefs and application. Just as a mother holds and feeds her newborn child, a disciple who is teaching a baby Christian must provide security, an atmosphere of acceptance, see that proper food and drink is given, cleans up his messes and gradually begins to teach him how to take care of himself. However, several things may need to be taught over and over. Babies and children in Christ tend to forget or even rebel at times. They need to be reminded or learn:

- How important a growing faith is in Christianity.
- About security, reconciliation, love, propitiation, forgiveness, redemption and other elementary principles that are foundational in Christianity.
- About temptation and the reality of how it impacts the Christian life.
- The goodness of God and how He wants to take care of us.
- About prayer and how it is the way to plug into an inexhaustible power source.
- All of the vital relationships that a Christian must have to function as God intends.
- About brokenness and the necessity of death to self.

As this teaching or training process advances, the disciple needs to develop a deeper understanding of what the God Man relationship is truly about.

What does God expect of us? What kind of relationship does He want us to have with Him? Let's take a deeper look at what God wants from us.

The Greatest Relationship of All

You begin to know another when you have gone beyond the fact (knowing about them), and begin to understand, relate and become involved with that person or entity. The question then is, 'How can you turn your knowledge about God into something that will actually help you know God personally?' The answer comes through the Word. As you Internalize and make each truth part of you, it will be easier to learn about God and His will. In thought, word and deed, you are beginning to truly know Him. The greater your obedience, based on a loving relationship to His will, the greater you will personally become acquainted with Him. The result of your personally knowing God has been summed up in John 17:3 when he stated,

"Now this is eternal life; **that they may know you, the only true God, and Jesus Christ,** whom you have sent."

It is for this reason that we continue our Journey Into Discipleship. To become a mature disciple, you must have a close communion with God; you must know Him well. And that leads you to the continued promise of eternal life with God.

Grace and the Heart Relationship

Several elements are needed if you are to develop a relationship with God. Obviously, knowledge is needed about God and His will for you. You also need to develop a strong faith in Him. However, God calls you to relationship. He wants you to be connected to Him.

In Matthew 23 the writer explains very specifically what God does not want and gives a warning to those who would be external Christians only. In verse 33 he states,

"You serpents, you brood of vipers, how are you to escape being sentenced to hell?"

So, what is he referring to? What would cause Jesus to make such a statement to the Scribes and Pharisees that were listening to him? Look at the general content of several of the Matthew 23 verses.

Verse 3 For they preach, but **do not practice**. He calls them hypocrites.

Verse 4 **Lay heavy burdens** on people's shoulders, but they themselves are not willing to move them with their finger.

Verse 5 They do all their deeds **to be seen by others**.

Verse 6 They **love the place of honor** and the best seats.

Verse 7 They **love to be seen and greeted** in the marketplaces and being called rabbi by others.

Verse 13 They **shut the kingdom of heaven** in people's faces. Keeping themselves and others entering it.

Verse 15 They travel across sea and land to make a single proselyte, and when he becomes a proselyte, they **make him twice as much a child of hell as they are**.

Verse 23 They tithe mint and dill and cumin and have **neglected the weightier matters of the law**: justice and mercy and faithfulness.

Verse 25 They clean the outside of the cup and the plate, but inside they are **full of greed and self-indulgence**.

Verse 27 They are like whitewashed tombs, which outwardly appear beautiful, but within are **full of dead people's bones and all uncleanness.**

After looking at this you should ask, 'Well I have a better idea as to what God doesn't want, but what does God want from me?' The important question is how do we obtain Grace and the Righteousness of Christ so that we can truly be saved? Is it by Law keeping? Are we to follow the laws found in the Bible at a level that allows us to obtain that Grace and Righteousness? Are we following commandments or doing good works that will allow us to obtain Grace and Righteousness that God wants to give us? It certainly doesn't look like that is the direction God wants us to take. We are to build a covenant or heart relationship with God. One that helps us become like the Father and like his Son. The answer is found in Matthew 23:26. It states,

"You blind Pharisee! **First clean the inside of the cup and the plate**, than the outside also may be clean."

So, God and Jesus do not want us to simply follow laws or commands; even the New Testament Law of the Spirit or many commands found in the New Testament. He doesn't want you to simply look the part of a Christian. He doesn't want you to just be a Christian on Sunday Morning, sometimes Sunday night or Wednesday night. He doesn't want you to look good for your own benefit. He wants you to change on the inside. He wants you to clean out the old self that has carnal wants needs and desires and focus on dying to self (Galatians 2:20) so that you can become Christ like in all that you are and all that you do. It is a choice you make minute by minute, hour by hour, day by day and you use self-discipline to choose to be and do as God wills. To accomplish this, you have to know what it means to be like Christ, or you will fail.

Basically, this means that you should be seeking to put on the very nature of Jesus. This is what leads you to saving Grace. This is what places you in God's care and provides you with a relationship that places you in His eternal Kingdom.

How does this start? Well, you have to make contact with God. You have to believe He exists. You have to believe that He has an eternal plan for you. You must be willing to follow His scheme of redemption and to do that you must know His Will. The Bible has that message. If you believe what the Bible says, the first thing you must do is develop a saving faith that leads you to relationship with God. Book one in this series, Grace and Salvation covers this beginning point of this relationship with God in detail.

Faith: The Foundation

The very foundation of our relationship with God is based on faith. "The word faith suggests the idea of trust, commitment and connection.....True Biblical faith leads to a change in behavior, a change of your internal self and commitment to the God-man relationship" (Crites, 2022). At conversion you began this intimate faith walk that lasts throughout your life, as long as you choose to remain one of God's children. It is important to note that your faith should grow as your relationship with Him develops and as you mature spiritually. The writer of Hebrews chastised the readers because they had not grown.

The Hebrews writer said,

> "About this we have much to say, and it is hard to explain, since you have become dull of hearing. For though by this time you ought to be teachers, you need someone to teach you again the basic principles of the oracles of God.
> You need milk, not solid food, for everyone who lives on milk is unskilled in the word of righteousness, since he is a child.
> **But solid food is for the mature, for those who have their powers of discernment trained by constant practice to distinguish good from evil. Therefore let us leave the elementary doctrine of Christ and go on to maturity, not laying again a foundation of repentance from dead works and of faith toward God,"**
> (Hebrews 5:11-14; 6:1).

To better understand the importance of your faith relationship we will discuss six major concepts. First, we will discuss the substance of saving faith. Second, we will determine the importance of fact in the faith system. Third, we will discuss the place of feeling in the belief system. Fourth, we will discuss faith as it relates to levels of maturity. Fifth, we will discuss faith as it relates to assurance. Last, we will discuss the benefits of faith.

Saving Faith

To many, faith is nothing more than a false sense of security. Often it is a mental phenomenon that is based on self-established perceptions that are more in tune with perceived self-wants or needs than doctrinal truth founded in the Scriptures. This variety of faith is a product of todays 'do your own thing' society, where the foremost standard for determining moral-ethical conduct is 'if it feels good – do it.' It is also seen as a smorgasbord approach to choosing doctrine you will accept or reject. Such faith is based on selected Scriptures, while at the same ignoring others. That's not how God wants it. He wants you to base your faith on all that He has given you, not just selected Scriptures. A good resource for understanding specific Bible doctrine can be found in the book titled, Comparative Doctrine (Crites, 2022) It discusses over fifty areas of doctrine in detail. No opinions, just Scriptures that show what the Bible teaches about specific doctrines.

Jesus and His Apostles did not think of faith in those terms. Jesus identified the faith of those who would come to believe in Him, without ever having seen Him, with the faith Thomas acquired through seeing and touching (John 20:26-30). Peter said of Jesus, "We believe and know" (John 6:69). Paul also affirmed, "I know whom I have believed" (2 Timothy 1:12). The writer of Hebrews calls faith the assurance, the confirmation, of the things we hope for and being certain of what we do not see—by having faith we are convinced of their reality.

These Scriptures are not expressions of uncertainty, but affirmations of unwavering conviction, not doubt or wishful thinking, but inescapable certainties based on compelling evidence. The overwhelming majority of everything you know is derived from reason, testimony, and 'evidence', not from personal experience. You must believe in God and Christ, not because you have seen them, but because evidence and reason compel you to do so.

As a New Testament Christian, you must understand that faith is the foundation upon which your Christianity is built, for 'without faith it is impossible to please Him' (Hebrews 11:6). Without this solid foundation of faith one can never have a covenant relationship with God—you can never be His son or daughter in Christ, nor can you understand what God can do for you. Albert Lemmons stated in his book Dynamic faith (1981), "Faith is the key that opens the door that has a God on the other side of that door who is able to do exceeding, abundantly above all that you can ask or think (Ephesians 3:20)."

Five Elements of Saving Faith

Many people in the religious world think they have faith, but in truth it is only an inadequate or false concept of a 'saving' faith. The Bible states that there are four elements to a saving faith. They are:

- It is by grace, not by works (Ephesians 2:8-9).
- There must be faith (Hebrews 11:6).
- This faith must express belief in Jesus (John 8:24).
- Love will be seen through faith as you obey (John 14:15; James 2:26).

- That obedience calls for you to be baptized Acts 2:38 and for you to have a complete change of life as you seek to be Christ like.

If you exclude any of the above elements you only deceive yourself into thinking that you have a Biblical faith (Romans 10:3). You can know about something without having faith in it. For example, Jesus lived, died and rose again. Many people suppose that this knowledge is faith. But this is merely an intellectual assent to certain historical facts. It is not what the Bible means by faith; saving faith (James 2:19; Matthew 8:29). Several Scriptures in the New Testament tell us that our faith is a faith of obedience.

"Whoever believes in the Son has eternal life; **whoever does not obey the Son shall not see life,**
but the wrath of God remains on him."
John 3:36

"If you **keep my commandments**, you will abide in my love, just as I have kept my Father's commandments and abide in his love."
John 15:10

"And by this we know that we have come to know him**, if we keep his commandments**."
1 John 2:3

"Whoever says "I know him" but **does not keep his commandments is a liar**, and the truth is not in him,"
1 John 2:4

"And whatever we ask we receive from him, because **we keep his commandments and do what pleases him**."
1 John 3:22

"**Whoever keeps his commandments abides in God**, and God in him. And by this we know that he abides in us, by the Spirit whom he has given us."
1 John 3:24

"For this is the love of God, that **we keep his commandments.**
And his commandments are not burdensome."
1 John 5:3

When you read the Scriptures it is evident that God expects us to keep his commandments. Some Christians feel they have a saving faith when they trust in the Lord for temporal security, but still trust in themselves for eternal life. Saving faith is trusting Jesus Christ alone for your salvation (John 14:6). You should be able to say, "God saved me by his grace when I trusted, fully believed, obeyed in love and continually sought to be what He wants me to be." In the gospels the very first step a disciple must take is an act of obedience which proves to be an act of faith. So many people believe that they have taken the step of faith that places them in Christ's body. Often such a step only amounts to cheap grace, faith without obedience through love, or salvation through works alone. Faith is only saving faith when there is obedience, never without it. Faith only becomes saving faith in the act of obedience (see 'The Foundation of Spiritual Maturity' in this work).

What is this obedience that the Bible speaks about? This was addressed in detail in the book titled, 'Grace and Salvation'. Obedience means that we do something that God wants us to do both before and after Salvation. Here are some examples:

Obedience or Gospel Commands	
Choose to have Belief and Faith	Hebrews 11:1; 6
Choose to Repent and turn from a Sinful life	Romans 3:23; Acts 3:19; Acts 17:30
Choose to Confess Jesus as your Lord	Matthew 10:32; Romans 10:9; 1 John 4:15
Choose to be Baptized	1 Peter 3:21; Acts 2:38; Acts 22:16
Choose to die to self daily	Galatians 2:20
Choose to be self-controlled	2 Timothy 1:7; Titus 1:8
See Chapter Eight 'Sanctification and External Change'	

Yes, having faith is an act of obedience. It is something you choose. However, all of the other things listed are also acts of obedience that God wants from us. God expects us to do or follow all of his commands, both before we become a Christian and after. Baptism is one of those Gospel commands that is specifically communicated over and over. Faith without following God's Commands is not a saving faith. Let's talk more about faith.

One more thought must be considered here. There were times when Abraham doubted; he did not have sufficient faith. However, because of his desire for a relationship he kept on going; he kept trying even though he was weary and questioned. So, you can see his faith and obedience to God's will kept him on the road that eventually led to a greater, stronger faith.

By this faith, he trusts in Jesus Christ alone for His salvation, surrenders to the Lordship of Jesus, becomes more like Him and as a result Christ's nature is seen in the believer.

In review, man is saved by the grace of God given in Jesus Christ's atoning death. Man's response is that of faith that leads to obedience, or non-faith. Saving faith is man's appropriate obedient response to the facts God has given him. By this faith, he trusts in Jesus Christ alone for His salvation, surrenders to the Lordship of Jesus, is buried in baptism to receive both the forgiveness of sins and to receive the gift of the Holy Spirit and chooses to become more like Him and as a result Christ's nature that is within the believer. This nature should be evident and growing as he listens to the Word and to the Holy Spirit as He seeks to direct every Christian in God's ways.

It is in the merit of Christ that salvation is available. When you come into contact with his blood through faith in baptism you are saved (you are justified or declared not guilty and given Christ's perfect righteousness). Because of Christ's sacrifice, your guilt disappears in the eyes of God. This will allow you to come to a proper relationship with God. It will lead you to a personal covenant relationship that will bring about personal fulfillment and spiritual growth. It is only through this relationship that man may find saving faith.

Scriptural Study

Read the following Scriptures to see how they relate to your personal faith. To assist in your study, you may underline these Scriptures in yellow.

Faith	Scripture
Definition	Hebrews 11:1
Evidenced by	James 2:17-25

Through it	Ephesians 3:12 John 3:15-16 Galatians 3:25 Romans 3:25 Mark 16:16 Acts 15:9 Galatians 2:20
Without Faith	Hebrews 11:6
Produces	1 Peter 2:6 Romans 5:2 Romans 15:13
Trial of	James 1:3
Christians Should	2 Corinthians 8:7 Colossians 1:23 2 Timothy 1:19 Luke 17:5 1 Corinthians 16:13
Commanded	Mark 11:22 1 John 3:23
STS: These Scriptures may be underlined in yellow.	

Don't Fall Off the Wall

As you continue your Journey Into Discipleship, you find that there is an important relationship between faith, fact and feeling. We are not suggesting that faith in itself is not key or even foundational. It indeed is one of the most important aspects of Christianity that we can experience. We must have faith. However, we must also keep in mind that in our world today there are those who would alter what faith looks like. They would seek to change the faith that we should have into something that it is not. Because of this we must also be able to identify fact from fiction when it comes to faith. How do we do that?

In Hosea 4:6 we have a clue. God stated, "My people are destroyed for the lack of knowledge." Your New Life must begin with a true understanding of faith that is based on Scripture and the life of Christ. A close friend shared this poem. We don't know where it came from, but we appreciate the content. We believe that it expresses the proper relationship between faith, fact and feeling in our Christian walk.

Three men were walking on a wall,
feeling, faith and fact.
Feeling got an awful fall,
and faith was taken back.
So close was faith to feeling,
he stumbled and fell, too.
But fact remained and pulled faith back,
and faith brought feeling too.

Fact or Feeling

The Christian belief emblazoned in the Bible can be proven through historical documentation. In other words, you can find many facts in the Bible that are supported by other historical documents or findings and vice versa. It's interesting to note that as time goes by, more and more archeological proof is being discovered that supports the Bible (see Titus M. Kennedy's book titled, Unearthing the Bible: 101 Archaeological Discoveries That Bring the Bible to Life). The Institute for Creation Research in Dallas, Texas has a vast amount of information that shows the truth about creation, man and many Biblical events. There are many other works that clearly show how the Bible is an accurate historical document as well as being God's written word. Facts abound that support the Bible and its message if you simply look for them. When possible, it is very encouraging to find that your faith is supported by factual data, not myth, legend or by other people's beliefs. It should also be pointed out that feelings are an important part of our religious experience, but they are inappropriate as a measure for determining right from wrong, good from bad or whether something is from God or Satan. Many have allowed their feelings to guide them in their religion. This desire to have an emotional religious experience has permeated Christianity. A Christian must base his beliefs on established truths. However, mere intellectual acquaintance or knowledge of the Word of God, without a true faith, lacks the joy and blessings of Christianity. As we have already stated, it is important to have true or saving faith in God. Actually, it is essential.

Feelings are an important part of our religious experience, but they are inappropriate as a measure for determining right from wrong, good from bad or whether something is from God or Satan.

As a Christian you must be willing to, 1) accept fact, and 2) rejoice over the beautiful feelings that come from a Biblical faith. So, you can see that facts as well as feelings, are important elements in the faith concept. You must be willing to accept Biblical fact as truth and most of all, accept the unseen as reality (Hebrews 11:1). Albert Lemmons (1981) has defined such a faith as, "...the capacity or ability of the human heart which, when activated by the Word of God, enables a man or woman who as yet has not seen God to know that God is real." So, the key to true saving faith is not the mere acknowledgement of the facts that lead you to faith. It occurs as a result of a powerful internal change that compels you to accept Jesus, become a Christian and strive to become less of self and more like Him as you walk through life. It is a belief in fact that takes man out of himself and puts him into a heart relationship with Christ. In this sense faith is not just intellectual assent to fact, but rather a cleaving to and trusting of the man Jesus the Christ for all that you are and can become.

Faith is the capacity or ability of the human heart which, when activated by the Word of God, enables a man or woman who as yet has not seen God to know that God is real."

Scriptural Study

The Scriptures below indicate the differences, and necessity of having fact, faith, and feeling in proper perspective in your Christian life.

Fact: Scriptural Documentation	
Historical Data	
Genesis 1:1	In the beginning, God created the heavens and the earth.
Mathew 2:1	Now after Jesus was born in Bethlehem of Judea in the days of Herod the king, behold, wise men from the east came to Jerusalem,
Mathew 27:26	Then he released for them Barabbas, and having scourged Jesus, delivered him to be crucified.
Matthew 27:50	And Jesus cried out again with a loud voice and yielded up his spirit.
Matthew 28:1-7	Now after the Sabbath, toward the dawn of the first day of the week, Mary Magdalene and the other Mary went to see the tomb. And behold, there was a great earthquake, for an angel of the Lord

	descended from heaven and came and rolled back the stone and sat on it. His appearance was like lightning, and his clothing white as snow. And for fear of him the guards trembled and became like dead men. But the angel said to the women, "Do not be afraid, for I know that you seek Jesus who was crucified. He is not here, for he has risen, as he said. Come, see the place where he lay. Then go quickly and tell his disciples that he has risen from the dead, and behold, he is going before you to Galilee; there you will see him. See, I have told you."
Acts 2	Peter's sermon and God's will for all mankind in found this chapter.
Commandments and Principles	
Matthew 22:37-39	And he said to him, "You shall love the Lord your God with all your heart and with all your soul and with all your mind. This is the great and first commandment. And a second is like it: You shall love your neighbor as yourself.
Matthew 28:18-20	And Jesus came and said to them, "All authority in heaven and on earth has been given to me. Go therefore and make disciples of all nations, baptizing them in the name of the Father and of the Son and of the Holy Spirit, teaching them to observe all that I have commanded you. And behold, I am with you always, to the end of the age."
John 13:34	A new commandment I give to you, that you love one another: just as I have loved you, you also are to love one another.
1 John 3:24	Whoever keeps his commandments abides in God, and God in him. And by this we know that he abides in us, by the Spirit whom he has given us.

It is a belief is the evidence, the facts that can be found in the Bible about God, the life of Christ, the teachings showing his will and more that give us what we need to have an undying faith. Without those facts and the truth behind them Christianity would not even exist.

Faith: Belief in Facts which Result in Obedience	
Hebrews 1:1	Long ago, at many times and in many ways, God spoke to our fathers by the prophets,
2 Corinthians 8:7	But as you excel in everything—in faith, in speech, in knowledge, in all earnestness, and in our love for you — see that you excel in this act of grace also.
James 2:21-25	Was not Abraham our father justified by works when he offered up his son Isaac on the altar? You see that faith was active along with his works, and faith was completed by his works; and the Scripture was fulfilled that says, "Abraham believed God, and it was counted to him as righteousness"—and he was called a friend of God. You see that a person is justified by works and not by faith alone. And in the same way was not also Rahab the prostitute justified by works when she received the messengers and sent them out by another way?

Feeling: Biblical Feeling is the Result of Faith in Combination with Works	
John 15:11	These things I have spoken to you, that my joy may be in you, and that your joy may be full.
2 Thessalonians 3:16	Now may the Lord of peace himself give you peace at all times in every way. The Lord be with you all.

Feeling in the Faith Experience

We have already stated that feeling should not be the foundation for belief or obedience. In the faith process, there are three important elements that must be in proper alignment for Christians to have spiritual joy. Feeling is an essential element but should never be the basis for our faith. The proper alignment is as follows:

Fact	These are God-given truths.
Faith	Saving faith is man's appropriate response to the facts God has given him. By this faith, you trust in Jesus Christ alone for our salvation, surrender to the Lordship of Jesus and obediently expresses our faith through love resulting in a changed nature that seeks to think, speak and act as Jesus would. It is by this kind of faith that God works in and for you.
Feeling	This is often experienced as a natural by-product of your obedience or non-obedience to fact and faith

When your feelings are not in proper alignment with your obedience, spiritual dissonance occurs. Dissonance is defined as the degree of difference between obedience and desire to obey. The greater the difference between obedience and desire to obey, the greater the dissonance. Negative spiritual dissonance produces:

- Unhappiness.
- Spiritual confusion.
- Mental confusion.
- Spiritual unfulfillment.

Positive spiritual dissonance is usually found among those who have 'Charismatic' experiences. Feeling becomes a very important element for them. Sometimes feeling becomes more important that Biblical fact. This is where the danger lies. Positive spiritual dissonance produces:

- Extreme emphasis on emotionality.
- Numerous feeling level experiences.
- Sensationalism.

Any spiritual dissonance is undesirable and must be addressed or it can cause problems in your spiritual life. Spiritual stability comes when feelings are in harmony with what we believe, and we exhibit actions that are Christlike. One who has spiritual stability has little, if any, dissonance. This is where we all should be in our Christian lives. Such harmony produces in various degrees:

- Joy.
- Peace of Mind.
- Fulfillment.

- Happiness.
- Fruit of the Spirit.

However, not everyone has this kind of faith yet. Many Christians experience spiritual dissonance. Many of us 'do', but really don't feel like it. We obey Biblical fact, which results in obedience (not always based on faith). The resultant feeling is not joy. On the contrary, those who are on the negative side of the dissonance scale experience feelings of confusion, turmoil, and unhappiness. This is why there are Christians who are not really happy. They have no real joy or peace. Such Christians find more apparent happiness, fulfilled lives, and joy in the world. Such 'worldly happiness' is often due to a seared conscience (1 Timothy 4:2). A seared conscience covers or masks negative dissonance. Worldly or terminal happiness is desired, easily found and clung to by those who experience negative spiritual dissonance. Again, such happiness is terminal, but fulfilling at times and preferred over a life filled with unhappiness, spiritual confusion, mental confusion and spiritual unfulfillment (negative spiritual dissonances).

Humans are goal seeking by nature. They desire comfort, love and happiness. If a need cannot be met in a spiritual way, we have a tendency (because of our fleshly nature) to meet it in a fleshly or carnal way. Spiritual forces of darkness work overtime to direct us towards our fleshly nature. This can occur when we are hurt, confused, unhappy and unfulfilled, when dissonance is high. When our 'needs' are not being met, our conscience can easily become seared. At the very least we try to ignore that what we are doing is actually ungodly. After all, we are taking care of ourselves; right? We seem to feel better, right? With this in mind, we can see why many Christians follow the way of the world, the worlds path to happiness. Such happiness is more readily found, more immediate, but fleeting. You can have 'fun and happiness' in the world even if it is terminal and illusional in nature. However, that's the problem; it's not real. It won't last. It doesn't have the eternal value that you get from spiritual joy that comes from saving faith and by living a Godly, Sanctified life.

Overcoming Negative Spiritual Dissonance

Horizontal Godly relationships are key in developing and maintaining spiritual health. Practical human love is essential in overcoming negative spiritual dissonance. Think about it! God made us. He knows what we need. He understands that we need each other. Human beings, especially our brothers and sisters in Christ, are key in identifying how we can meet many of those needs. ***The important thing is that the fulfillment of these needs is of major importance in producing happiness in every human.*** God intended us to have close fellowship in order that we might meet each other's needs.

One key benefit of meeting daily in the early church was that they could lift each other up or help each other (Acts 2:46). There are four basic psychological needs that must be fulfilled through our fellowship, if we are to remain spiritually and psychologically healthy. All of these needs are met through fellowship. They are:

- We need to develop a relationship with a significant someone; someone who is spiritual in nature.
- We need an intimate few; a close spiritual group we can share with.
- We need activity with Christians who are close.
- We need affection, both emotional and physical. We must know that we are cared for; that we are loved. Touch is a very powerful tool in health care.

If you have all four of these needs met in your life, you are well on the way to becoming spiritually healthy. There should be little, if any, negative spiritual dissonance. If you are lacking in any of these areas, then you undoubtedly feel unsure of your Christianity. Doubt, anxiety, frustration and possibly anger may be evident. However, if you want to overcome these feelings, you must develop relationships from within God's body.

Personal Reflection

List three things that you learned or that were reinforced that could help you better connect with God.

1.

2.

3.

Growing Your Faith

Chapter Five

Does faith grow? Should it? Scriptures support that we all should grow in our faith. Abraham struggled with faith for many years. However, his life can provide a wonderful example of what faith looks like through a person's stages of spiritual growth. You can actually see three different stages of his faith when you look at the Scriptures. What's interesting is that you can see where you are in the faith process when you look at what Abraham experienced in his life.

- Stages of Faith and Abraham
- The God Can Stage of Faith
- The God Will Stage of Faith
- The God Does Stage of Faith
- Promises: The Benefits of Faith

Stages of Faith and Abraham

If you look closely at Abraham's life you will see three basic stages of faith. Abraham's faith growth is our illustration. We call the first stage the 'God Can' stage (Genesis 12; & Genesis 20:1-13). Abraham had enough faith to leave his homeland, but not enough to trust God when his life was in danger. The second stage is the 'God Will' stage (Genesis 17:15-21). This faith increased to the point that he fainted not at the promise of God though his reproductive capacity was dead. He waited in faith. The last stage is the 'God Does' stage (Genesis 22:1-19). When Abraham was about to take Isaac up the mountain to sacrifice him, his servant asked what he should do. Abraham told him to wait, he and Isaac would be back. The third stage is the highest and most desired stage of faith. Those who are at this stage of faith accept the reality of God's promises.

A quick review of these three stages will help us see the faith process that most of us go through. As we look at the Scriptures, it appears that we must be in the 'God Will' stage of faith if we are to expect to receive the abundant life in all its fullness. The interesting point to this is that you can also compare your stages of faith to Spiritual Maturity. Spiritual babies and children are often found in the God Can stage of Faith. Spiritual adolescents may often be found in the God Will stage and Spiritual Adults would most often be found in the God Does stage. We will discuss the stages of spiritual maturity in a later chapter. Challenge yourself to determine which stage of faith you often find yourself in right now. It you are not in the God Does stage, what's holding you back? Think about it as you read.

The God Can Stage of Faith

The 'God Can' stage of faith is characterized by the story of Abraham that is found in Genesis 12: and in 20:1-13. Practically speaking, Christians at this stage of faith are very child-like in their spiritual life. They don't know what is best for them, so they focus on what they want; their wants, needs, desires and preferred way of life. Another example of someone at this stage of faith is that they have a tendency to hold on to a commandment oriented or a legal system for their Christianity. Such Christians are more often than not motivated by self rather than by relationship with Jesus. The abundant life is given to those who have a relationship with Jesus. So, we can see the frustration, the lack of power, and overall spiritual confusion that would be evident in one at such a stage in his spiritual growth. It is our responsibility to help each other grow beyond this stage. Regardless, God still can work in their lives. Even as baby Christians we should believe that God can do anything! However, we often wonder if He really will do all that He says He will do for us. The following is a list of characteristics that can be seen in this stage.

- You know God can, but will he?
- You are guided by circumstances!
- You have self on the throne of life.

- There is doubt.
- There is fear.
- There is failure.

The God Will Stage of Faith

Christian faith that believes that God will act occurs as we develop a stronger faith in God and what He has promised us. The 'God Will' stage of faith is characterized by the story of Abraham as found in Genesis 17:15-21. Practically speaking this stage is where Christians begin to see the real blessing of the abundant life. They have developed a relationship with the Lord through faith and have begun to be more victorious in their Christian walk. Such Christians have come to understand that Christianity is not so much a set of commands or laws but is a completely new way of living.

It is also a new way of thinking, because of their death to life relationship with the Lord. In this stage you should believe that God wants to help you and has your best interest in mind. The following characteristics can be seen in this faith stage.

- Unsure or confused at times.
- Victory occurs.
- Strength in self-weakness.
- Adventure in Christian Living.
- Inner Peace.
- Humility.
- Thankfulness.

The God Does Stage of Faith

The 'God Does' stage of faith is characterized by the story of Abraham as found in Genesis 22:1-19. This third stage is where we should all want to be in our faith walk. Those who attain this stage of faith experience the abundant life to the fullest (John 10:10). They have died to self. It is no longer they who live, but Christ truly lives and reigns in them (Galatians 2:20). Practically, this means that you have faith even if things don't go as you want or pray for. You must understand that there will be times when God is doing what is best for you when He answers prayers. Sometimes God is glorified when His answer is not what you really wanted. Regardless, His decision is always best for you, if you can just see past the moment. The following characteristics can be seen in this faith stage.

- Constant in praise.
- Constant in prayer.
- Ability to stand firm against the world.
- Bearing much fruit of the Holy Spirit
- Selfless lifestyle and attitude.
- Knows how God wants them to function in the body.
- Functions in the body where God Placed them.
- Accepting of God's answer or response.

Knowing that the presence of God is constant and that He will watch over us while we are in this body is at the very least reassuring. So, no matter how difficult things become, keep in mind that you are never alone and He does have a plan for you.

Promises: The Benefits of Faith

God's promises are both important and faith building for a Christian. There are many promises that were made for all Christians so that we can have a deeper faith and hold on to a greater assurance of what God has prepared for us. A promise is defined as an assurance given by one person to another that the former will or will not do a specific act. It also suggests reasonable grounds to hope or expect that such an act or event will or will not take place. As a child of God, you can look forward to, and thank God for His promises that He Gives to all would become believers.

All we need to do is believe in Him and follow His will and we will receive what He has promised. However, many of us do not even know what God has promised us.

Promises to Believers

The following promises are granted to all believers as they accept God's will in their lives. If you simply watch as you read the Bible you will find many promises that God has made to his people. You might want to keep track of all of God's promises by simply putting the letter 'P' next to those Scriptures. As you read you will have a constant reminder that God has made promises to you and will fulfill them.

Promises to All Believers	
Acts 2:38	The Promise of forgiveness of sins and the reception of the Holy Spirit.
Luke 24:49	The Promised of the Holy Spirit.
John 3:15	The Promise of Eternal Life.
John 8:32	The Promise that if you know the truth, the truth will set you free.
John 10:10	The Promise of an Abundant Life.
John 14:23	The Promise that God will love you if you love Jesus and keep his word.
2 Peter 1:3-4	The Promise that we will receive all things that pertain to life and Godliness.
1 John 5:14	The Promise that we will receive answers to our prayers.
James 2:5	The Promise of the Kingdom.
James 1:12 & Revelation 2:10	The Promise of receiving the Crown of Life for those who endure.
2 Peter 3:13	The Promise of a New Heaven and Earth
John 14:1-3	The Promise of a home in heaven for believers.

Cause and Effect Relationship

There are many other promises that can be found in the Bible. The point is that God did make promises and He has fulfilled His part of the bargain throughout time. He made many promises to Israel and all of those promises were fulfilled. However, He wasn't done yet. He has truly made some fantastic promises emphasizing His love and concern for each of us today. If we follow God's plan and if we fulfil our responsibility, these new promises that are found in the New Testament will come to fruition for us. To help you see the impact of these promises, let's consider the law of cause and effect. Remember, all of God's promises are conditional on your faith as it is manifested by obedience to the will of God. In essence this obedience is the cause of an effect (promise given in these cases). Let's look at some examples:

Acts 2:38-39 tells us to, "Repent and be baptized every one of you in the name of Jesus Christ for the forgiveness of your sins, and you will receive the gift of the Holy Spirit."

Cause: When you repent and are baptized in the name of Jesus Christ.

Effect: You will receive forgiveness of your sins and You will receive the gift of the Holy Spirit.

John 8:32 states: "and you will know the truth, and the truth will set you free."

Cause: When you now the truth

Effect: You will be set free.

John 14:23 states: "Jesus answered him, "If anyone loves me, he will keep my word, and my Father will love him, and we will come to him and make our home with him."

Cause: When you really develop a love relationship with Jesus.

Effect: The Father will love you.

We encourage you to look back at any of the promises that are shown in this chapter and that are important for you at this moment. Look at the cause and effect for each one. Do you have a role in the promise? If so, what is it? God's promises are there for the taking. It's up to you.

The point of looking at promises is that God provides them for us. If we are not mature enough to see what our response should be we can lose out of some very special blessings that God is offering. The saddest of all is that He is offering Salvation for all but if we do not 'keep His word', even after we have become a Christian, we may not receive the promise of an eternal home with Him. That is why it is important to get to a God does stage in your faith walk. You must know that He will do exactly as He has said if you simply follow the plan.

Scriptural Study

The following Scriptures may be underlined in yellow. Read each Scripture and determine the cause-and-effect relationships that exist. Make it personal.

Matthew 4:19	Mark 9:23	John 3:15-16
Matthew 5:3-9	Mark 11:22-23	John 6:35-37
Matthew 6:3-4	Mark 11:24	John 6:54
Matthew 7:8-9	Mark 16:16	John 7:17
Matthew 7:24-25	Luke 6:30	John 10:10
Matthew 10: 22	Luke 6:35	John 11:40
Matthew 11:28-30	Luke 11:8	John 14:13
Matthew 16:24-25	Luke 12:8	John 15:11
Matthew 16:27	Luke 18:7-8	Acts 20:35
Matthew 17:20		Revelation 22:14

Personal Reflection

List three things that you learned or that were reinforced that will help you see what you may need to do to grow your faith and/or enjoy the promises that God has given you.

1.

2.

3.

Part Three: Spiritual Growth

Your spiritual growth is one of the most important aspects of Christianity. God expects that you grow and become more mature spiritually. It's not really an option. You should be growing. Part three of this work will help you understand what needs to happen for you to grow. It will describe how your growth must be both internal and externally based. It will also provide you with information regarding stages of spiritual growth so that you can see where you are in that process at this moment.

- Brokenness and Christianity
- Sanctification, Holiness and Inner Change
- The Foundation of Spiritual Maturity
- Sanctification and External Change
- Keys to Spiritual Growth
- Stages of Spiritual Growth
- Does God Judge a Christian by His Work

Brokenness and Christianity

Chapter Six

When we speak of brokenness, we are speaking of that moment where you realize that you are sinful in nature and your only hope is if God will accept and forgive you. A very important part of the salvation process is called repentance. In the New Testament, the key Greek term for repentance is metanoia or μετάνοια. Mounce (2006) defines repentance or metanoia as "a radical, moral turn of the whole person from sin and to God." He says it is a radical turn. What does radical mean? The dictionary defines radical as, "change or action, relating to or affecting the fundamental nature of something; far-reaching or thorough." That means that repentance calls for a 'radical change within you', if you are to become one of God's children. What does that have to do with brokenness? Brokenness is evident when, as a non-Christian, you see that you have no chance at eternal life with God. You see that you are living a life in darkness and there is no spiritual life within you. All of your sin becomes evident, because even one sin can keep you out of heaven. Your only chance is to admit your weaknesses, your carnality, your sin and tell God that you want to live a new life in the light. When you become a Christian your ongoing 'job' is to recognize how there are still parts of your life that are dark. It should pain you to see those parts, but you should also have joy because God knows that you are continuing to ger rid of the old brokenness that caused you so much pain. Now you are on a journey towards minimizing your fleshly nature as you become more Christ like.

The catch is that you must want to step into his loving arms. You can no longer depend on your self-will, strength, might or anything else to develop or maintain your relationship with God. You must be willing to break yourself of all self-issues. The moment you believe you can maintain your relationship with God based on your self-will, etc. you have arrived at a critical moment in time where you will either accept that you need be broken or you will be distanced from the Father. You can't have it both ways. Before you became a Christian you were broken. You were in darkness and nothing you did was acceptable to God. When you become a Christian God expects that you will constantly seek to be broken. To understand this better, let's look at different aspects of brokenness.

- Symptoms of Not Being Broken
- Brokenness and Eden
- Brokenness and Spiritual Maturity
- The Holy Spirit and Brokenness

Symptoms of Not Being Broken

God seeks man's heart, he desires a broken heart (Psalm 51:16-17), not just a life of good works. There are several symptoms that can tell you if you haven't become broken. God wants you to acknowledge your pain, your sin, your self-wants, needs and desires and then give them all to Him. He can then make you a new creature; one of light instead of darkness. We only ask that you prayerfully consider your relationship to God in these areas and then seek to change if you truly desire God's life and holiness to flourish inside of you. You are not yet broken of self if:

- You trust in your own righteousness rather than in God's (Luke 18:9).
- You think you or your group are the only ones doing God's will (Luke 9:49).
- You are more interested in doctrinal correctness than in serving others (Mark 10:45). This does not mean that doctrinal correctness is not important, because it is vital. It does mean that love should be the focus when you are speaking or helping others regarding doctrine.
- You are more dedicated to recruiting than you are to redeeming the lost (Matthew 23:15).

- You major in minors. You make a big deal over issues that are really not that important or that are very difficult to take a true Biblical stand on, e.g., traditions.
- You are more concerned with image than you are with Christ-like character (Matthew 23:27ff).

If the above is what brokenness is not, then what needs to happen? The plan for brokenness began in Eden.

Brokenness and Eden

What does the Garden of Eden have to do with brokenness? It was in the Garden of Eden that man broke his relationship with God. Before the relationship was damaged man didn't know light from darkness or good from evil. All Adam and Eve knew was goodness. Their minds were set on God and Godliness in their lives. And then, man fell and starting with Adam and Eve man now knew good from evil. What were their thoughts like before they fell. In James it reviews what God's wisdom looks like. I suspect that is also what Adam and Eve believed and thought. In James 3:17 we are told,

> "But the wisdom from above is first pure, then peaceable,
> gentle, open to reason, full of mercy and good fruits,
> impartial and sincere."

This must be what their thoughts were like before the fall. Many other Scriptures identify the way God thinks and for a period of time man enjoyed such thinking. From the day of the fall onward God has wanted His people to have that same kind of mind again, but it could never happen again unless something dramatic happened. There had to be a new way to provide perfection. There had to be a new way that would produce not just outward obedience, but inward change that would lead man towards a perfect heart and mind.

In Genesis 3:15 God says,

> "I will put enmity between you and the woman,
> and between your offspring and her offspring;
> he shall bruise your head, and you shall bruise his heel."

This can be taken several ways. However, many scholars believe that this refers to the idea that Satan will damage Christ (bruise his heel), to the point of seeing Him die on the cross. However, the story doesn't end there. Jesus (the Son of God and the ultimate offspring of Eve) is raised from the dead and crushes Satan's head. He wins the age-old battle that began in Eden. Man now has an opportunity to become Godlike in purity and holiness once again and Jesus has provided a way for that to occur. Galatians 2:20 helps us see that more clearly.

"I have been crucified with Christ.
It is no longer I who live, but Christ who lives in me.
And the life I now live in the flesh I live by faith in the Son of God,
who loved me and gave himself for me."

Now that Christ has crushed Satan's hopes and aspirations to doom all men to hell, we now have an opportunity to become unblemished before God, if we truly become his child. One important piece to this puzzle is that we must die to our old carnal nature, the nature that knows sin and wrongdoing, and put on the very nature of Christ. It's no longer I, but Christ in me. This is the bottom line for brokenness. We must start by acknowledging that in and of our selves we have no relationship with God, nor can we be the person we need to be without Christ living through us. Our very nature without God causes damage to us and without God it can never be fixed. We were utterly broken.

Victory over self begins as we follow Biblical command and principle. We learn that there is one name above all others that can offer us victory supreme (Acts 4:12; Matthew 17:5). If you are to overcome yourself, you must have a true desire to make Jesus Christ Lord of your life (1 Peter 3:15). You make Jesus your Lord and Master by counting the cost and then by breaking yourself of all self-will and self-desire. You make Jesus' will your own by yielding yourself to Him. However, it is often difficult to overcome self. In the author's experiences, we have found that the more we understand something the easier it becomes to deal with it. As a result, we felt it would benefit you if you more clearly knew what you were trying to put into subjection; just what you were dealing with as you tried to become broken.

Specifically speaking it is the fleshly or lower nature (σάρξ or sarx in the Greek language) that is put into subjection when you put on Christ. As you put this nature into subjection through Christ, you develop spiritually (see 'The Holy Spirit and Brokenness in this work). As you allow God to will and work within and without for

His good pleasure and glory you begin to experience the Holy Spirit working to break the fleshly nature that is comprised of self-love, self-strength, self-will, self-confidence and self-cleverness (1 Peter 5:10). Each disciplinary working of the Holy Spirit is aimed at breaking your fleshly nature, the old nature, or as some stated your carnality (Philippians 2:13). Brokenness is the way of blessing, the way of fragrance, the way of fruitfulness where personal ministries, fruit of the Spirit and spiritual fellowship are set into motion.

Let's break down this concept of brokenness further so that we can have a greater understanding of it. Within the concept of brokenness there are two specific areas that we can look at. First, there is an external area of brokenness that tells us that we are to put away sins such as fornication, lying stealing, adultery, and such like. Most of us have heard preachers and teachers tell us how important it is to keep such things out of our lives. The reason we kept struggling so much with such sins is that we have been taught to deal with symptoms of spiritual disease and little has been said on how to effectively deal with the cause of such disease.

The second area of brokenness deals with the cause. To truly be an overcomer, you must deny self. You must die to self and let Christ reign in your life (Galatians 2:20). This is the most important thing that you could ever do. Many Christians can put away obvious sin of the first type, but often find it difficult or seemingly impossible to truly deny self and become Christ powered. The reason more Christians aren't experiencing the abundant life (John 10:10) is because they have not truly died to self. How can we expect to receive God's blessings when we seek those blessings on our own merit, through our own self-power and will. That was never God's intent. He wants us, not just what we can do. When you truly begin to grow spiritually you are finally allowing God to purge you and direct your life in the way He would have it go (Hebrews 12:5-6). This purging and direction are made evident in His Word and through the Spirit (Hebrews 4:12).

Brokenness and Spiritual Maturity

Many Christians today hold on to an illusion of spiritual maturity. This is one of the major problems that each of us must deal with in our Christian lives. True spiritual maturity cannot occur until we deny self. This occurs when we have put away self-direction, confidence, will, and strength and have given Christ control of our lives. The more we die to self and allow Christ to rule, the more we develop spiritually. Our spiritual maturity increases in direct proportion to the decrease we have in our focus on self, or how much we have died to self.

You should not allow yourself to be guided by our own desires for you are now a servant of the Master, by choice, and there can be only one head to rule (Ephesians 1:22). Are you to dictate your own lifestyle? Are you to make decisions based on your carnality? God forbid! Your entire life, second by second, should be Spirit guided. You should think as Jesus thought. If you by your will and might, live your life as 'God Wills', you are still living as a carnal Christian, one who has not yet died to self (John 12:25). In John 12:24-25 we are told,

"I tell you the truth, unless a kernel of wheat falls to the ground
and dies, it remains only a single seed.
But if it dies, it produces many seeds.
The man who loves his life will lose it,
while the man who hates his life in this world
will keep it for eternal life."

How do you become broken? How do you become like Jesus? The bottom line is that you must die to self, so that everything you internalize, think, do and say will be based on the will of the man and deity of Jesus Christ. You must radically turn from sin and all the hurt that it causes. You must turn to God. Now, let's get practical for a moment. If you are struggling with the die to self-concept but want to get there, you can do several things that will help you get started.

1. First, you must stop internalizing darkness, sin, or unholy characteristics. Keep in mind that what you read, what you see, what you hear eventually becomes part of you. When it becomes part of you, it is something that you think about; a lot (1 Thessalonians 5:21-22).
2. To truly die to self, you must acknowledge that you can't just put new wine (God like Characteristics) into an old wineskin (on top of our carnal nature). You must die to self. You must put away human weaknesses (Galatians 2:20).
3. You must also intentionally cut out dead works. Old ways must be put away (John 15:2). Sometimes it will take the help of others to accomplish this. That's okay. As

Christians we are here to help each other and build each other up.

4. You must seek to be good soil so that the very nature of Christ can grow inside of you. As you hear or learn of God's will, retain it and consistently make it part of your life (Luke 8:15). Think about it. Read it over and over. Pray about it a lot.
5. Develop a hunger for the Word. As you internalize His will, you will begin to mature into the likeness of Christ (John 15:7). This also means that you cannot be stagnant. You should be growing or maturing in Him (Hebrews 5:11-14).
6. Have a continuing desire to seek, serve and support your brothers and sisters and in your own way share this wonderful life with others (Galatians 35:13; 1 Peter 4:10).

The key to brokenness or true change occurs when you change from within. Without this change you are literally seeking be a Christian using your own power. That is not what God wants from us. There are several Scriptures that communicate this essential component to living the Christian life. Here are a few:

Concept	Scripture
Die to self and let Christ live inside of you.	Galatians 2:20
Renew your mind so as to better understand God's will.	Romans 12:2
Put others before self and look to what is best for them.	Philippians 2:3-4
Develop a servant heart as you humble yourself before God.	Philippians 2:5-8
Set our mind on Godly things, e.g., truth, honor, just, purity, lovely	Philippians 4:8
Seek out and allow the Fruit of the Spirit in your life, e.g., love, joy peace, patience, kindness, goodness, faithfulness, gentleness, self-control.	Galatians 5:22-23
Abide on the vine, bear much fruit and keep His commandments (summary).	John 15:
STS: These Scriptures may be underlined in yellow.	

All of the above are examples of what the internal aspect of a Christian should be like. The more you internalize these aspects or qualities, the more you will become like Jesus. In addition, as you internalize these qualities in your life journey you will begin to spiritually mature as you die to self.

The Holy Spirit and Brokenness

All Christians are sealed by the Holy Spirit when they respond in obedient faith to God's grace (Mark 16:16; Ephesians 1:13-14). Though all baptized believers possess the indwelling Holy Spirit, not all are spiritually mature. Many remain in an extremely carnal state, leading to a frustrating, self-defeated life (1 Corinthians 3:1). Yet the goal and ideal of the Christian life is to constantly be controlled by the Spirit. Christians as a whole know the relationship of the Inner man to man in general, but:

1. Fail to realize the function of the Spirit (see chapters in Part Four of this work), or
2. Interpret their own feelings or thoughts to be functions of the Spirit. This can lead to carnal thinking.

For inroads to thinking spiritually, you must realize that only spiritual understanding can penetrate the spiritual realm. Spiritual truths must be explained with spiritual phrases. You must employ spiritual means to reach spiritual ends. Your spirit's relationship with God's Spirit is the foundation for pleasing Him and bearing fruit. Even though you have already been delivered from sin, you must recognize that the Holy Spirit alone can grant you the strength required by your inner person. Any deception of self-pride, egotism or ignorance only grieves the Holy Spirit and yields continued immaturity (See the chapters on the Holy Spirit). God considers your inner man all important. It is not terminal like your outer body. He especially cares for your inner man by providing growth-oriented circumstances that:

1. Reveal who is genuinely Lord.
2. Breaks each individual of a self-reliant habit.
3. Causes us, whether sooner or later, to depend upon the Holy Spirit working through each individual's inner man.

We should all desire to become spiritually mature. In Luke 6:40 we are told that one of our primary objectives in life is to be like Christ. This is accomplished through the Holy Spirit. The Holy Spirit helps us mature as we follow God's guidelines so to speak.

Keep in mind that, we develop spiritual maturity in direct proportion to the degree we resist Satan who wants us to live life based on our carnality (self-wants, needs, desires, etc.). The more we listen.

to the Holy Spirit, the more we mature. Often Christians feel that they can make use of all the power that is available from the Holy Spirit when they are newborn Christians. This is not so! We must realize that the maturing process comes through testing and then resisting the temptations of spiritual forces of darkness.

Personal Reflection

List three things that you learned or that were reinforced that will help you understand and learn how to be broken in your life.

1.

2.

3.

Sanctification, Holiness and Inner Change

Chapter Seven

We know that Sanctification is an important part of our salvation process. It is something that the Holy Spirit does in Baptism when He Regenerates and Sanctifies you. It is where the seal of the Spirit is placed on you making you a child of God (See Grace and Salvation, 2022). But does sanctification stop there? Many struggle with the apparent truth that Sanctification has two basic meanings. First, Sanctification is something that is done to you when you are saved. That is discussed in greater detail in the work, Grace and Salvation, the first work of this series. Second, Sanctification is something that God calls for us to grow into. Many have chosen to call this Progressive Sanctification. This simply means that once we have become a Christian we should be seeking to become a holy or sanctified vessel for God. We must continue to seek out His nature and become more like Him. That is progressive sanctification or in other words, it is our seeking to be holy as He is holy.

Jesus expects man to focus on the internal-heart relationship and then the outside will be as God wants it (Matthew 23:26). When the focus is on the outside, you are simply seeking to look Godly, not be Godly. That does not mean that you shouldn't strive to do good. God expects right behavior or deeds. The point is that you should focus on the internal change and the external should become evident. Look at this Scripture.

"Strive for peace with everyone, and for the holiness
without which no one will see the Lord."
Hebrews 12:14

So, we are tasked with striving for holiness. There are a multitude of Scriptures that address this. We will share several of them in this chapter.

- Sanctification is a Process
- Desiring the Holy or Sanctified Life
- Heart Relationship
- Developing a Right Heart
- The Importance of the Heart or Mind
- The Holy Spirit Helps You

Sanctification is a Process

The word translated sanctification in the Bible also means a separation. It is used in the New Testament, according to Vine's Expository Dictionary of New Testament Words, of the separation of the believer from evil, and it is the result of obedience to the Word of God. Progressive Sanctification or spiritual growth is what gradually separates the people of God from the world and makes them more and more like Jesus Christ.

Everything we think (internal) and do (external) should be aimed at glorifying God in some way.

This aspect of Sanctification or holiness differs from justification in several ways. Justification is a one-time work of God, resulting in a declaration that you are "not guilty" or pardoned because of the work of Christ on the cross. Progressive Sanctification is a process that starts at salvation and continues throughout your life. Justification is the starting point of the line that represents one's Christian life; progressive sanctification (seeking to be holy) is the spiritual growth that begins at salvation and continues until you die.

There are several essential elements that must be present if you are to mature spiritually. We have already spoken of how faith plays a most vital role. It is because of this faith and resultant covenant relationship that you should have a desire to please your God and Creator through a lifetime of daily worship (Romans 12:1). What is the most primary and foundational element of worship that

God expects from His children? In Isaiah 43:7 we are told that we were created to glorify God. That means that everything we think (internal) and do (external) should be aimed at glorifying God in some way. This is the foundation, the bottom line for those desiring long-term relationship with God. With this in mind, there are four basic areas of spiritual worship you should consider in your daily life.

First, you need to work on being broken of self (dying to self) so that you can truly put on Christ-like qualities in thought, word and deed. The more you die to self and put on Christ, the more you will internalize Godly attributes. The more you internalize Godly attributes the more you will think about them. The more you think about them, the more you will speak about them. The more you speak about them, the more you will do or take action regarding that attribute. Think of it as a constant circle. If you keep this process up you will gradually become more holy or grow spiritually. Brokenness or dying to self appears to be the most difficult, yet most critical element of Christianity in the spiritual growth process. Yet, God expects us to follow His will not our own. The Proverb writer stated,

> *Brokenness or dying to self appears to be the most difficult, yet most critical element of Christianity in the spiritual growth process.*

"There is a way that seems right to a man,
but in the end, it leads to death."
Proverbs 14:12

Second, you must internalize the will of God by studying His Word, the Scriptures. You must know the Word so that you can learn how to live the life that God wants you to live. It also helps you see what you need to become and how to prepare for every spiritual battle that you will face. Actually, you face this battle more often than you realize. We all do. The work, Temptation and Testing (Crites) explains this in great detail and provides you with the ways you can be prepared to battle these spiritual forces of darkness. The chapter titled, *Knowing God's Word* in this work addresses this second step in the cycle of Spiritual Growth in detail. Understanding specific doctrine found in the Word is a very important step in the spiritual growth process (See Comparative Doctrine, Crites).

Third, you need to let God and the Holy Spirit direct your thoughts, words and deeds (Romans 21:28-29). You need to desire to live the holy or Sanctified Life. When you become a Christian you should want to be holy in everything you internalize, think, do and say because of what God has done for you. If you have faith in God and what He has offered, and have chosen to become a follower of Jesus, you should be excited. When you know that your eternal life is lined up with God's purpose and when you realize He has a home prepared for you, you should want to live a life of light, goodness and holiness. You should want to fill your holy and sanctified vessel by becoming more like Jesus; by inputting, thinking, speaking and doing those things that are Christ like.

When the Holy Spirit makes you holy; when He sanctifies you, you were given the opportunity to live a life of obedience to God with the Holy Spirit helping you. You have Christ as a model to live by. As a result, you should seek to internalize or become like Jesus and as you do you will grow in holiness; you will mature spiritually. As believers we are told to 'throw off everything that hinders and run with perseverance, 'fixing our eyes on Jesus' (Heb 12:1-3). Your response to your loving God for saving you should be your daily work of seeking to be holy. You need to want to be holy. You need to want to live a Sanctified life because of what He has given you. You should desire to grow spiritually. As we have already discussed, the becoming process is brought about by the gracious and continuous operation of the Holy Spirit who helps you to live the holy or sanctified life. In other words, sanctified living occurs as a result of action faith that comes from you wanting to present yourself as a holy instrument to God for the accomplishment of His holy purpose (Hebrews 12:14).

Sanctified living occurs as a result of action faith that comes from you wanting to present yourself as a holy instrument to God for the accomplishment of His holy purpose (Hebrews 12:14)

Last, you need to act with self-discipline or self-control to choose to do what the Bible teaches you to internalize, think, do and say (Titus 1:8). See the Cycle of Spiritual Growth chart on the next page.

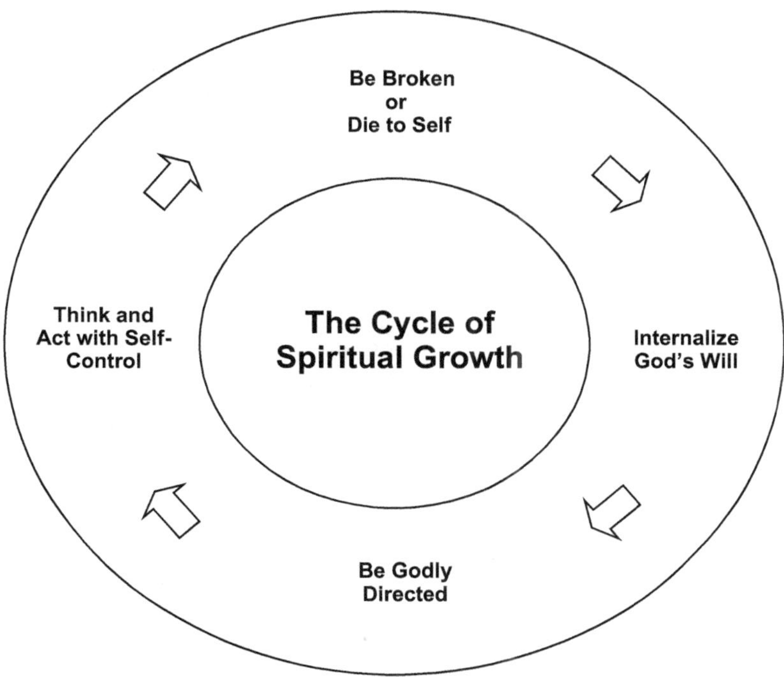

This process of spiritual maturity begins as you die to self and put on a Christlike nature. That is what the process of Sanctification is all about. If you look at the Cycle of Spiritual Growth shown above you will see that it actually continues on throughout your life if you are truly seeking to grow spiritually. With each cycle you should, 1) become more effective in dying to self wants, needs, and desires and focus more on Godly qualities. 2) develop a deeper understanding of the Bible; a deeper understanding of God's will for you as you study and grow, 3) become increasingly Godly directed. Instead of listening to your fleshly nature that calls you to sin, you listen more and more to God through the Word and as the Holy Spirit seeks to direct you in ways that lead toward a greater holiness. 4) Become more self-controlled in what you choose to internalize, think, say and do. Why? Simply because you are gradually putting on more and more of Christ's nature and it becomes easier and easier to think and act as God wants you to, based on the Scriptures that we all have access to.

Desiring the Holy or Sanctified Life

With this process in mind, let's take a closer look at this process of internal change that is necessary if you are to live a Holy life that God expects of all of us. To truly understand the importance of internal change in the Sanctification process, a good place to refer to is Jesus' conversation with the Pharisees as shown in Matthew 23:25-26.

> "Woe to you, scribes and Pharisees, hypocrites!
> For you clean the outside of the cup and the plate,
> but inside they are full of greed and self-indulgence.
> You blind Pharisee! First clean the inside of the cup and the plate,
> that the outside also may be clean."

Your internal change or development is a product of your covenant relationship with Christ and is not necessarily due to anything you do externally. However, it is the first thing that must be addressed, just as Jesus suggested to the Scribes and Pharisees. The good news is that you are given Jesus' righteousness and the Holy Spirit regenerates you and makes you a sanctified vessel for God (See Grace and Salvation by Crites). They do that for you when you become a Christian. It is a blessed gift bestowed upon all of us when we choose to be one of God's children. However, once they provide those wonderful gifts God does expect that we respond. What does that look like internally?

Simply stated, you must internalize the mind of Christ. This will occur as you grow into His likeness or put on His nature, which in turn is expressed in your behavior; how you act. In Philippians 2:5-8 we are told to be like Jesus. In the process of seeking to become more like Jesus we want to share four foundational areas that we all need to address. There are many others, but these are obviously a good start. They are:

1. As previously discussed, we must be broken, become nothing and die to self so that the nature of Christ can live through us (Galatians 2:20).
2. We must develop an attitude of humility, becoming like a servant just as Jesus did (Philippians 2:5-8). Servant attitudes was a quality that Jesus taught over and over. It was very important to Him.
3. We must become all things to all men looking to the interests of others rather than self (Philippians 2:3-4).

Putting the best interests of others above selfish wants, needs or desires is also extremely important.

4. As fellow Christians we must be of the same mind, have the same love, be in full accord and of one mind (Philippians 2:1-2). Being unified with brothers and sisters for a common goal or building each other up and sharing the life of Jesus is an important part of being a Christian.

Heart Relationship

God does want man to behave rightly (Deuteronomy 6:25 Luke 1:6), however, to maintain relationship, your behavior must be external evidence of your internal change.

God seeks relationship with man. It is due to God's initiative that the gracious gift of relationship was granted. He wants above all else a right heart relationship from man that will produce 1) a heart that seeks to be like his Son, and 2) a desire to consistently seek to be like Him in what you internalize, your thoughts, words and deeds as we follow the guidance of the Holy Spirit. To God, law or commandment keeping is only meaningful when it is an expression of an existing relationship with Him. However, just following laws or commandments without internal change will never bring about the relationship. Outside this covenant relationship with God, obedience to law or command has no meaning or validity whatsoever. As seen in Matthew 23 the Pharisees were following law but had no real heart relationship. They were only seeking to fulfill the law or commandments. God does want man to behave rightly (Deuteronomy 6:25 Luke 1:6), however, to maintain relationship, your behavior must be external evidence of your internal change.

Just as with Sanctification, there are two aspects of righteousness. First, it is a call for you to internalize the righteousness of Christ and then let what you learn be reflected in your behavior. In 1 Timothy 6:11 we are told, "But as for you, O man of God, flee these things. Pursue righteousness, godliness, faith, love, steadfastness, gentleness." Several other Scriptures speak to the point that we should seek to be or pursue righteousness, e.g., 1 John 3:7; 2 Timothy 2:22; Matthew 6:33. So, this form of righteousness is not Jesus' righteousness that we get when we become a Christian. It is different.

However, it is important to realize that in and of ourselves we will never be truly righteous. It is essential that we seek to be righteous, but true righteousness can never be obtained by what we do. In Romans 3:10 it says, "As it is written: "None is righteous, no, not one."

But, in 1 John 1:9 we are told that, "If we confess our sins, he is faithful and just to forgive us our sins and to cleanse us from all unrighteousness."

So, if no one is righteous, but God will forgive us and cleanse us of all unrighteousness, can we get some kind of righteousness that makes us perfect in His eyes? Let's take a closer look at this.

The first way some seek to be righteous is by the works of the Law; following the old law. To be justified, and declared righteous by the Law, is to seek to be righteous before God by keeping the Law of Moses. In other words, it is to be righteous by your own works. And the Bible says that no man can be justified before God by his own works. You can never do enough.

Nor can you maintain your righteousness by trying to please God by following Works of the Law or Works of Law (See Grace and Salvation by Crites for a deep explanation). Since utter perfection is beyond any human being, no one therefore can be righteous before God by works.

The other way, which is the only way, is to be justified by God through faith.

The more you go about internalizing Scriptures that talk about your righteousness because of Christ, the more you'll experience life spiritually, physically, and in your every area of life (see Proverbs 12:28).

The opposite is also true. The more you obey so as to be righteous, the more you'll experience death in your every area of life.

Back to our question: "How then can man be righteous before God?"

The answer: By becoming a child of God through faith as you follow God's will and seek to become like Jesus.

Developing the Right Heart

As previously discussed, brokenness is one of the hardest concepts to understand, yet it is one of the most fundamental and essential qualities for true spiritual growth. Before you can grow you must be willing to give Christ control of your heart. The church has far too often been more concerned with numbers of converts rather than in the training up of mature, Biblically sound, faith-oriented disciples. The result has been disastrous. Commitment has become the exception, not the rule. We feel that commitment, brokenness or a right heart that leads to Discipleship is absolutely essential for a growing Christian. Without this proper relationship converts are in danger of becoming one of many who claim Christianity in word and deed just as the Pharisees did in Matthew 23, but Jesus was not happy with them. Jesus called such men hypocrites; men who had a bad heart, they were not broken to self. They were not changed on the inside.

Now, let's take a look at two examples of man, sin and attitude of heart and how God has responded to these different situations in the past.

First Scenario: For the full story read 2 Samuel Chapters 11 and 12. It's the story of Bathsheba and David. How did God punish David for what he did?

Here we find David, a man after God's heart, committing two sins, **adultery and murder**. He had previously shown his love for God as well as a penitent, broken heart.

God forgave him!

Second Scenario: Read the story of Ananias and Sapphira who **lied** to God and the Holy Spirit. It's found in Acts Chapter 5. How did God punish them?

Ananias and Sapphira wanted to follow in the steps of Barnabas (Acts 4:36-37), by giving the money they received from the sale of their land; however, they gave only a part of the money and said they gave it all. It appears that they were motivated by pride or were seeking recognition for their act of good will. There is a suggestion that they wanted to appear more righteous than they really were.

They both died when the lied to God and the Holy Spirit.

Now you have to ask yourself, 'Why do you think God was less severe with David?' Maybe it had to do with his heart. Think about it. We suspect that was the case.

The Importance of the Heart or Mind

Consider these Scriptures that address how our heart or mind and what we think has an impact on being holy, living the sanctified life and seeking to be righteous as He is righteous.

Proverbs 23:7 (ASV) For as he thinketh within himself, so is he:
(American Standard Version)

What you think, which is defined by what you internalize on a day-by-day basis, determines your holiness and character. The more you think about something, the greater the likelihood it will become second nature for you. It will define you. That is why Paul was so specific about what Christians should do in Romans 12: 2. He wrote,

"Do not be conformed to this world,
but **be transformed by the renewal of your mind,**
that by testing you may discern what is the will of God,
what is good and acceptable and perfect.

Paul tells us that, as Christians we must be transformed by putting on the mind of Christ and denying self. It is through temptation and testing that we can grow. The more we are tested, the greater our ability will be to discern God's will in our lives.

It's extremely important to understand that when you are tempted to lie, gossip, speak harshly towards another, or any other sin you are in spiritual warfare. However, God and the Holy Spirit will turn temptation into a time of testing where you can grow spiritually if you make right choices. Testing is what allows you to grow. It also teaches you to better discern good from evil or godly from ungodly (see Temptation and Testing by Crites). This Scripture has also been shared before, but it is also important in context here. In Hebrews 5:13-14 we are told,

"for everyone who lives on milk is unskilled in
the word of righteousness, since he is a child.

But solid food is for the mature,
for those who have their powers of discernment trained
by constant practice to distinguish good from evil.

How does this Scripture apply in this situation? Simply stated, as you spiritually grow and mature when you face evil or temptation and make a godly decision. Whey you practice distinguishing good from evil and make proper choices, your ability to discern right from wrong is honed and becomes clearer for you in your day-to-day life. An important aspect of this is that you must develop a deeper understanding of the Word of God, which in turn helps you make spiritual decisions when you are tempted and tested.

The Holy Spirit Helps You

You must want to spiritually mature. You must be willing to transform your mind as shown above. You can accomplish this by walking in step with the Holy Spirit. If any change is to occur, if you are to grow spiritually, you must allow the Holy Spirit to work inside of you. We have already mentioned the concept of brokenness and it applies here. You cannot walk in the Spirit and depend on self. You must die to self so that Christ and the Holy Spirit can live in you (Galatians 2:20). One way to look at this concept is to see how this death relates to the fruit or the characteristics of the Holy Spirit.

The fruit of the Spirit is not just evidenced by your self-desire or self-power to act or become like Jesus. This fruit is evidenced when you give up self and let Christ and the Holy Spirit make minute by minute, day-by-day decisions in your life. The becoming process is not just acting, thinking or talking like Jesus and following the leading of the Holy Spirit. It's more than that. It is a dying to self in all areas of life so that Jesus can rule and the Holy Spirit can exhibit his character within you. Never allow yourself to be fooled into believing that you can become like Christ or exhibit the fruit of the Spirit without first dying to self. It you attempt to do this you are simply putting new wine in a nasty old wineskin. The end result is just not what God wants you to be.

With the above in mind, each type of fruit has a purpose, a role in the development of the new nature of a believer. As you grow and mature the fruit of the Spirit should be evident in your life as you die to self and let God and His Spirit work within you. Take a quick look at yourself. Have these become obvious in your life? Are you struggling with them? Look inside and see how much you are letting God and His Spirit work inside of you. To do that you need to understand what the fruit of the spirit looks like. What is the fruit of the Spirit and what does each Fruit mean as it relates to how God can work through you? In the next chapter we will specifically address what the Fruit of the Holy Spirit is and how it can be seen in your life.

Scriptural Study

Read each of the Scriptures and see how they apply to internal development. These Scriptures deal with Instruction or Christian Living and may be underlined in Yellow based on the Sharpening the Sword Study System.

Sanctification, Holiness and the Right Heart	
Matthew 5:8	"Blessed are the **pure in heart,** for they shall see God.
Luke 8:15	"As for that in the good soil, they are those who, hearing the word, hold it fast in an **honest and good heart**, and bear fruit with patience."
Acts 8:37	And Philip said, "If you believe **with all your heart,** you may." And he replied, "I believe that Jesus Christ is the Son of God."
Romans 2:28-29	"For no one is a Jew who is merely one outwardly, nor is circumcision outward and physical. But a Jew is one inwardly, and **circumcision is a matter of the heart**, by the Spirit, not by the letter. His praise is not from man but from God."
Romans 10:9-10	because, if you confess with your mouth that Jesus is Lord and **believe in your heart** that God raised him from the dead, you will be saved. For **with the heart one believes** and is justified, and with the mouth one confesses and is saved."
Galatians 2:20	"I have been crucified with Christ. **It is no longer I who live, but Christ who lives in me**. And the life I now live in the flesh I live by faith in the Son of God, who loved me and gave himself for me."

Ephesians 3:17	"So that **Christ may dwell in your hearts** through faith—that you, being rooted and grounded in love,
Ephesians 6:5-6	"Bondservants, obey your earthly masters with fear and trembling, **with a sincere heart,** as you would Christ, not by the way of eye-service, as people-pleasers, but as bondservants of Christ, **doing the will of God from the heart,"**
Philippians 2:3-5	Do nothing from selfish ambition or conceit, but in humility count others more significant than yourselves. Let each of you look not only to his own interests, but also to the interests of others. Have this mind among yourselves, which is yours in Christ Jesus,
1 Peter 3:15	but **in your hearts honor Christ the Lord as holy,** always being prepared to make a defense to anyone who asks you for a reason for the hope that is in you; yet do it with gentleness and respect,
STS: The Scriptures above may be underlined in yellow.	
Warning	
Hebrews 3:10	Therefore I was provoked with that generation, and said, 'They always go astray in their heart; they have not known my ways.'

So, in summary, the Bible does teach that what you put in your mind is important. When we become Christians, our minds should be transformed whereby we focus on thinking Godly thoughts which would create Godly actions. We should be watching out for unwanted, unspiritual or unhealthy thoughts that could bring you down or in time alter how and what you think. One step further suggests that you should want to think such spiritual thoughts for they bear fruit that shows you have truly sought to die to self and put on Christ's nature.

Dying to Self

When you are forgotten or neglected, or purposely set at naught, and you don't sting and hurt with the insult or the oversight, but your heart is happy, being counted worthy to suffer for Christ, that is dying to self.

When your good is evil spoken of, when your wishes are crossed, your advice disregarded, your opinions ridiculed, and you refuse to let anger rise in your heart, or even defend yourself, but take it all in patient, loving silence, that is dying to self.

When you lovingly and patiently bear any disorder, any irregularity, any impunctuality, or any annoyance; when you can stand face to face with waste, folly, extravagance, spiritual insensibility....and endure it as Jesus endured it, that is dying to self.

When you are content with any food, any offering, any raiment, any climate, any society, any solitude, any interruption by the Will of God, that is dying to self.

When you no longer care to hear yourself in conversation, or to record your own good works, or itch after commendation, when you can truly love to be unknown, that is dying to self.
When you can see your brother prosper and have his needs met, and can honestly rejoice with him in spirit and feel no envy nor question God, while your own needs are far greater and in desperate circumstance, that is dying to self.

When you can receive correction and reproof from one of less stature than yourself, and can humbly submit inwardly as well as outwardly, finding no rebellion or resentment rising up within your heart, that is dying to self.*

*Used with permission. Commitment to God's Design, Carl Brecheen and Paul Faulkner.

Personal Reflection

List three things that you learned or that were reinforced that will help you change internally as you seek to be holy in your day-to-day life.

1.

2.

3.

Sanctification and External Change

Chapter Eight

When you become a Christian, the Holy Spirit Sanctified you and made you holy. He made a holy vessel out of something that was dark and ungodly. Then he asks you to live a holy life, to press on, to seek to be holy as He is holy. Wait a minute. You are already sanctified and holy. Does something else need to happen so that I can be sanctified or holy? The key is that after you are saved and given the gifts of Adoption, Justification, Righteousness and Sanctification (made holy), you should want to seek holiness or righteousness in your behavior. You should desire to be more holy as you grow in Christ. You should want to listen to the Holy Spirit as he helps you see how you should be living your life each day. You should honestly seek to be what God has already made you; Justified (not guilty or pardoned), perfect because of Jesus' Righteousness, and Sanctified because the Holy Spirit has made you a holy vessel. Because of what God and the Holy Spirit have done for you, right living should naturally be evident in your life. That is part of what happens when you truly die to self and live for Christ.

You certainly can't sanctify or become holy by yourself. However, you can seek to live the holy or sanctified life. So, how do you do that? How do you live a sanctified life if you are already Sanctified? This is confusing for many. We have referred to sanctification as God and the Holy Spirit Sanctifying your vessel. At salvation you become a sanctified or holy person. However, New Testament writers then tell you that you must seek to be holy. What does that mean? It certainly appears to be obvious that God wants you to fill that vessel with holy living. He wants you to seek to be and act sanctified or holy. Why? Because your eternal life depends on it. Do the scriptures discuss this concept at all? Actually, there are multiple Scriptures that teach you to seek or strive to be holy. Hebrews 12:14 is a good example. It says,

"**Strive for peace with everyone, and for the holiness**
without which no one will see the Lord."

As a Christian you must strive for peace and holiness. That sounds like something you must do. The word for strive in the Greek is poudazo. In the New Testament Greek Lexicon, it means "to hasten, make haste to exert one's self, endeavour, give diligence." In Mounce's Expository Dictionary the word strive "generally indicates to strive to give one's best effort to do something." Several other works give the same kind of definition. This certainly communicates that the word strive is something that you do; diligently. Let's take it one step further. What does the word diligent or spoudazo mean in the Greek. In Mounce's Expository Dictionary the word spoudazo or diligent "indicates to strive to give one's best effort to do something." It's certainly eye opening when you dig into the Greek to understand words. In this case it makes it clear that striving is something that you do. It is something you attempt and work at because you know it is what God wants from you. Whatever Godly behavior you attempt to exhibit, is the right thing to do, based on Scriptures. You should be striving to understand what Godly behavior looks like, simply because your inner self is attempting to become what God wants you to become. That becoming should be evidenced in what you do, or how you speak and act.

That's an important statement because you are supposed to be allowing the Holy Spirit to work in you. It is clear that He works in you through your knowledge of the Word and through His providential working. If you don't have the knowledge of what God wants you to be like, it is difficult if not impossible to be and then do what He expects. Jesus made it clear that if you abide in Him you should be bearing (exhibiting) good fruit (John 15:4-5). Understanding what this looks like can help all of us as we seek to externalize our holy inner nature. Let's see at what this would look like in your behavior. There are six areas we will cover to help communicate this.

- Holiness is also a Behavioral Process
- Striving to Be Holy
- The Importance of Self-Control
- External Evidence of an Internal Change
- External Side of Bearing Fruit

Holiness is Also a Behavioral Process

After you become a Christian holiness and living the sanctified life is both an internal and external process. It begins when you become a Christian and doesn't end until you die.

Since we have these promises, beloved, let us cleanse ourselves from every defilement of body and spirit, bringing holiness to completion in the fear of God.
2 Corinthians 7:1

It is something that you seek to internalize and exhibit each day of your life. It is also a growth process. That is what 'striving' is all about. You don't go from being totally sinful in nature to fully mature spiritually when you are saved. There are multiple steps to growth along the way. You may fail at times, but you shake off the sin and seek or strive to do better with God's help. The more often you make decisions (Self-Control) that are holy, the more you will grow spiritually. It really is a spiritual maturational process that you are going through.

"For the grace of God has appeared, bringing salvation for all people, training us **to renounce ungodliness and worldly passions,** and to **live self-controlled, upright, and godly lives** in the present age."
Titus 2:11-12

Self-control is actually a fruit of the Holy Spirit that we all really need to have working inside of us as we make decisions each day of our lives. With self-control we have a much better chance of living a sanctified and holy life.

Sanctification is a Journey	
2 Corinthians 7:1	"Since we have these promises, beloved, let **us cleanse ourselves from every defilement of body and spirit, bringing holiness to completion** in the fear of God."
Ephesians 4:15	"Rather, speaking the truth in love, we are to **grow up in every way into him** who is the head, into Christ,"
Philippians 3:14	"I **press on toward the goal** for the prize of the upward call of God in Christ Jesus."
Colossians 2:7	"rooted and **built up in him** and established in the faith, just as you were taught, abounding in thanksgiving."
STS: The above Scriptures may be underlined in yellow.	

After looking closely at the Scriptures listed above what do you see? Are the Scriptures a suggestion of something you should think about doing or are they guidance that tells you what you should be doing? We think it's evident that the Scriptures are telling us what we need to do, or not do, if we truly love God and want to be like His Son. The more we are built up in him it will become more evident to ourselves and others that we are dying to self, being self-controlled and living the holy life.

Striving to Be Holy

You now have the opportunity to live a life of obedience as you 'listen' or pay attention to the nudges the Holy Spirit gives you. You have a model to live by and should seek to both internalize and externalize that model. In other words, seeking to be holy should occur daily in our lives as a result of action faith that comes from you wanting to present yourself as a holy instrument to God for the accomplishment of His holy purpose. Hebrews 12:14 suggests that if we don't strive to live a life of holiness we may not 'see the Lord'.

"Strive for peace with everyone, and for the
holiness **without which no one will see the Lord**."

The suggestion here is that we would not be accepted into heaven on the day of Judgment if we have not sought to be holy. That is a choice on our part. We should be making every effort, based on our level of spiritual maturity, to live a holy life, say, 'No' to ungodliness and seek to exhibit Godliness in our lives.

"For God has not called us for impurity, but **in holiness**."
1 Thessalonians 4:7

In Titus 2:11-12 we are told to renounce ungodliness and worldly passions (things we should not be doing). Let's look at the Greek language again. What does renounce or arneomai mean in the Greek. In Mounce's Expository Dictionary the word renounce or arneomai means "to deny," although it's wider range of meaning covers "disown, fail to confess, reject, say 'No,' refuse." It certainly sounds like we are to choose to not exhibit ungodly behavior. It is not consistent with the Holy and Sanctified life if we have truly changed inside. Christianity cannot just be an acknowledgement of Godliness. We must strive to remove ungodliness from our inner and outer selves and allow Godliness to become our daily norm.

The development of your internal holiness that leads to Holy or Godly behavior is a lifelong process. Let's take a closer look at self-control and how it plays a role in this process.

The Importance of Self-Control

One of the greatest problems many Christians have to deal with is that they know what they should believe, but for some reason they can't give their whole self to Christ. Feelings or attitudes for some reason or another keep them from giving up self completely. Some who are in this situation may have been 'devoted' Christians earlier in life, others may never have had that joy. At any rate, those who are at this point often consider the 'gifts of the world' as an alternative to what appears to be a miserable life as a Christian. They don't feel religious. At times they don't even want to be religious in any way. It's obvious that those who feel this way have been hurt, and that they continue to hurt in their daily life. They know enough about hypocrites to not want to be one. The problem is that we all sin and that doesn't make us hypocrites. That's important to understand. According to the Holman Bible Dictionary, hypocrite or hypocrisy is defined as, "(hih pahc' rih ssee) Pretense to being what one really is not, especially the pretense of being a better person than one really is." A Christian who is seeking to live the holy life but makes mistakes and sins is not a hypocrite. At the very least when we sin and fall, we should be facing the right direction. We get up and seek to be better. We desire to grow spiritually but we all will struggle at times.

You want to exhibit the right behavior based on Godliness. Yet sometimes you struggle with sin. Consider this. Should you try to be something on the outside that you really don't feel like on the inside? In regard to Christianity, the answer is YES! Keep in mind that you are constantly in a spiritual war and Satan's minions will do all they can to cause you to question yourself and yes, help you make poor decisions. Just remember that you have God's Spirit inside of you. He is seeking a way to work in your life. You have to be willing to search and discover God's will. You need to listen to the nudges of the Holy Spirit when you consider taking an action. Using self-control, you must constantly seek to make the decision to allow the Spirit to work even when you don't feel like it. Don't let Satan and his dark spiritual forces control you. God expects all of us to live a self-controlled godly life even when it is hard to do so. So, what do you do? The answer is in the Scriptures. Let's look at a few Scriptures that address this issue. You can find additional Scriptures that address this if you search the Bible.

Self-Control	
Galatians 5:23	Gentleness, **self-control;** against such things there is no law (Fruit of the Spirit).
2 Timothy 1:7	for God gave us a spirit not of fear but of power and love and **self-control.**
2 Peter 1:5-6	For this very reason, make every effort to supplement your faith with virtue, and virtue with knowledge, **and knowledge with self-control**, and self-control with steadfastness, and steadfastness with godliness,
Titus 1:8	but hospitable, a lover of good, **self-controlled,** upright, holy, and **disciplined**
Titus 2:11-12	For the grace of God has appeared, bringing salvation for all people, training us to renounce ungodliness and worldly passions, and to live **self-controlled,** upright, and godly lives in the present age,
Proverbs 25:28	A man without **self-control** is like a city broken into and left without walls.
STS: The above Scriptures may be underlined in yellow.	

Being disciplined and self-controlled is what God expects of all of us. Yes, we must seek to make decisions to do what is right and behave in right or Godly ways. The Holy Spirit does not force us to behave correctly. He can help, just as knowledge of right and wrong behaviors is evident if you read the Bible.

External Evidence of an Internal Change

Some people state that you cannot work to get your salvation, nor should you have to work to maintain your salvation. We focused on the first part of the statement in the first book Grace and Salvation. Let's look at the second part of this belief; you should not have to work, do or follow commands to maintain your salvation. Is that true or not? What does the Bible say? In the process of sanctification or holiness, external change should be occurring as a result of internal change. In other words, people should see you grow in how you act towards them and others. So, Holiness and living the sanctified life is not just an event, it truly is a process. It is something that you seek to internalize and if you have it should be evidenced each day of your life by how you act. That is the process of spiritual growth. Keep in mind that we all have bad days, but we acknowledge them, confess our sins and grow from our mistakes. There are several Scriptures that describe a process or ongoing actions that we should intentionally be taking as a Christian. External evidence is secondary, but just as important to God as is your internal change. If you don't show your internal qualities by your actions you may not have truly changed. They are connected. They are inseparable. You can't just internalize these Godly qualities; they need to shine forth into how you speak and act in your day-to-day life. Here are some Scriptures that discuss the need to exhibit Godly behaviors or qualities in your life.

> *In the process of sanctification or holiness external change should be occurring as a result of internal change.*

External Evidence or Sanctification Made Visible	
Concept	**Scriptures**
Two Types of External Evidence	
1. Verbal: Through him then let us continually offer up a sacrifice of praise to God, that is, the **fruit of lips** that acknowledge his name.	Hebrews 13:15
2. Behavioral: Do not neglect to **do good** and to share what you have, for such sacrifices are pleasing to God.	Hebrews 13:16

Verbal Evidence	
To **speak evil of no one, to avoid quarreling,** to be gentle, and to show perfect courtesy toward all people.	Titus 3:2
Know this, my beloved brothers: let every person be quick to hear, **slow to speak, slow to anger.**	James 1:19
Rejoice in the Lord always; again I will say, rejoice. **Let your reasonableness be known to everyone.** The Lord is at hand; do not be anxious about anything, but in everything by prayer and supplication with thanksgiving let your requests be made known to God.	Philippians 4:4-6
Behavioral Evidence	
Repay no one evil for evil, but give thought to do what is honorable in the sight of all.	Romans 12:17
You yourselves are our letter of recommendation, written on our hearts, to be known and read by all.	2 Corinthians 3:2
Let not sin therefore reign in your mortal body, to make you obey its passions.	Romans 6:12
Every athlete **exercises self-control in all things**. They do it to receive a perishable wreath, but we an imperishable. So I do not run aimlessly; I do not box as one beating the air. But I **discipline my body and keep it under control,** lest after preaching to others I myself should be disqualified.	1 Corinthians 9:25-27
Whoever **humbles himself** like this child is the greatest in the kingdom of heaven.	Matthew 18:4
STS: The above Scriptures may be underlined in yellow.	

God does want you to change when you become a Christian. The Holy Spirit regenerates you and makes you a holy vessel when he sanctifies you. We like to say that you become a Holy Vessel for God, whereas before you became a Christian your vessel was filled with darkness. You are now of God, and He wants your holiness to shine for all to see in how you speak and act in your life.

There are several other Scriptures that address how we should act, simply because it is the Godly thing to do. Here are a few examples that can help you see how God wants you to act or behave in your day-to-day life. Here are some other Scriptures that can help you see how if you have truly changed on the inside, you should be exhibiting it on the outside.

Sanctification Made Practical	
Concept	**Application**
Unselfishness	Help one another (Galatians 6:2; Romans 15:1-3). Edify, help others grow spiritually (1 Corinthians 8:9-13; 9:10).
Humility	Count others better (Romans 12:3; Philippians 2:13). Consider all others as equals (Romans 12:16; Hebrews 12:14).
Peace	Live peaceably with all men, give no occasion for offense (Romans 12:18; 2 Corinthians 6:3; Hebrews12:14).
Love	Bless your enemies, be tenderhearted and forgiving as Christ forgave and pray for all men (Matthew 5:44).
Purity	Guard your thoughts, no corrupt words, I hate evil (Philippians 4:7-8; Ephesians 4:29; Jude 23).
Joy and Contentment	Continually give thanks in all things, rejoice in your eternal hope, be content (Romans 8:28; Philippians 4:4-6).
Deportment	Live blamelessly before the world, being an example of Christ's life (Romans 12:17; 14:162 Corinthians 3:2).
Words	Speak evil of no one. Believe the best of everyone. Be swift to hear, slow to speak. Praise God verbally (Titus 3:2; James 1:19; Hebrews 13:15-16).

Temperance or Self-Control	Not obeying the dictates of the flesh. Instead, have such under control (1 Corinthians 9:25-27; Romans 6:12).
Good Works	Zealous in the practice of doing good unto all men (Galatians 6:9-10).

There is a great psychological truth that applies to such situations. If you wish to change an attitude or feeling confront it behaviorally. That is, you must act in a way that is conducive to mature Christianity. You must act out what you believe is right, even if you don't 'want' to do the right thing in the moment. That's self-control or self-discipline. It is your fleshly nature that is pulling you away from doing what is good and right. You may not feel like following the nudges of the Holy Spirit who is trying to help you but it will make you and those around you feel better once you've begun the journey and have given it time to work.

Let's look at the external side of bearing Fruit of the Holy Spirit. This is actually very important. Most of us have heard the phrase bear fruit. As a Christian you should be bearing fruit. What does that mean and how does that apply to how we act or behave as Christians. Let's go to the Scriptures again to find out more about fruit bearing.

The External Side of Bearing Fruit

We have already discussed internal change. However, addressing the Fruit of the Spirit is an important aspect of change; both internal and external. So, does bearing fruit have anything to do with how we act or behave? Yes, it does. However, those external actions should be based on the internal fruit you have allowed to grow within you as you die to self and allow the Holy Spirit to work inside you. Should we be doing good things, acting in certain ways based on what we are becoming mentally or spiritually? Of course, you should. The behaviors others see is the actual fruit. The spiritual and mental change is the seed that allows the fruit to be evident in your life. If you are not planting the seeds of love peace patience, kindness and much more there is a good chance you will not exhibit it. The seeds are often the Scriptures that address the fruit of the Spirit. You must die to self and plant those seeds with the

> *The Holy Spirit can only work through you as you die to self and allow Him to guide you towards a Godlike nature.*

Holy Spirit's assistance so that you can change internally. If you simply exhibit these Godly behaviors but don't change internally, you are just acting out God's commands. God expects your actions to be a result of your internal change. Let's assume that since you are reading this work, you truly have begun the process of dying to self and are seeking to let God work on your life so that your behavior will represent Him.

The key Scripture that addresses the Fruit of the Holy Spirit is found in Galatians 5:22-23. Paul writes,

> "But the fruit of the Spirit is love, joy, peace, patience, kindness, goodness, faithfulness, gentleness, self-control; against such things there is no law."

Fruit of the Spirit The External Evidence		
Love	**Greek: Agape**	**Scriptures**
Unconquerable benevolence, undefeatable good will. Seeks only the highest good of its fellowmen.		1 Corinthians 13:13 Colossians 3:14 Romans 13:10
Goodness	**Greek: Agathosun**	**Scriptures**
Generosity that flows from the heart that is kind. Being generous and liberal even to those who don't deserve it.		Ephesians 5:9 2 Thessalonians 2:17
Joy	**Greek: Chara**	**Scriptures**
The distinguishing atmosphere of the Christian life. It fills every circumstance every characteristic of man at all times because of his eternal hope.		Philippians 4:4 1 Thessalonians 5:16 John 15:11
Kindness	**Greek: Chrestotes**	**Scripture**
Treating others the way God has treated us.		Ephesians 4:32 Colossians 3:12 Romans 2:4
Self-Control	**Greek: Egkratela**	**Scriptures**
That which makes a man capable of living in the world, yet able to remain unspotted by it.		1 Corinthians 9:25 2 Peter 1:6
Peace	**Greek: Eirene**	**Scriptures**
Serenity, tranquility, and contentment, of a life that is completely happy and secure in God. It is right relationship in every life relationship.		1 Peter 3:11 2 Peter 3:14 John 15:11

*Patience	Greek: akrothumia μακροθυμία	Scriptures
Patience and endurance. To delay one's anger. An attitude toward people and events. Never losing patience with people, always holding hope. Never admits defeat, but holds to hope and faith as God works.		Ephesians 4:2 Colossians 1:11 2 Peter 3:15
Faithfulness	**Greek: Pistis Πίστις**	**Scriptures**
Belief, trust, confidence....Faithfulness, trustworthiness (Mounce).		1 Corinthians 4:2 Luke12:42 Luke 19:17
Meekness	**Greek: Praotes πραότης**	**Scriptures**
Meekness....is the fruit of power. Meekness is the opposite of self-assertiveness and self-interest; it is equanimity [poise, self-control, calmness] of spirit that is neither elated or cast down, simply because it is not occupied with self at all (Vines).		2 Timothy 2:25 Titus 3:2 James 3:13 1 Peter 3:4

Definitions come from Mounce's Complete Expository Dictionary of Old and New Testament Words & Vines Complete Expository Dictionary of Old & New Testament Words, by Vine, Unger and White.

Obviously, the Holy Spirit is attempting to lead us to exhibit the qualities or behaviors listed above. Each of the fruits mentioned above is from the Holy Spirit. It is His character so to speak. Since He is within you He will seek to urge you exhibit those wonderful traits. However, the Holy Spirit can only work through you as you die to self and allow him to gently guide you towards a Godlike nature. Are you listening to Him and what the Bible teaches or are you focusing on your personal wants, needs, or desires. Look back over these characteristics and try to determine how well you are allowing these to be part of your everyday life.

A Lack of Fruit Means

What does a lack of fruit mean? Christians who do not produce the kind of fruit that is shown above can be setting themselves up for spiritual problems. Often such Christians are either focusing on self or are babies as Christians. They are still in the learning stage and simply need guidance. If someone were to disciple the young

Christian, he could grow and become a mature disciple who exhibits the fruit of the spirit daily.

What about the person who either doesn't want to grow or who doesn't have the help he or she needs? There are numerous Scriptures that speak about growing in your Christianity. How does Jesus respond to those who don't grow or who alter his plan in some way? Let's see his response to the Pharisees who were claiming to know and follow God but in reality were not. Read Matthew 23 when you have time. Jesus communicates clearly what he wants and doesn't want from us. We want to focus on three of the 'Woe's' found in this chapter. Read each one of the Scriptures shown and determine what the underlying teaching that Jesus is teaching. It is critical for all Christians to understand this principle. Look at the following Scriptures and look for the underlying Principle communicated by Jesus in each of the verses.

Internal and External Growth Necessary **Application for All Christians**	
Matthew 23:23	"Woe to you, scribes and Pharisees, hypocrites! For **you tithe mint and dill and cumin, and have neglected the weightier matters of the law: justice and mercy and faithfulness.** These you ought to have done, without neglecting the others.
Matthew 23:25	"Woe to you, scribes and Pharisees, hypocrites! For **you clean the outside of the cup and the plate, but inside they are full of greed and self-indulgence.**
Matthew 23:27	"Woe to you, scribes and Pharisees, hypocrites! For you are like whitewashed tombs, which **outwardly appear beautiful, but within are full of dead people's bones and all uncleanness.**

We believe the Scriptures above and below accurately share God's truth about internal and external growth. It also suggests that if we don't strive to live a life of holiness we may not 'see the Lord'. The Scriptures clearly state that if we exhibit 'good' behavior for the 'wrong' reason we are not acceptable to God. It also states that we must be growing spiritually. It is an expectation. As Christians, we should be making every effort, based on our level of spiritual maturity, to live a holy life and say, 'No' to ungodliness (Hebrews 12:14; 1 Thessalonians 4:7; Titus 2:11-12). As we grow into a

Godly nature we should also be exhibiting more Godly behavior. That's God's plan. He wants all of us to become mature Christians.

Key Information Found in this Chapter

1. When you become a Christian, the Holy Spirit Sanctified you and made you holy. He made a holy vessel out of something that was dark and ungodly.
2. The key is that after you are saved and given the gifts of Adoption, Justification, Righteousness and Sanctification (made holy), you should want to seek holiness or righteousness in your behavior. You should desire to be more holy as you grow in Christ.
3. After you become a Christian holiness and living the sanctified life is a process. This aspect of sanctification or holiness is often called Progressive Sanctification by many.
4. Christianity cannot just be an acknowledgement of Godliness. We must strive to remove ungodliness from our inner and outer selves and allow Godliness to become our daily norm.
5. Using self-control you must constantly seek to make the decision to allow the Spirit to work even when you don't feel like it.
6. In the process of sanctification or holiness external change should be occurring as a result of internal change.
7. If you wish to change an attitude or feeling confront it behaviorally. That is, you must act in a way that is conducive to mature Christianity. You must act out what you believe is right, even if you don't 'want' to do the right thing in the moment.
8. External actions should be based on the internal fruit you have allowed to grow within you as you die to self and allow the Holy Spirit to work inside of you.
9. As Christians, we should be making every effort, based on our level of spiritual maturity, to live a holy life and say, 'No' to ungodliness.

Personal Reflection

List three things that you learned or that were reinforced that helped you understand the importance of both God and others seeing your acts of holiness or the Fruit of the Spirit in your daily life.

1.

2.

3.

Keys to Spiritual Growth

Chapter Nine

In the previous chapter we mentioned spiritual growth or maturity several times. Now it's time to look at this important aspect of Christianity more closely. We believe that Sanctification after salvation is a process, but how does it work? How does spiritual growth apply to all of what you have read up to this point? Does God really expect us to grow or is it okay to stay where you are spiritually for a long time? Does he just want us to accept Jesus into our lives and then be apathetic, non-involved, not maturing? We believe that the Bible does teach us that God wants us to grow spiritually. He not only wants you to grow. He also expects it. He expects that all Christians will grow up and become a mature Christian. This maturation process is you seeking to become more holy as you mature. It occurs as you daily live the sanctified life allowing the nature of Christ to live in you and become more like you as time goes by. It occurs as you use self-discipline to put off your sinful life and seek to truly be the holy vessel of God that He made you. And yes it occurs when you take actions or follow God's will in your daily life. We must do what the Bible tells us to do. The following will be covered in this chapter.

> *God doesn't expect you to be Perfect, because He has already given you His Son's perfect righteousness. What He wants is for you to Grow and Mature. He wants you to seek to become what He has already made you.*

- Before Thought is What's Most Important
- Thought and Spiritual Growth
- Capturing Unwanted Thoughts
- Words and Spiritual Growth
- Actions and Spiritual Growth
- Self-Judgment and Self Control
- Christian Confession and Spiritual Growth

Before Thought is What's Most Important

You may be asking what we mean by this. If so, it's a good and very important question. This was discussed in the Grace and Salvation book, but it also fits perfectly here. I want to talk about your mind and how it works. This is actually very important. Keep in mind that God created how your mind works. He knew there were both benefits and some pretty significant negatives that could come into play because you have choice in what you think, so He addressed how we should use our mind in the Bible. To begin with, where do you think your thoughts come from? The question you need to ask is, what triggers, or in a sense directs, what you think on a minute by minute, day-by-day basis? Do you know where what you think comes from? The answer is that it comes from what you internalize. What you become, what you are on the inside, occurs as a result of everything that you read, listen to and watch. Yes, it comes from the radio, television, movies or anything else that you see or hear in your everyday life. It also includes what you hear when you listen to others. That is why it is important to read the Scriptures, study them, meditate on them more often than you internalize that which is not Godly. We are flooded by ungodly messages daily. For most people it would be an impossible task to not be faced with unhealthy or unholy messages multiple times in a day. God knew this also, so He gave us some ways to counter this.

> *What you become, what you are on the inside, occurs as a result of everything that you read, listen to and watch.*

In Psalms 119:1-3. It says, "Blessed are those whose way is blameless, who walk in the law of the Lord. Blessed are those who keep his testimonies, **who seek him with their whole heart**, who also do no wrong but walk in his ways!"

How does that apply here? What does 'who seek him with their whole heart' mean? It simply goes along with the premise that you need to put God's Word in your heart, or in your mind. Think of your mind as being a plowed field ready to have something planted in it that will grow. If you plant ungodly, carnal, fleshy thoughts, images or words in your mind, those thoughts, images or words will grow and you will see them come to fruition in how you speak and act. If you plant Godly characteristics or Scriptures that help you deal with life, that is what the garden in your mind will grow. Let's look and see what God wants us to be thinking.

Thought and Spiritual Growth

What we feed our mind or plant in the garden of our mind determines what our thoughts will be. So, yes you must clean up your garden. It is essential that you stop planting seeds of carnality. In other words, we cannot continue to choose to internalize ungodly beliefs, teachings, etc. The Bible is filled with Scriptures that tell us to think Godly or spiritual thoughts. The reason these Scriptures were written is because what you become is predetermined to a great degree by what you have sent your brain over time. Whatever is planted in the garden of your mind is what you will automatically think, say and ultimately do. Even more important, what you plant in your garden defines who and what you are becoming. If you think Godly thoughts you are setting yourself up to grow spiritually. Let's look more closely at this concept.

> *Whatever is planted in the garden of your mind is what you will automatically think, say and do.*

Paul addressed this important issue in Romans 12:2. He wrote,

"Do not be conformed to this world, **but be transformed by the renewal of your mind**, that by testing you may discern what is the will of God, **what is good and acceptable and perfect.**"

Let's focus on the phrase transformed by the renewal of your mind. How does that occur? Here is the key. You must seek to be transformed into the likeness of Jesus as you internalize His characteristics and His will. How do you transform? First, you must die to self wants, needs, desires, (Galatians 2:20). Self-will or power is not the solution. Second, you must 'set your mind on things above, not on earthly things' (Colossians 3:1-2). What are the Scriptures that communicate this belief? Let's start with a closer look at Colossians 3:1-2.

Since, then, you have been raised with Christ, [have become a Christian], [then you should] **set your hearts on things above**, where Christ is, seated at the right hand of God. **Set your minds on things above, not on earthly things.**
Colossians 3:1-2

"Finally, brothers, whatever is **true**, whatever is **honorable**, whatever is **just**, whatever is **pure**, whatever is **lovely**, whatever is **commendable**, if there is any **excellence**, if there is anything **worthy of praise, think about these things**."
Philippians 4:8

Why do you want to follow the advice of the Scriptures shown above? The answer is that God expects a transformation. He wants you to think Godly thoughts, not carnal thoughts. He knows that what you think you become (Proverbs 23:7) and that's why He wants you to 'think' Godly thoughts.

God knows that whatever you set your mind on or think about, you will become. Whatever you choose to plant in the garden of your mind is what defines what you become. So, ultimately one of your greatest goals for spiritual growth is to flood your mind with Godly, spiritual thoughts and knowledge. As much as is possible, you must avoid reading, listening to or seeing anything that is ungodly. You should be focusing on images and words that transform your mind into a mind that is Christlike.

Capturing Unwanted Thoughts

None of us are perfect. What happens if you think thoughts that you shouldn't? What if you have allowed something into the garden of your mind and it is damaging you spiritually? How do you deal with that? Does the Bible suggest a course of action? Are there any suggestions or strategies that you can use to help you rid your mind of ungodly beliefs, ideas, etc.? Yes there is! God shares that you must take captive unwanted or ungodly thoughts.

"We destroy arguments and every lofty opinion raised against the knowledge of God, and **take every thought captive to obey Christ**,"
2 Corinthians 10:5

So, you must intentionally take every thought captive to obey Christ in your daily life and in doing so you destroy such thoughts or arguments. It is essential that you fill your mind with Scriptures that can help you minimize the negative impact of dark and unhealthy thoughts. You must be careful about what you plant in the garden of your mind. Obeying Christ, filling your mind or garden with Godly, spiritual, healthy thoughts will make you healthier physically, mentally and spiritually. Earlier in this chapter we discussed that what you think, you become. What you focus on, you become. So, when you capture an unwanted spiritual thought, it is not best to 'think about it a lot'. However, that doesn't mean that you shouldn't do something about it. When a thought crosses your mind or if it is an ongoing unspiritual thought that seems to stick in your mind you must capture it. Once captured or identified you must determine how to address it.

Unless you live a perfect life in your thoughts and actions, you will experience unwanted unspiritual thoughts. So, what do you capture? What do you ignore? What do you do with a thought that is damaging or unspiritual? Let's take a closer look at capturing unwanted thoughts and what can be done with them.

Do Not

Do not keep thinking about the carnal, unspiritual thought you have identified and hopefully captured. Keep in mind that if you continue to think about the unwanted thought you are planting unspiritual weeds that grow up and become harder to deal with.

Do not visualize your sin or carnal thought even when you are trying to be rid of it. It causes you to desire them more or at the very least distorts your spiritual perspective. You must stop visualizing sin.

Do not try to change your behavior unless you change your thinking first. Romans 12:22 Your behavior will be transformed as you renew your mind.

Do

Look at the thought. Identify how it is unspiritual or unhealthy. Use a Scripture if possible. Acknowledge that the thought as being unhealthy, carnal, unspiritual. If it is truly unhealthy or unspiritual, pull it out of your garden, get rid of it and think the Godly opposite (Philippians 4:8).

You could also visualize the spiritual opposite. What does that look like? What is the spiritual application that takes the place of the unspiritual thought. See it in your mind. Use a technique called 'Going to the Movies' (Foundations, 2016). Simply see the spiritual opposite played out in your mind over and over. If the issue is a serious problem. Play it out each morning several times before you get out of bed. Play it during the day. Play it at night before you go to bed. This is a visual flooding technique that helps you destroy the old unspiritual thought. In Joshua 1:8 we are basically told that if we don't put the Word of God into practice in our minds, our actions will never be Godly.

You must also identify where the unspiritual thought originated in your life. If it is a person, a book, an author, a presenter, etc. you should minimize your contact. You may want to remove that person from your social circle.

To truly deal with this, you must not just be willing to focus on righteousness instead of sin in your thinking. You should desire it. In 2 Corinthians 5:21 we are told that because we are in him, Jesus, we can become the righteousness of God. We can think what we ought to think and be what we ought to be. He has shown us through His word what that looks like.

As stated before, you will see and hear many things in a given day that are ungodly, negative and hurtful in one way or another. In psychology a method called flooding is very useful in helping people address multiple issues. In this case you could use flooding to intentionally internalize more positive or Godly messages for your garden than negative or messages of darkness. Five godly to one ungodly would be a great ratio. For every ungodly message your brain acknowledges, attempt to find five Godly messages. For example, say a Scripture five times to counter a negative or ungodly thought.

One of your greatest goals for spiritual growth is to flood your mind with Godly, spiritual thoughts and knowledge.

Another way of dealing with unwanted sinful, carnal thoughts is to utilize the Refocus Strategy shown on page 270 of this work.

Here is an adaptation of the Refocus Strategy. If a carnal, fleshly, sinful thought comes into your mind you can immediately capture or demolish it by using one of several possible strategies. Using the Refocus Strategy you would simply focus on a selected Scripture or statement that you can say over and over to help you keep the garden of your mind free of carnal 'weeds'. As soon as an unwanted, ungodly thought emerges say,

God, may your light shine through me destroying darkness and filling me with light.

Pick a Scripture, create your own statement. You could also create an image of Jesus sending a beam of holy light that covers you and destroys darkness. Whatever works for you. Say it over and over until you overcome the unwanted thought. Just remember, DO NOT tell the intrusive thought or image to go away. DO NOT talk or reason with the image. DO NOT argue with or get disturbed by the thought or image. WHY? Because every time you talk to the thought or image you make it more powerful....more real. Simply replace it with a Godly image, Scripture or statement.

Keep in mind that your mind is the battlefield where your spiritual life is won or lost. You must capture or destroy unholy thoughts. Cast them down and make sure that your thoughts are obedient to Jesus (2 Corinthians 10:5).

There are several other Scriptures that suggest other ways you can capture and get rid of unwanted or ungodly thoughts. Here are a few: The bold is for emphasis.

"**Be still** and know that I am God."
Psalm 46:10.

Being still is hard to do, but it provides mental, physical and spiritual benefits when you stop and focus on being still. How can you do that? There are several ways. There are two that obviously benefit you spiritually. First, you could pray. Identify the righteous opposite of your captured thought or behavior and pray for God to help you increase that righteous thought in your daily life. (See the chapter on prayer). Second, meditate on God's word (See the chapter on meditation). Pick a scripture that counters the captured thought and memorize it. Or you can put it on your phone and read it several times a day. As opportunity arises, say the verse over and over in your mind. You could also simply think about one of

God's amazing attributes. There is research that shows that what you actively put in your mind becomes more and more a part of you as you internalize it. So, if you are going to think something over and over, make sure that it is something that is going to benefit you spiritually, mentally or physically. If you want to better understand this concept the workbook titled, Foundations (Crites, 2016) addresses this in detail.

Words and Spiritual Growth

You also need to be careful with your words. Words that you use actually shape you. They can draw people to you and help them or your words can be damaging to self or others. Let's look at some of the Scriptures that discuss how your words can cause difficulties.

"but no human being can tame the tongue. **It is a restless evil, full of deadly poison.**"
James 3:8

"Do you see a man **who is hasty in his words**? There is more hope for a fool than for him."
Proverbs 29:20

"The one who **conceals hatred has lying lips**,
and whoever **utters slander** is a fool.
Proverbs 10:18

"If one **gives an answer before he hears**,
it is his folly and shame."
Proverbs 18:13

"Even a fool who keeps silent is considered wise; when he closes his lips, he is deemed intelligent."
Proverbs 17:28

"Whoever keeps his mouth and his tongue
keeps himself out of trouble."
Proverbs 21:23

"Whoever guards his mouth preserves his life;
he who opens wide his lips comes to ruin.
Proverbs 13:3

"Whoever restrains his words has knowledge, and he who has a cool spirit is a man of understanding."
Proverbs 17:27

"The lips of the righteous know what is acceptable, but **the mouth of the wicked, what is perverse."**
Proverbs 10:32

"A soft answer turns away wrath, **but a harsh word stirs up anger."**
Proverbs 15:1

The Bible also discusses what you should be doing with your words. Let's look at some of the Scriptures that discuss how your words can be beneficial or Godly.

"And let the peace of Christ rule in your hearts, to which indeed you were called in one body. And be thankful. Let the word of Christ dwell in you richly, teaching and admonishing one another in all wisdom, singing psalms and hymns and spiritual songs, with thankfulness in your hearts to God. **And whatever you do, in word or deed, do everything in the name of the Lord Jesus, giving thanks to God the Father through him**."
Colossians 3:15-17

"Know this, my beloved brothers: let every person **be quick to hear, slow to speak, slow to anger;**
James 1:19

"Let your **speech always be gracious,** seasoned with salt, so that you may know how you ought to answer each person."
Colossians 4:6

"Rather, **speaking the truth in love**, we are to grow up in every way into him who is the head, into Christ,"
Ephesians 4:15

"Therefore, having **put away falsehood**,
let each one of you **speak the truth** with his neighbor,
for we are members one of another."
Ephesians 4:25

"Let **no corrupting talk** come out of your mouths, but only such as is **good for building up,** as fits the occasion, that it may **give grace to those who hear."**
Ephesians 4:29

"Let no one despise you for your youth, but **set the believers an example in speech,** in conduct, in love, in faith, in purity."
1 Timothy 4:12

"Therefore **encourage one another** and build one another up, just as you are doing."
1 Thessalonians 5:11

"**Rejoice always, pray without ceasing, give thanks in all circumstances;** for this is the will of God in Christ Jesus for you."
1 Thessalonians 5:16-18

How would you rate yourself? Are you thoughtful and considerate? Are you really focusing on the words that are loving, kind, and that show thankfulness and graciousness? Do you speak the truth in love? Do you only speak in ways that build others up? That should be the goal for all of us. To speak in negative or hurtful ways damages you spiritually and hurts others.

Actions and Spiritual Growth

Are our actions or deeds that we perform important to God? The Bible certainly indicates that it is important. As Christians we are called to be holy. That holiness must be reflected in our behavior or what we do. Simply stated, we are called to act and live the Sanctified life. We are told to live a self-disciplined life that is focused on becoming like Jesus. We are to seek to do as Christ did when he was on earth. It is a choice we must make each day, each week, each year of our life. In 1 Peter 1:15 Peter states,

"but as he who called you is holy,
you also be holy in all your conduct."

The question you must ask is, "Was that a suggestion or was it something God expects of you?" We believe that it is an expectation. Why? Because if you have changed inside or have cleaned out the inside of the dish (Matthew 23:25-26) then good works or deeds will be evident in your life. With that in mind, what does that look like and how important is it to be holy in how you act? Let's look at some Scriptures that address this.

"By this all people will know that you are my disciples,
if you have love for one another."
John 13:35

"**Keep your conduct among the Gentiles honorable,** so that
when they speak against you as evildoers, they may **see your**
good deeds and glorify God on the day of visitation."
1 Peter 2:12

"But be **doers of the word**, and not hearers only,
deceiving yourselves."
James 1:22

"Who is wise and understanding among you**? By his good**
conduct let him show his works in the meekness of wisdom."
James 3:13

"Only **let your manner of life be worthy of the gospel of Christ**,
so that whether I come and see you or am absent, I may hear of
you that you are standing firm in one spirit, with one mind striving
side by side for the faith of the gospel,"
Philippians 1:27

"Do nothing from selfish ambition or conceit, but **in humility count**
others more significant than yourselves.
Philippians 2:3

Whoever **pursues** righteousness and kindness
will find life, righteousness, and honor.
Proverbs 21:21

"So if there is any encouragement in Christ, any comfort from love,
any participation in the Spirit, any affection and sympathy,
complete my joy by being of the same mind, having the same love,
being in full accord and of one mind. Do nothing from selfish
ambition or conceit, but **in humility count others more**
significant than yourselves. Let each of you look not only to
his own interests, but also to the interests of others. Have this
mind among yourselves, which is yours in Christ Jesus,"
Philippians 2:1-8

For “Whoever desires to love life and see good days,
let him keep his tongue from evil and his lips from speaking deceit;
let him turn away from evil and do good;
let him **seek peace and pursue it**.”
1 Peter 3:10-11

Strive for peace with everyone, and for the holiness without
which no one will see the Lord.
Hebrews 12:14

“I call heaven and earth to witness against you today, that I have
set before you life and death, blessing and curse.
Therefore choose life,
that you and your offspring may live,”
Deuteronomy 30:19

What does the Deuteronomy Scripture have to do with actions? It's actually a very interesting verse and it deals with how your actions can cause not just problems for yourself, but it could trigger problems for your children. It deals with our choices in life. Do we choose life that is healthy, good and spiritual or do we choose something that is destructive or ungodly. There is a relatively new field of science called Epigenetics. This new field is showing how your environment and your choices can influence your genetic code — and that of your kids (See Time review under Bible). This obviously gives us even more motivation to be and do all things in a Godly way.

As you can see from these Scriptures God does not expect you to be perfect, but he does expect you to Internalize the right information for the garden of your mind. If you plant the right fruit, you will think, speak and act in a Christ-like way. He wants you to do this because as you think, speak and act as Jesus did, you will have a positive impact on the Kingdom and will ensure for yourself a place that He has prepared for you. Keep in mind that the Apostles who walked and talked with Jesus did not immediately became mature Christ followers. In time they grew, but it was often difficult for them.

Now with this in mind let's look at how Christians may act as they grow up into becoming Christlike. Some of us grow fast, some slow. Some quit or give up. Some get stuck but keep working toward the goal. See if you can see where you are as we look at the possible stages of spiritual growth.

The question then is, what does Spiritual Growth look like? How can we see if we are growing and maturing spiritually? To help you see this we are going to look at spiritual growth and compare it to our human condition. We hope this helps as you explore what spiritual growth and maturity mean to you personally.

We have continued to refer to Galatians 2:20 that says, "I have been crucified with Christ. It is no longer I who live, but Christ who lives in me. And the life I now live in the flesh I live by faith in the Son of God, who loved me and gave himself for me." This scripture is foundational for spiritual growth. The need to die to self is key to spiritual growth and maturity. The good news is that the Spirit works with you to help you grow and mature spiritually. However, this journey towards maturity is not necessarily short lived. It takes time. When you successfully, and sometimes gradually, mature in Christ with the Spirit's help, you will be able to see a difference in how you think, speak and act. You will also be able to do something else that is extremely important. Carefully read this scripture!

In Hebrews 5:14 the author says, "But **solid food is for the mature**, for those who have their **powers of discernment trained by constant practice to distinguish good from evil.**" There are three very important messages in this verse. First, we need to be eating solid food (deeper principles beyond the basics of Christianity). We need to mature to the point that we are learning deeper principles. Second, we need to be internalizing and practicing those deeper principles in our lives. Third, the major benefit is that as we mature, use and internalize what we learn, we will be able to distinguish good from evil (right and wrong, Spiritual or Non-spiritual, Godly or ungodly). To sum it up, consider the three points shown below. To grow spiritually:

1. You must learn and go beyond the milk of the word so that you can start eating solid food (deeper Biblical Principles).
2. You must make constant use of that learning. You must make it part of your daily life as a Christian.
3. If you do this, you will have trained yourself to distinguish good from evil.

1 Thessalonians 5:21-22 we are told to,

"...test everything; hold fast what is good.
Abstain from every form of evil."

To effectively do that, we must mature and truly understand God's will or we might be pulled into darkness.

Obviously, all that above is extremely important to a Christian. However, Spiritual maturity does not happen immediately. That's why the mature should take care of the less mature. God wants us to take care of each other. Why? Because it takes time to mature and everyone grows at different rates. Babies don't immediately become mature, fully functioning, reasonable, individuals right after they are born. In time and with experience, they grow in knowledge and ability to use that knowledge. They learn by experience. Were you ever told to not touch a hot stove? You probably were. So, what happened? You touched it anyway. What did you learn? Obviously, not to touch a hot stove because it hurts. So, it is with spiritual babies and children. Sometimes they need to make mistakes to learn. That's okay, as long as they keep learning and keep working towards maturity. Growth can occur as we learn from our mistakes as well as our successes.

As they learn God's will, they learn better self-judgement. Self-judgement occurs when a person has internalized a believe system that includes values and spiritual beliefs that help them determine right from wrong, good from bad, spiritual from carnal. All Christians desperately need good self-judgment. Christian self-judgement is based on Biblical teachings or doctrine. It has to be learned and internalized. It becomes part of your very nature. That takes time. That is why it is important to study the Bible. You have to know something before you can make it part of you. If you don't know doctrine and other spiritual truths how can you determine right from wrong, spiritual from unspiritual?

Self-Judgment and Self-Control

The New Life God imparts to you is indeed most powerful with its heavenly nature, desire, light and thought. However, when man inherits eternal life with God he is still a babe, newly born, very weak and not able to understand by faith God's complete truths. He needs meat and not just milk of the word. In 1 Corinthians 3:1-3 a newly regenerated believer is compared to a baby. His level of spiritual maturity is as tiny and weak as a baby naturally born. Because of this he often unintentionally, and sometimes intentionally, acts very carnal when he begins his New Life. At your New Birth your spirit life could be compared to a spark of fire, the very beginning of your new life. At this stage in your spiritual life, your tendency is to yield to your old nature (flesh or carnal nature). This is because you have not yet developed good spiritual self-judgment, nor have you developed good self-discipline. It takes time, learning and practicing self-control or self-discipline, but it is something that God wants you do to. Actually, He expects you to grow Spiritually by being self-controlled. Consider the two following Scriptures.

- Titus 1:8 we are told to be, "hospitable, a lover of good, **self-controlled,** upright, holy, and **disciplined."**
- Titus 2:11-12 "For the grace of God has appeared, bringing salvation for all people, **training us** to renounce ungodliness and worldly passions, and to live **self-controlled**, upright, and godly lives in the present age."

Without good self-judgment (Knowledge of God's Will) and self-control (the act of making Godly choices) it is difficult to make good spiritual decisions. As a result, you more readily revert back to your old nature for daily decision making. In Hebrews 5:13-14 we are told,

"For everyone who lives on milk is unskilled in the word of righteousness, since he is a child. But solid food is for the mature, for those who have their powers of discernment trained by constant practice to distinguish good from evil."

The writer is clearly communicating that the only clear and decisive way to truly be able to consistently discern good from evil. How? You must eat solid food so that you can learn how to distinguish good from evil as you practice good self-judgment and self-control. That requires a deeper knowledge of God's word and spiritual growth that should accompany it. As time goes on you should gradually increase in knowledge and in spiritual maturity as you continue to learn and grow in relationship with God.

Practically speaking, how does this knowledge help you in your spiritual growth? If you are to ever develop spiritually you must have goals. You must know what you want to become. With this in mind, you can see how important it is for you to understand both what you need to grow spiritually and what that process looks like. You must read the Bible, study the Scriptures and identify how those Scriptures shape what you believe and how you are to think, speak and act. In another work titled, Comparative Doctrine (Crites, 2022), you can see over fifty doctrinal beliefs that are found in the Bible. Each of these areas are important in their own way. It's up to you to learn what the Bible teaches and then make those teachings part of your personal spiritual value system. You need to know what the Bible teaches. You need to internalize those teachings into your very core. You also need to know how to find information about core doctrine so that you make good decisions for yourself and eventually help others who are without Christ or who are struggling with finding truth. As you learn these Biblical truths and make them part of your life you too will have a greater chance to grow spiritually and mature in Christ.

When you become a Christian, you begin this new life. This life consists of a spiritual spectrum starting at a level which is often very carnal up to a level that is highly spiritual or spiritually mature. All Christians are somewhere between these two levels. The good news is that God accepts you where you are as long as you are seeking to grow and become more like Jesus. That's the process of Sanctification or Holiness that you should be seeking in your life.

Christian Confession and Spiritual Growth

Confession seems to take on two basic meanings in the New Testament. First, is when you confess Jesus as Lord of your life as you begin your life as a Christian. This was discussed in the work titled, *Grace and Salvation* (Crites, 2022). Second, the Bible teaches that we should confess our sins to one another. This aspect of confession needs to be a part of the new Christian's life. Why does the Word of God tell us to confess?

Confession is a way for the Christian to address his sins, weaknesses, frustrations and get help from both God and fellow Christians. Confession actually helps you grow spiritually as you seek to help each other on this spiritual journey. As a child of God, you have conditions that must be met in order to go to heaven for eternity. Contrary to the belief of many, a child of God can sin in ways that can cause him to be eternally lost. Peter said,

> "For if after they [Christians] have escaped the pollutions of the world through the knowledge of the Lord and Savior Jesus Christ, they are again entangled therein, and overcome, **the latter end is worse with them than the beginning.**"
> 2 Peter 2:20

And this is why Paul said in Colossians 1:22,

"he has now reconciled in his body of flesh by his death,
in order to present you holy and blameless
and above reproach before him."

And then Paul says, in verse 23,

"if indeed you continue in the faith, stable and steadfast, not shifting from the hope of the gospel that you heard, which has been proclaimed in all creation under heaven, and of which I, Paul, became a minister."

The Scriptures on the previous page simply help us understand why God wants us to get help from each other. In James 5:16 we are told,

"Therefore, **confess your sins to one another and pray for one another,** that you may be healed. The prayer of a righteous person has great power as it is working."

Healing is not just about physical or psychological ailments. It's also about spiritual weaknesses or for a sharing of a burden.

The Christian Confession: Confession of Sins	
James 5:16	Therefore, **confess your sins to one another and pray for one another, that you may be healed**. The prayer of a righteous person has great power as it is working.
1 John 1:8-9	If we say we have no sin, we deceive ourselves, and the truth is not in us. **If we confess our sins, he is faithful and just to forgive us our sins and to cleanse us from all unrighteousness.**
STS: The Scriptures above may be underlined in yellow.	

Without your initial confession that you believe that Jesus is the Christ and that you want to make him Lord of your life, you had no chance of becoming a Christian. However, once you made that decision, God provides you with a plan that will help you with your sinful nature. In addition, while living the Christian life, you will sin. As you find yourself failing to live up to the perfect standard that was set by your Lord in His life on earth, you can get help.

Confessing your sins so that you can get support from your brothers and sisters is one powerful method. It is not applied nearly enough in the church today. We are convinced that God would be pleased if more people were confessing sins to one another and helping each other as He intended. Confession is one of our most powerful methods to help us when we are having any kind of problem in our life.

We are convinced that God would be pleased if more people were confessing sins to one another and helping each other as He intended.

Personal Reflection

List three things that you learned or that were reinforced that helped you understand the importance of spiritual growth and how to accomplish it.

1.

2.

3.

Stages of Spiritual Growth

Chapter Ten

The New Life God imparts to you is indeed most powerful with its heavenly nature, desire, light and thought. Though man inherits eternal life he is still a babe, newly born, very weak and not able to understand by faith God's complete truths. In 1 Corinthians 3:1-3 a newly regenerated believer is compared to a baby. His level of spiritual maturity is as tiny and weak as a baby naturally born. Because of this he is very carnal when he begins his New Life. At your New Birth your spirit life could be compared to a spark of fire, the very beginning of your new life. At this stage in your spiritual life, you have a tendency to yield to your old nature (flesh or carnal nature). This is because you have not yet developed good spiritual self-judgment, which means it is difficult to make good spiritual decisions. As a result, you more readily revert back to our old nature for daily decision making. However, as time goes on you should gradually increase in knowledge and in spiritual maturity as you continue to learn and grow in relationship with God.

Practically speaking, how does this knowledge help us in our spiritual growth? If you are to ever develop spiritually you must have goals. You must know what you want to become. With this in mind, you can see how important it is for you to understand, 1) that you need to grow spiritually and 2) what that process looks like. To help you with Spiritual Growth we want to discuss the following:

- Who is your Discipler
- Stages of Spiritual Growth
- Baby Stage of Spiritual Development
- Child Stage of Spiritual Development
- Youth Stage of Spiritual Development
- Adult Stage of Spiritual Development

Who is Your Discipler

A key word in the title of this work is Discipleship. However, it's just not a word. It is a lifestyle. So, how do you become a disciple? Obviously, you have to become a Christian. Then what? Is there some kind of system that is supposed to be set up so that we can all become Disciples or people who promote Discipleship?

The most important question for you at this moment is, 'Do you have someone teaching you?' Do you have a fellow Christian who you go to, who wants to help you learn and become a more spiritual being? Are there people in your church who are supposed to help you grow spiritually? You should have that person and there should be people who are specifically helping you grow. Years ago, a gentleman by the name of Juan Carlos Ortiz wrote a book called, Call to Discipleship. In his book he made a statement in response to the Scripture Ephesians 4:11-12,

> "And he gave the apostles, the prophets, the evangelists, the shepherds and teachers, [What are they supposed to be doing?] to equip the saints for the work of ministry, for building up the body of Christ,"

If we read it correctly, it sounds like there are two extremely important things that should be happening on an ongoing basis. Which of those two things are most important?

1. The Equipping the Saints or members for the work of ministry.
2. The building up or helping each member grow spiritually.

It certainly appears that both of them are extremely important for the spiritual leadership in a congregation to accomplish. Actually, it appears that the Equipping the Saints must be accomplished so that the second can occur. Ortiz believed that it was the leadership's role (Preachers, Teachers, Elders) to make sure that new Christians and non-growing baby Christians get past the milk of the work and become more mature and active in the body. He stated that,

> "The purpose of preaching and teaching in the church is to perfect (bring to maturity) the saints for the work of ministry. The one learning today is to become the teacher of tomorrow. The pastors are not to entertain or maintain the believers, but to mature them. In other words, shepherds are not placed in the flock to give milk to the sheep. God provides milk to every mother to give to her child. Ministers take the sheep to maturity" (Ortiz, 1975).

The only reason numerical growth should be focused on is so that you will have more opportunity to truly focus on the spiritual maturity of new converts and current members of the body. Leadership should provide multiple ways in which a person can spiritually grow. Don't take this wrong, but a Bible class that teaches the basics over and over doesn't address the deeper spiritual needs of some maturing Christians. When Russ was working for one congregation he convinced the elders to have a learned man in the church teach Greek. It was amazing how many people showed up because they wanted to have a better understanding of what the Bible taught and to investigate specific meanings of Scriptures. It helped them develop a deeper meaning of some Scriptures. Classes on Grace, identifying personal ministry, gifts for service, a class on spiritual growth, building a deeper faith, understanding meatier doctrine and so much more would help people grow spiritually. And yes, classes that actually provide service in some way can be exciting and can be growth producing. We digress. So, what should our spiritual leadership be doing? Ortiz summed it up when he said,

> "We are supposed to go about leading the people from being milk-drinkers, to being meat eaters."

Leadership should be personally helping some members actually grow and become meat eaters. They could help people identify ministry that they can be involved with and ultimately those being helped would become disciplers themselves. That should be the ultimate goal of every preacher, teacher and elder in the church. That may very well be the most important thing that leaders in the church can do today. We know of several churches where each person on staff is taught that they should be discipling at least three people in their lives, through one-on-one time, group time and social time. Each person they are discipling ultimately was to do the same. This process should continue on indefinitely. Hundreds could eventually become involved. Remember, the goal is the world. The impact of doing this can be staggering if we actually did what Jesus asked us to do.

With the above in mind, leaders of the church should be promoting a Discipleship mindset to everyone in the flock. Those who live the Discipleship lifestyle will also help others grow spiritually and develop personal or communal ministry that will benefit the body.

That includes you. You are not in this alone. You should not face the battle against spiritual forces of darkness alone. You should have a person or persons around you who can help you spiritually grow and get through the pitfalls of life. Even if you are a teacher, a preacher, or an elder, you too need others to help you grow and fight this ongoing battle that you face against Satan's spiritual forces.

So, with all of this in mind, you need to have a spiritually mature person in your life who can help you grow. You need to become part of a group that helps you grow. But the group needs to be relational. It also has to be application based and it has to deal with real life issues that you face as a struggling Christian. We all need that. You also need to find a teacher, elder, or another Christian that can help you become more spiritually mature. If you do, your spiritual growth will be accelerated.

Keep in mind that we all go through a growth process in our Christianity. The speed at which we grow is determined by many things. Some of what we have discussed, if properly dealt with, will help you grow faster. Let's look at what the journey to spiritual maturity might look like. We want to compare spiritual growth with the physical growth we all go through from birth to adulthood.

Stages of Spiritual Growth

When you become a Christian, you begin this new life. This life consists of a spiritual spectrum starting at a level which is highly carnal up to a level that is highly spiritual or spiritually mature. All Christians are somewhere between these two levels. To better understand this spectrum, we have identified four stages of spiritual development.

These four stages are:

- The Baby Stage of Spiritual Development
- The Child Stage of Spiritual Development
- The Youth Stage of Spiritual Development
- The Adult Stage of Spiritual Development

You should be able to determine the spiritual stage you are in by the characteristics you exhibit. It's interesting to note that you can equate your spiritual state to the corresponding life state and its inherent characteristics. Let's take a look at each stage.

Baby Stage of Spiritual Development

Newborn Baby: A newborn baby is totally dependent upon his parents for all his needs. He needs others to care for him, because he is not yet ready to take care of himself. He is very selfish and often wants things his way. He needs others to feed him, change his diapers, watch over him and protect him. He cannot sit, crawl, walk or run. He often lets others know that he needs something by crying, throwing a fit or by being upset. He doesn't know how to express himself well yet. Wherever he is, he seems to be the focus of attention. A baby is not yet old enough to serve or do things for others; he lives to be served. He has to learn what is best for him and often must be corrected. Such an infant must be fed milk for he is not ready for solid food. This is exactly how a new babe in Christ functions.

> *But I, brothers, could not address you as spiritual people, but as people of the flesh, as infants in Christ. I fed you with milk, not solid food, for you were not ready for it. And even now you are not yet ready, for you are still of the flesh. For while there is jealousy and strife among you, are you not of the flesh and behaving only in a human way? For when one says, "I follow Paul," and another, "I follow Apollos," are you not being merely human?"*
> *1 Corinthians 3:1-4*

Spiritual Baby: With the above in mind, what should we do when we convert someone to Christ? It's obvious that we must feed them milk or the basic teachings regarding Biblical truth. Deeper Biblical principles are often much too difficult to grasp. A new convert must be taught how to study and read the Bible. He does not have the ability to 'feed himself.' As poor choices are made, we need to teach them necessary Scriptural information and then steer them toward right choices. We need to be patient, kind and loving as we help them develop a strong, solid belief system that helps them make right spiritual decisions. It takes time and effort. As a result, it is important that the new babe in Christ be surrounded by those who will help him grow in Christ. He must be taught how to communicate with God, just as a natural baby must be taught to communicate with people. He must be taught how to talk and walk with God, the same as a natural baby must learn to sit up, stand, eventually walk and communicate wants, needs and desires. It is through this training that the new Christian can develop the strong spiritual character and values they need to become fully functional disciples of Christ. The following is a list of the qualities or characteristics that often can be found in baby Christians:

- Thinks about self.
- Wants his own way.
- Feelings easily hurt.
- Often jealous.
- Lives to be served.
- Never or rarely serves.
- Stuck on the milk of the Word.
- Makes a lot of bad decisions.

Scriptural Study for Baby Stage	
Book	Scripture
1 Corinthians 3:1-4	But I, brothers, could not address you as spiritual people, but as people of the flesh, as infants in Christ. I fed you with milk, not solid food, for you were not ready for it. And even now you are not yet ready, for you are still of the flesh. For while there is jealousy and strife among you, are you not of the flesh and behaving only in a human way? For when one says, "I follow Paul," and another, "I follow Apollos," are you not being merely human?

1 Peter 2:1-3	So put away all malice and all deceit and hypocrisy and envy and all slander. Like newborn infants, long for the pure spiritual milk, that by it you may grow up into salvation— if indeed you have tasted that the Lord is good.
1 Corinthians 14:20	Brethren, do not be children in your thinking; yet in evil be infants, but in your thinking be mature.

Child Stage of Spiritual Development

Natural Child: Children love to be praised. They will do most anything for attention and approval. When they do get attention, they feel very important. They are often envious of others who receive or have things they don't have. As a result, some children have temper tantrums or lie to get what they feel they deserve or just want. They also lie in an attempt to stay out of trouble. Often such children don't realize that they are really hurting others by what they say and do. They know what they like to eat, but it is usually not healthy for them. Candy, chips, popcorn, ice cream and such like would be their preferred breakfast, lunch and dinner if they were the one choosing what they would eat.

Spiritual Child: The spiritual child also needs a lot of attention and support. As a result, he can be channeled into a spiritual direction if you take time with him. Without trying he can be sinful, simply because he still doesn't truly have a firm grip on what the Bible teaches. Sometimes, he tests the boundaries of right and wrong spiritually, because he isn't convinced that it is the right thing to do or be. He may lie about being caught up in doing unspiritual things in hopes that he won't get in trouble with those he is learning from. He will be a bit confused about what he is supposed to be learning in the Bible. Sometimes he may express an interest and other times he may be too busy doing other things with his life. The following is a list of the qualities or characteristics that can often be found in Christians who are in the childhood stage of development:

- Often untruthful.
- Envious.
- Gossips.
- Becomes a martyr when rebuked or corrected.
- Emotional outbursts.
- Easily puffed up.

- Loves praise.
- Resentful when crossed.
- Selfish.
- Wants things his way.
- Still not completely sure what he believes is right.
- Rebels at times.
- Easily pulled into sin.
- Has some understanding of spiritual values or teachings.
- Struggles with self-judgment, knowing right and wrong. He's still learning.
- Has some self-control or self-discipline, but often wavers between good decisions and poor ones.

How many Christians are stuck in this stage of spiritual development? If we listed some of the major problems in the church today, we might very well find that the issues are often caused by people who are stuck in the child stage of spiritual development. Being in the child stage is not the problem. However, staying in the child stage is a problem. Who's fault is it? Actually, the fault lies in two places. First, the individual is responsible for his or her own salvation and Christian life. Each person must seek to learn more and become more like Jesus. However, children often will make poor choices. Second, those who are more mature should be helping the young Christian. If they do not have a person and/or a group of people around them who are correcting and teaching, their chance of growth is minimized.

Scriptural Study for Child Stage	
Book	Scripture
Hebrews 5:12-13	For though by this time you ought to be teachers, you need someone to teach you again the basic principles of the oracles of God. You need milk, not solid food, for everyone who lives on milk is unskilled in the word of righteousness, since he is a child.
Leave Elementary Doctrine Hebrews 6:1-3	Therefore let us leave the elementary doctrine of Christ and go on to maturity, not laying again a foundation of repentance from dead works and of faith toward God, and of instruction about

	washings, the laying on of hands, the resurrection of the dead, and eternal judgment. And this we will do if God permits.
1 John 2:12	I am writing to you, little children, because your sins are forgiven for his name's sake.
1 Corinthians 13:11	When I was a child, I spoke like a child, I thought like a child, I reasoned like a child. When I became a man, I gave up childish ways.

Youth Stage of Spiritual Development

Natural Youth: During this stage a teenager often acts like an adult at times and then reverts back to the irresponsible actions of a child. They get upset when you don't treat them as adults, but often exhibit behaviors that are irresponsible and sometimes dangerous. They don't like to be told what to do and want to make their own decisions.

Spiritual Youth: During this stage we find the young spiritual youth trying to act like a mature spiritual adult. He is attempting to attain true maturity, but he all too often allows self and the world to get in the way. He is trying to put childish things away (1 Corinthians 13:11) but is having difficulty doing it at times. Sometimes he becomes very frustrated fluctuating between adult and childlike characteristics. He often rebels, because he lacks understanding and patience. He's trying to grow and at times it is very painful. Christians who are at this level of spiritual development have begun to really understand the difference in a religious life and true spirituality. They understand the need to count the cost and then put self away so that Christ can really live in them. However, because of their continuing hold on childish ways they often struggle with self and fail to yield to the Spirit on a minute-to-minute basis. The following is a list of the qualities or characteristics that can be found in Christians in the youth stage of development:

- All of the childlike qualities.
- All of the adult qualities.
- A fluctuation between being a child and an adult spiritually.
- The gradual putting away of childish things and the development of adult qualities.

- Usually knows what is right but struggles to make right decisions. Sometimes successful, sometimes not.
- The fleshly nature has a strong lure.

Scriptural Study for Youth Stage	
Book	Scripture
1 Corinthians 13:11	When I was a child, I spoke like a child, I thought like a child, I reasoned like a child. When I became a man, I gave up childish ways.
1 John 2:13	I am writing to you, fathers, because you know him who is from the beginning. I am writing to you, young men, because you have overcome the evil one. I write to you, children, because you know the Father.

Adult Stage of Spiritual Development

Natural Adult: This is the stage that most of us get to physically. All we have to do is live long enough and we will age. The hope is that as you get older, you will learn how to live life in a responsible way. Wisdom is often a result of experience. The natural adult learns about life and how to navigate it. Hopefully, such an adult is prepared to teach and train his children how to live a healthy, Godly life as a result of what he has learned and experienced in his life.

Spiritual Adult: This is the stage that most of us get to physically but is hard to get to spiritually. Adult maturity comes when we finally give up our childish ways and let the Lord rule supremely in our lives. Those who truly seek to become like Jesus eventually allow the characteristics of the Spirit (Galatians 5:22-23) to become more evident in their lives. When this happens, when you really give control of your life to Jesus and the Holy Spirit, you will begin to enjoy the full blessings of the abundant life (John 10:10) and will also begin to understand more fully what peace with God really means.

Christians at this stage do not try to develop the qualities of the Spirit with their own self-power or strength. They understand that the Spirit's qualities are already part of their internal makeup because they are Christians. Because of their maturity they are allowing the Spirit's qualities to be evidenced in their lives. The following is a list of some of the qualities or characteristics that can be found in spiritually mature Christians in the Adult stage of development:

- Peace with God.
- Looks to the future.
- All things work for the good.
- Agape love.
- Has identified and is using his spiritual gifts.
- Rejoices in spiritual children.
- Has joy.
- Has patience.
- Has kindness.
- Is good.
- Is faithful.
- Is gentle.
- Practices self-control or self-discipline.

Scriptural Study for Adult Stage	
Book	Scripture
Ephesians 4:11-13	And he gave the apostles, the prophets, the evangelists, the shepherds and teachers, to equip the saints for the work of ministry, for building up the body of Christ, until we all attain to the unity of the faith and of the knowledge of the Son of God, to mature manhood, to the measure of the stature of the fullness of Christ
1 John 2:13	I am writing to you, fathers, because you know him who is from the beginning. I am writing to you, young men, because you have overcome the evil one. I write to you, children, because you know the Father.

Scriptural Study

What are some key Scriptures about spiritual growth and what we must do to accomplish it?

Scriptures that Address Spiritual Growth	
Growth Needed Hebrews 5:12-13	About this we have much to say, and it is hard to explain, since you have become dull of hearing. For though by this time you ought to be teachers, you need someone to teach you again the basic principles of the oracles of God. You need milk, not solid food, for everyone who lives on milk is unskilled in the word of righteousness, since he is a child. But solid food is for the mature, for those who **have their powers of discernment trained by constant practice to distinguish good from evil.**
Leave Elementary Doctrine Hebrews 6:1-3	Therefore let us **leave the elementary doctrine of Christ and go on to maturity,** not laying again a foundation of repentance from dead works and of faith toward God, and of instruction about washings, the laying on of hands, the resurrection of the dead, and eternal judgment. And this we will do if God permits.
Transform Your Mind Romans 12:2	Do not be conformed to this world, but be **transformed by the renewal of your mind,** that by testing you may discern what is the will of God, what is good and acceptable and perfect.
Grow up into Him Ephesians 4:15	Rather, speaking the truth in love, **we are to grow up in every way into him** who is the head, into Christ,
Grow in Grace and Knowledge 2 Peter 3:18	But **grow in the grace and knowledge of our Lord and Savior Jesus Christ**. To him be the glory both now and to the day of eternity. Amen.
Gain Knowledge of Him 2 Peter 1:3	His divine power has granted to us all things that pertain to life and godliness, **through the knowledge of him who called us** to his own glory and excellence,
Supplement your Faith 2 Peter 1:5-7	For this very reason, **make every effort to supplement your faith with virtue, and virtue with knowledge, and knowledge with self-control, and self-control with steadfastness, and steadfastness with godliness, and godliness with brotherly affection, and brotherly affection with love.**

Fruit of the Spirit Galatians 5:22-23	But the fruit of the Spirit is **love, joy, peace, patience, kindness, goodness, faithfulness, gentleness, self-control;** against such things there is no law.
Have Mature Thinking 1 Corinthians 14:20	Brethren, do not be children in your thinking; yet in evil be infants, **but in your thinking be mature.**
STS: The Scriptures above may be underlined in yellow.	

Personal Reflection

List three things that you learned or that were reinforced that helped you understand the stages of Spiritual growth and where you are in the growth process at this point in time.

1.

2.

3.

Does God Judge a Christian by His Work

Chapter Eleven

Well, the answer is yes and no! We obviously need to take a closer look at judgment and its role in how a Christian lives. So, is work as related to daily Sanctification or holiness a good thing or a bad thing. Does God judge us by what we do or by who we become? Are both essential or is just one necessary? Let's look at four things that will help you see what God does and does not want from you. Each of these might help you determine how Sanctification or Holiness and works relate. First, the Divine-human relationship was and still is due to God's initiative. It is a gracious gift of God. He has offered us a relationship with him, all we have to do is accept it. The question for many is how do we accomplish that? Second, law keeping or doing works is only meaningful when it is an expression of an existing relationship with God. However, law keeping or good works could never bring that relationship about. Third, outside of the covenant (relationship), 'obedience' to law has no meaning or validity whatsoever. Fourth, we really need to understand who Paul is speaking to in order to get a better handle on what he is communicating. We will cover the following in this chapter:

- Covenant Concept
- Perversion of the Work Ethic
- God's Judgment and the Work Ethic

- Who is Paul Speaking to
- Right Behavior or Deeds
- Getting Judgment for Your Sinful Nature

Covenant Concept

When you became a Christian you were adopted by God. Adoption or υιοθεσία or yiothesía in the Greek explains what God does when you chose to become a Christian. What does He do? God gave you the right to become one of His children. When you chose him, He accepted you into his family and He gives you all the rights that being in His family provides. He promised to love you, to help you live a good and holy life, to help you in times of trouble, to provide you with a home with Him when you die and much more. What's the catch to get all of this? With the Holy Spirit's help, you must also commit to living the holy life. You must commit to growing into the Christian man or woman that He wants you to become. You must seek out and follow His will. You must commit to an inner change that is Christ like that also exhibits Christ like behavior. That is the covenant. To say it in different words, He promises to take care of you, if you promise to live a holy life serving Him in who you are on the inside and what you say and do on the outside. You became one of His children. With this in mind, a covenant simply is sacred promise between God and you. In making this covenant with you, God promises to bless you for the internal change and obedience to his will.

- It is a Covenant made by God for man.
- He promises to love and bless you.
- You must fulfill your promise to follow God's will and grow Spiritually.

Perversion of the Work Ethic

The work ethic has been perverted by many people. Let's take a closer look at this. First, legalism occurs when you follow commands with no real relationship. You are taught to only to keep the law or commandments. The Pharisees were a good example of this (Matthew 23). The second common reaction is that some people say that God does not judge the deeds of man. However, there are Scriptures that state that God does judge man based on his works. We will discuss this soon. Last, some say that God is not concerned with whether or not man keeps His law. All the above are incorrect and is a perversion of the work ethic found in the Bible. As a Christians you must exhibit good deeds. Keep in mind that good deeds are not what saves you. Good deeds are a response to a loving God who has saved you. You should want to think like him, talk like him and act like him because of what He has done for you. So, there are three basic ways that man has perverted God's work ethic. They are:

- When you follow Commands with no real relationship.
- The belief that God Does not judge man by his deeds or works.
- God is not concerned with whether or not man keeps His law.

God's Judgment and the Work Ethic

It is very important that you realize that when he talks about judging works in this scripture, he is not talking **about what is needed for you to become a Christian.** This scripture is directed to those who are already Christians. He is saying that all Christians need to be doing good works or deeds. However, even more important is that those works should be a result of what you are becoming. Are you dying to self? Are you putting on the attributes of Christ? Are you becoming more Christlike in your thoughts, words and yes deeds? If so, then that is what God expects. With that in mind, does God really judge a man based on his work? In Romans 2:6-16 we are told that *God will judge the works of man.* In verse 6 Paul states,

"He [God] will render to each one according to his works:"

People will often say, "That's not what that Scripture means." Our question is how can it possibly mean anything else. It is as clear as it can be and is supported by other Scriptures. Let's continue to look at this.

In verse 10 it says, "but glory and honor and peace for **everyone who does good**, the Jew first and also the Greek."

What was the precedent that Jesus set for exhibiting good deeds or works? In Matthew 23:26-28 Jesus said,

"You blind Pharisee! **First clean the inside of the cup and the plate**, that the outside also may be clean.

"Woe to you, scribes and Pharisees, hypocrites! For you are like whitewashed tombs, **which outwardly appear beautiful, but within are full of dead people's bones and all uncleanness.** So you also outwardly appear righteous to others, but within you are full of hypocrisy and lawlessness."

He was trying to help them see the truth in what God wanted from man. He does want man to obey and do good works. However, he doesn't accept them if they are just for show. You can't just act like a Christian in what you do. You must change on the inside. That journey should have begun as soon as you decided you wanted to be a Christ follower. When you followed God's plan for becoming a Christian you repented of your sins. In doing so, you hopefully made a choice to make a radical turn from sin and darkness and to Godliness and light. You began your journey to become a New Testament Christian. Each day you should be choosing to put off self and seek to become more like Jesus in thoughts words and deeds. God knows that it is a process. The road to being all that you can be for God takes a lifetime for many. And that's okay, as long as you are faced toward God. You should be seeking to be more Christlike as you learn more about God's will in your life. This is called Spiritual Growth and God expects that as you learn and internalize His will you will become more and more like His Son. That means you become more like Jesus in who you are on the inside and how you act on the outside. Both are important.

This is called Spiritual Growth and God expects that as you learn and internalize His will you will become more and more like His Son.

God does expect good works from man, and they must be Godly works. It can't be done out of duty. Your works cannot be just actions that show others that you are a Christian. Your actions must be a result of a change in your nature. Your works are judged based on the heart or 'real' relationship you have with God. However, the ultimate concern is not whether you or your deeds are good or right, but whether or not your deeds are external evidence of your faith and loyalty to Jehovah God. As shown above Jesus addressed this with the Pharisees in Matthew 23.

Who is Paul Speaking To

Paul is clearly speaking to Christians, Christ followers. He is telling them that they cannot obtain salvation apart from God. However, after you have become a Christian there are expectations. There are specific things a Christian must do and not do. God's reward is determined by whether or not a Christian fulfills God's expectations. Let's be clear again. The Scriptures will tell us the truth. Opinion matters little. Let's look at two Scriptures where Paul communicates this.

Scriptures will tell us the truth. Opinion matters little.

God's Expectations	
Romans 14:10-12	Why do you pass judgment on your brother? Or you, why do you despise your brother? For we will all stand before the judgment seat of God; for it is written, "As I live, says the Lord, every knee shall bow to me, and every tongue shall confess to God." So then **each of us will give an account of himself to God**.
2 Corinthians 5:10	For we must all appear before the judgment seat of Christ, so that each one may receive what is due for **what he has done in the body, whether good or evil.**
Revelation 20:12	And I saw the dead, great and small, standing before the throne, and **books** were opened. Then another book was opened, which is the book of life. **And the dead were judged by what was written in the books, according to what they had done.**

So, in terms of reward, it is absolutely true that God judges each person on the basis of their deeds. You can't just claim that you are good and acceptable to God on the inside and external evidence is not evident (Matthew 6:1). You must have a right heart. With no right heart any work to maintain salvation is null and void. Works with no internal change is not what God wants (Matthew 23).

Right Behavior or Deeds

Let's look at how works are important in another way. God does expect you to exhibit right behavior. There are simply too many Scriptures that communicate this to us for us to say it is not important to God. However, as previously stated those works must be a result of a heart that is in relationship with God. Internal change is essential. Let's look to the Bible again to see what it says about God expecting us to behave right or do good deeds.

Examples of Righteousness

Matthew 6:1	**"Beware of practicing your righteousness before other people in order to be seen by them,** for then you will have no reward from your Father who is in heaven
Romans 2:13	For it is not the hearers of the law who are righteous before God, but **the doers of the law who will be justified.**
Romans 6:16	Do you not know that if you present yourselves to anyone as obedient slaves, you are slaves of the one whom you obey, either of sin, which leads to death, **or of obedience, which leads to righteousness?**

Right Behavior or Deeds: God's Judgment

Luke 1:6	And they were both righteous before God, **walking blamelessly in all the commandments and statutes** of the Lord.
Romans 2:6-7	**He will render to each one according to his works: to those who by patience in well-doing** seek for glory and honor and immortality, he will give eternal life;

Getting Help for Your Sinful Nature

As you deal with sin, because of your fleshy or carnal nature, you must keep foremost in your mind that you lose your spiritual life in proportion to the degree you allow the flesh to rule. The more you allow the flesh to influence you, the more the spiritual man is damaged or minimized.

The ability to address sin on a moment-by-moment basis grows weaker as the fleshly nature gains greater control in your life. Unless you confess your sins and get help from God and your brothers and sisters in Christ, the fleshly or carnal nature will soon control your whole man, spirit and all, resulting in spiritual death (Romans 8:13). You must overcome, control the body of sin or flesh to the point that you render it unfruitful or dead. You have three avenues through which you can obtain help. Read the following Scriptures to see where your help can come from.

Scripture	Verses	Who Helps
Ephesians 3:16	that according to the riches of his glory he may grant you to be **strengthened with power through his Spirit** in your inner being,	Holy Spirit
Philippians 4:13	I can do all things through **him who strengthens me**.	Christ
Romans 1:12	that is, that we may be **mutually encouraged** by each other's faith, both yours and mine.	Help Each other

So, at the very least, help is available from three different sources as you seek to be the spiritual man and less of the carnal or fleshly man. You must be willing to constantly put yourself in situations where you can be supported or aided. You are in a war with spiritual forces of darkness for your spiritual life, and you must take advantage of the supports that God has provided you.

Who is your spiritual village? Who do you spend time with? Keep in mind that you often become like those you spend time with. It should be easy for you to answer when you are asked those questions. If not, you could be on the firing line facing the enemy without much support. That's dangerous. You should be spending time with Christians who are on the same spiritual journey that you are on so that you can support and encourage each other. God wants you to be around people of like-minded or spiritual, not with people who choose the ways of the flesh.

Personal Reflection

List three things that you learned or that were reinforced that helped you understand how God judges you as a Christian and what you may need to do to improve your situation.

1.

2.

3.

Part Four: The Holy Spirit

The Holy Spirit plays a much larger role than some believe he does. Part Four addresses many aspects of the Holy Spirit and how he can and does work in our lives.

- The Holy Spirit
- Indwelling and Work of the Holy Spirit
- The Holy Spirit and Spiritual Growth
- Works of the Spirit

The Holy Spirit

Chapter Twelve

We have mentioned the Holy Spirit several times up to this point, but now it's time to look more closely at who the Holy Spirit is and what his role is in your life. We will be discussing the following in this chapter:

- The Time of the Holy Spirit
- The Holy Spirit's Initial Work
- The Holy Spirit and the Bible
- The Holy Spirit is Promised
- The Holy Spirit is a Distinct Individual
- The Holy Spirit is Male
- The Holy Spirit has Godly Attributes
- Providential Working and the non-Christian
- Key Facts About the Holy Spirit

The Time of the Holy Spirit

What dispensation are we currently in according to the Bible? That may seem to be an odd question as we discuss the Holy Spirit, but actually it's not. May believe that there are three dispensations throughout time.

God's Dispensation

Each person in the Godhead has been in charge of a dispensation. In Old Testament times God directly led and directed his people.

- Hebrews 11:7 God led Noah to build the Ark.
- Hebrews 11:8-9 God led Abraham out of Ur of the Chaldees.
- Genesis 12:1-4 God told Abraham to go to the land that he had shown him.
- Deuteronomy 8:14-15 God led them out of bondage and while in the wilderness.
- Deuteronomy 29:4-5 Another time where God led his people while in the wilderness.

Second Dispensation

The second dispensation belonged to Jesus. He led them by example and with words. Here are some examples of some important things he taught and expected from those who followed Him. Keep in mind that these are Jesus' words and expectations, not another man's opinion.

Matthew 5:19 Therefore whoever relaxes one of the least of these commandments and teaches others to do the same will be called least in the kingdom of heaven, but **whoever does them and teaches them will be called great in the kingdom of heaven**.

Matthew 7:12 "So whatever you wish that others would do to you, **do also to them**, for this is the Law and the Prophets.

Matthew 7:21-23 "Not everyone who says to me, 'Lord, Lord,' will enter the kingdom of heaven, but **the one who does the will of my Father who is in heaven**. On that day many will say to me, 'Lord, Lord, did we not prophesy in your name, and cast out demons in your name, and do many mighty works in your name?' And then will I declare to them, 'I never knew you; depart from me, you workers of lawlessness.'

Mark 8:34 And calling the crowd to him with his disciples, he said to them, "If anyone would come after me, **let him deny himself and take up his cross and follow me**.

John 1:43 he directed them to 'follow him'.

John 3:16 "For God so loved the world, that he gave his only Son, that **whoever believes in him** should not perish but have eternal life.
John 14:23 Jesus answered him, "If anyone loves me, **he will keep my word**, and my Father will love him, and we will come to him and make our home with him.

John 15:2 Every branch in me that does not bear fruit he takes away, and **every branch that does bear fruit he prunes**, that it may bear more fruit.

John 15:10 **If you keep my commandments, you will abide in my love,** just as I have kept my Father's commandments and abide in his love.

Jesus' commandments or teaching apply to us today as much as they did the day he spoke to them. He expected that if people wanted to come to him they had to do so with the right heart and then follow his commandments and teachings. The Scriptures above clearly communicate this.

Third Dispensation

The third dispensation belongs to the Holy Spirit. He leads people today in his own way. God told and directed them. Jesus led by example and with words. The Holy Spirit leads man by speaking to them through the Scriptures and through providential working or urging the inner man. Let's take a much closer look at what the Holy Spirit does in his dispensation.

The Holy Spirit's Initial Work

The Word of the Gospel is powerful and is always the primary agent that leads to faith, repentance and ultimately to conversion. It is through the Word that God's will and His plan for humanity can be found. That makes His Word very important. It is through the Word that the Holy Spirit seeks to help each person connect with God. It's one of his greatest works. Here are some Scriptures that communicate this:

The Holy Spirit Works through the Word to Lead us to Christ	
Luke 8:11-15	Now the parable is this: **The seed is the word of God.** The ones along the path are those who have heard; then the devil comes and takes away the word from their hearts, so that they may not believe and be saved. And the ones on the rock are those who, when they hear the word, receive it with joy. But these have no root; they believe for a while, and in time of testing fall away. And as for what fell among the thorns, they are those who hear, but as they go on their way they are choked by the cares and riches and pleasures of life, and their fruit does not mature. As for that in the good soil, they are those who, **hearing the word, hold it fast in an honest and good heart, and bear fruit with patience.**
John 6:44-45	No one can come to me unless the Father who sent me draws him. And I will raise him up on the last day. It is written in the Prophets, 'And they will all be taught by God.' Everyone who has **heard and learned from the Father** comes to me—
John 20:21	but **these are written so that you may believe** that Jesus is the Christ, the Son of God, and that by believing you may have life in his name
Romans 1:16	For I am not ashamed of **the gospel, for it is the power of God for salvation** to everyone who believes, to the Jew first and also to the Greek.
Romans 10:17	So faith comes from hearing, and hearing through **the word of Christ.**
1 Corinthians 4:15	For though you have countless guides in Christ, you do not have many fathers. For I became your father in Christ Jesus **through the gospel.**
Hebrews 4:12	For the **word of God is living and active**, sharper than any two-edged sword, piercing to the division of soul and of spirit, of joints and of marrow, and discerning the thoughts and intentions of the heart.
James 1:18	Of his own will he brought us forth by the **word of truth,** that we should be a kind of first fruits of his creatures.
1 Peter 1:23	since you have been born again, not of perishable seed but of imperishable, **through the living and abiding word of God;**

The Holy Spirit and the Bible

How did the New Testament become a reality? The short answer is that the Holy Spirit provided many men the information they needed to write the words that would make up what our Bible is today. A very important Scripture addresses this. In John 16:13 we are told that, "When the Spirit of truth comes, **He will guide you into all the truth**, for he will not speak on his own authority, but whatever he hears he will speak, and he will declare to you the things that are to come." The Holy Spirit was to speak God's message to the writers of the New Testament. He was to guide them into all truth. Jesus also told them, "But the Helper, the Holy Spirit, whom the Father will send in my name, **he will teach you all things and bring to your remembrance all that I have said to you** (John 14:26). Paul also shared this in 1 Corinthians 2:13 when he wrote, "And **we impart this in words not taught by human wisdom but taught by the Spirit**, interpreting spiritual truths to those who are spiritual." With the above scriptures in mind, it becomes abundantly clear that it was through the Holy Spirit that the writers of the New Testament penned the different letters that became our New Testament today.

> *The Holy Spirit... will teach you all things and bring to your remembrance all that I have said to you.*

The Holy Spirit is Promised

The Holy Spirit is promised to those who believe and accept Jesus as their Lord and Savior. There are two important Scriptures in John that communicate this important truth. In John 7:37-39 he wrote,

On the last day of the feast, the great day, Jesus stood up and cried out,

"If anyone thirsts, let him come to me and drink.
Whoever believes in me, as the Scripture has said,
'Out of his heart will flow rivers of living water.'"

In the next Scripture John communicated another truth regarding the Holy Spirit. In John 4:15-17 he quoted Jesus who stated,

"If you love me, you will keep my commandments.
And I will ask the Father, **and he will give you**

another Helper, to be with you forever,
even the Spirit of truth, whom the world cannot receive,
because it neither sees him nor knows him.
You know him, **for he dwells with you and will be in you**."

The Holy Spirit is only promised to those who have become one of God's children. That simply means that all Christians have the Holy Spirit inside of them. He is there to help you with your daily walk.

The Holy Spirit is a Distinct Individual

Jesus' statement about the Holy Spirit communicates that He is a person, a personality. The Holy Spirit does things on His own at the behest of God.

The Holy Spirit is a Distinct Individual Scriptures	
Exhibits Intellectual Ability.	Romans 8:26-27; 1 Corinthians 2:10-11
Exhibits volitional activity such as choosing or making decisions.	Acts 13:2; 15:28; 16:6-7; 20:28; 1 Corinthians 12:11
Speaks.	John 16:13-14; Acts 8:29; 13:2; 1 Timothy 4:1
Teaches.	John 14:26; 1 Corinthians 2:13
Experiences emotions or feelings.	Romans 15:30
Grief (Distress, hurt, pain, sorrowful, displeased).	Ephesians 4:30; Isaiah 63:10
Is treated like a person: He is lied to. He is tempted. He is blasphemed (and other sins against Him). He is Insulted.	 Acts 5:3 Acts 5:9 Matthew 12:31 Hebrews 10:29
STS: Scriptures may be underlined in orange.	

Taken from Grace and Salvation by Crites 2022

As seen on the previous page, let's not forget that the Holy Spirit truly is a divine individual who has specific characteristics of a living being. He exhibits intellectual ability (Romans 8:26-27). He exhibits volitional activity such as choosing or making decisions (Acts 13:2; 15:28; 16:6-7; 20:28; 1 Corinthians 12:11). He speaks

(John 16:13-14; Acts 8:29; 13:2; 1 Timothy 4:1). He experiences emotions or feelings (Romans 15:30). He experiences grief, e.g., distress, hurt, pain, sorrow, displeasure (Ephesians 4:30; Isaiah 63:10). He is also treated like a person in the Bible. He is lied to in Acts 5:3, tempted in Acts 5:9, blasphemed in Matthew 12:31, insulted in Hebrews 10:29. All of these Scriptures lead us to believe that the Holy Spirit is indeed a distinct individual in and of Himself.

The Holy Spirit is Male

Did Jesus consider the Holy Spirit to be male or female? You would think that he knew the gender of the Holy Spirit. He knew him just as he knew the Father or God himself. If that's true how did Jesus refer to the Holy Spirit?

But the Helper, the Holy Spirit, whom the Father will send in my name, **he** will teach you all things and bring to your remembrance all that I have said to you.
John 14:26

"But when the Helper comes, whom I will send to you from the Father, the Spirit of truth, who proceeds from the Father, **he** will bear witness about me.
John 15:26

When the Spirit of truth comes, **he** will guide you into all the truth, for **he** will not speak on **his** own authority, but whatever **he** hears **he** will speak, and **he** will declare to you the things that are to come. **He** will glorify me, for **he** will take what is mine and declare it to you.
John 16:13-14

"If you love me, you will keep my commandments. And I will ask the Father, and he will give you another Helper, to be with you forever, even the Spirit of truth, whom the world cannot receive, because it neither sees **him** nor knows **him**. You know **him**, for **he** dwells with you and will be in you.
John 4:15-17

Let's look back and count how many times Jesus referred to the Holy Spirit using the masculine term he or his. In these four Scriptures Jesus calls the Holy Spirit he or his fourteen times. Was than an accident? We are convinced that Jesus knew exactly how to address the Holy Spirit. However, is there anything else that could suggest that the Holy Spirit is male or not?

A noted theologian by the name of Jack Cottrell stated this concerning the Holy Spirit's 'gender' after reviewing the Greek in detail. "What is relevant, though, is the fact that on a few occasions masculine pronouns are used to refer to the Holy Pneuma where we would have expected them to be neuter. Grammatically, they should be neuter..... In John 16:13-14 and Ephesians 1:14 the masculine Ekeinos ("He, that one") and the masculine relative pronoun hos ("Who") are used instead of neuter form of these words. This seems to be a deliberate assertion of the Spirit's personhood" (Cottrell, 2006). You can make your own determination, but there is some evidence that the Holy Spirit may very well be male in nature.

The Holy Spirit Has Godly Attributes

The Holy Spirit exhibits many of the qualities or attributes of God. There are three that we don't often consider, but in reality they are just as much a part of the Holy Spirit as they are to God Himself.

First, the Holy Spirit is **Eternal.** God had no beginning nor will He have an end. God is eternal. Eternal simply means forever. The Bible also states that the Holy Spirit is eternal and has always been with him . In Hebrews 9:14 we are told,

how much more will the blood of Christ,
who **through the eternal Spirit** offered himself
without blemish to God, purify our conscience from dead works
to serve the living God.

Second, the Holy Spirit is **Omniscient.** Just as God knows everything, including everything about us and what we think and do, the Holy Spirit can also search out and find anything that He desires to know. In 1 Corinthians 2:10 Paul writes,

these things God has revealed to us through the Spirit.
For the Spirit searches everything,
even the depths of God.

Third, the Holy Spirit is **Omnipresent.** Just like God, the Holy Spirit can actually be here with you at this very instant, yet at the same time be on the other side of the earth with others. The Holy

Spirit is in each and every Christian no matter where they are located. He too is everywhere. In Psalms 139:7-10 we are told,

Where shall I go from your Spirit? Or where shall I flee from your presence? If I ascend to heaven, you are there! If I make my bed in Sheol, you are there! If I take the wings of the morning and dwell in the uttermost parts of the sea, even there your hand shall lead me, and your right hand shall hold me.

Providential Working and the Non-Christian

The Holy Spirit seeks to save all non-believers! That means the Holy Spirit was at work in you even before you became a Christian. It that true? Let's take a look. In John 16:8-11 Jesus says,

"And when he [Holy Spirit] comes, **he will convict the world concerning sin and righteousness and judgment**: concerning sin, because they do not believe in me; concerning righteousness, because I go to the Father, and you will see me no longer; concerning judgment, because the ruler of this world is judged."

Let's look at two well-known commentaries addresses this issue.

Commentary on John 16: 8
The Holy Spirit is our Guide, not only to show us the way, but to go with us by continued aids and influences. To be led into a truth is more than barely to know it; it is not only to have the notion of it in our heads, but the relish, and savour, and power of it in our hearts. **Matthew Henry's Concise Commentary**
This conviction of the world is by witness concerning Christ (John 15:26). It is the revelation to the hearts of men of the character and work of Christ, and, therefore, a refutation of the evil in their hearts. The result of this conviction is two-fold, according as men embrace it, accept its chastening discipline, and are saved by it; or reject it, and in the rejection harden their hearts, and are thus condemned by it. **Ellicott's Commentary for English Readers**

We have to decide who the world is in this Scripture. Jesus was telling his listeners that when the Holy Spirit came **he would**

convict the world concerning sin and righteousness and judgment. In some way he would take action. It appears that Jesus is referring to all those who are not Christians. That includes everyone up to this very day. He literally means all mankind. "The word for convict (elencho or ἐλέγχω) refers to the act of making one's sins known to him in order to prompt him to feel a sense of personal guilt and then to correct his behavior" (Cottrell, 2002). Cottrell goes on to say that this is accomplished in two separate ways. The Holy Spirit communicates through the written word of God and through providential intervention in your life. The first is always true. The second may or may not be true in any given situation. John 16:8-11 literally tells you how the Holy Spirit worked in you before you became a Christian. He was to convict you of your sin, righteousness and judgment. Did you ever feel guilty about something you did before you became a Christian? Sometimes you have listened to your conscience and chose not to sin. Was it really just your conscience? Of was it the Holy Spirit urging or nudging you as he attempted to help you see your sin? We would like to think that the Holy Spirit does 'nudge us' to think before we sin. So, in fact the Holy Spirit does seek to aid non-christians in a providential way. He is not 'inside of them' but he does assist them to find God.

Resisting the Spirit and Providential Working

One of the ways non-Christians sin against the Holy Spirit is to RESIST him. So, if the Bible communicates a way to resist him then it would also suggest that someone must be able to resist something that is being 'communicated' in some way. Let's read Acts 7:51.

"You stiff-necked people, uncircumcised in heart and ears,
you always **resist the Holy Spirit.**
As your fathers did, so do you.

Luke was referring to people who refused to listen to the Word in order to be saved. They didn't want to accept it. As a result, they were resisting the Holy Spirit's message. To this very day people continue to resist the message of God. This resistance is fatal in the end. However, until that time the Holy Spirit seeks to urge the individual to believe in God and become part of His family.

Warning about Blasphemy

Blasphemy is an extremely dangerous thing to do. Everyone does agree that it separates you from God. There are many ideas regarding what Matthew 12:31-32 means and we will not be able to give you a solid answer. There are two basic ways to look at this issue. Let's look at the Scripture first.

"Therefore I tell you, every sin and blasphemy will be forgiven people, but the ***blasphemy against the Spirit will not be forgiven***. And whoever speaks a word against the Son of Man will be forgiven, but ***whoever speaks against the Holy Spirit will not be forgiven,*** either in this age or in the age to come."

The first way a person can blaspheme is when there is a malignant, persistent, and/or willful rejection of the Holy Spirit by a non-Christian. The point here is that you reject salvation from God, you are blaspheming the Holy Spirit as he is attempting to move you in some way to accept Christianity. That also means if you continue to reject the Holy Spirit who is trying to move you to accept the Gospel you can never be saved. As long as you blaspheme or reject the Holy Spirit there is no way you can obtain salvation. As a secondary note, it is important to understand that the Holy Spirit is indeed working in the lives of non-Christians to help them see the need for salvation. This is one clear example of the providential working of the Holy Spirit in non-Christians.

Matthew 12:31-32	"Therefore I tell you, every sin and blasphemy will be forgiven people, **but the blasphemy against the Spirit will not be forgiven.** And whoever speaks a word against the Son of Man will be forgiven, **but whoever speaks against the Holy Spirit will not be forgiven, either in this age or in the age to come."**
Mark 3:28-30	"Truly, I say to you, all sins will be forgiven the children of man, and whatever blasphemies they utter, **but whoever blasphemes against the Holy Spirit never has forgiveness,** but is guilty of an eternal sin"— for they were saying, "He has an unclean spirit."
Luke 12:10	"And everyone who speaks a word against the Son of Man will be forgiven, **but the one who blasphemes against the Holy Spirit will not be forgiven."**

Many scholars believe that this form of blasphemy is exhibited by someone who is not a Christian. They reject Jesus and salvation. As a result, they are rejecting or blaspheming the Holy Spirit.

Can a non-Christian change his mind and seek to believe in God at a later time after they have blasphemed? There is a Scripture that sheds some light on this. In 1 Timothy 1:13 Paul writes,

"though formerly **I was a blasphemer,** persecutor,
and insolent opponent. But I received mercy because I had acted
ignorantly in unbelief,"

We have to believe that Paul was forgiven and became one of the most impactful Apostles and writers of the New Testament. Jesus himself came to Paul and 'recruited' him. It would obviously suggest that if anyone today who had blasphemed the Holy Spirit but at some point chose to 'listen to Him' that he would be allowed to become a Christian. We simply can't imagine that God would not accept someone into his family.

Stepping Away From/Denying God

The second way blasphemy can be seen is when a Christian steps away from and denies God after they have been saved. This occurs when a Christian separates or severs his ties with God. Most people have known Christians who have severely damaged their relationship with God or have completely fallen away. Some have even become atheists. Some suggest that this too is akin to blasphemy. Let's briefly look at this situation. In 1 Timothy 1:18-20 Paul writes,

"This charge I entrust to you, Timothy, my child,
in accordance with the prophecies previously made about you,
that by them you may wage the good warfare,
holding faith and a good conscience. By rejecting this,
some have made shipwreck of their faith,
among whom are Hymenaeus and Alexander,
whom I have handed over to Satan
that they may learn not to blaspheme."

That is an interesting statement, but what does it mean? It certainly sounds like Hymenaeus and Alexander have lost their relationship with God. They have been severed or disconnected from Him. Let's look at two commentaries that address this issue.

Blaspheming GOD/Holy Spirit 1 Timothy 1:20 Commentary
Matthew Henry's Concise Commentary
"I rather think the sense is no more than, whom I excommunicated and cast out of the church, **making them of the world again**, (as the world is opposed to the church, and kingdom of Christ), which, for the greater terror, the apostle expresseth by this notion of **being delivered to Satan, who is called the god of this world....**"
How many masters can a man have? Matt. 6:24-26 "No man can serve two masters!"
Geneva Study Bible
Of whom is Hymenaeus and Alexander; {17} whom I have {n} delivered unto Satan, that they may {o} learn not to blaspheme. (17) Those who **fall from God,** and his religion, are not to be endured in the Church, but rather ought to be **excommunicated**. (n) **Cast out of the Church, and so delivered them to Satan.** (o) That by their pain they might learn how serious it is to blaspheme.

There is some discussion about what this Scripture really means in context with other Scriptures that deal with forgiveness. We will take this stance. If, as a Christian, you Blaspheme the Holy Spirit there is no forgiveness. Why? Because you have severed yourself from God. Both commentaries suggest that Hymenaeus' and Alexander's sin was so great (blasphemy) that they were 'delivered to Satan' who is the father of this world. Technically they had already delivered themselves. The point is that we cannot have two masters. If we serve Satan, then he is our master. If Satan is now our master then we no longer have connection with God. If we have no connection with God then we have chosen for Him to not save us. As long as we are blaspheming, forgiveness cannot occur. God can and will forgive your daily sin if you are His child and are seeking to live the holy life. However, if you commit blasphemy you have stepped away from God. Basically, you have said, "I don't want God in my life." When that happens and you are

> *If you do Blaspheme against the Holy Spirit there is no forgiveness. Why? Because you have severed yourself from God.*

no longer connected to God and there can be no forgiveness of sins. He will see every sin you commit and only one sin can keep you out of heaven. That's why having relationship with God is so important and why having his Son's righteousness is essential. If you step away from God, but came back to Him and say, "I messed up. Forgive me Father. I do believe in you and I want a relationship with you again." In such a case, we believe that God can and wants to forgive and make you His child again.

Key Facts About the Holy Spirit

1. The Word must be received and accepted before salvation and remission of sins.
2. The Holy Spirit regenerates and sanctifies or makes you holy during the salvation process.
3. The Holy Spirit is given to dwell in a Christian after you have been saved.
4. The Holy Spirit is a unique separate individual personality that is part of the Godhead.
5. The Spirit and the Word are not the same. However, the Word (Scripture) is the Spirit's main material tool to help you in your day-to-day life.
6. At the same time the Holy Spirit regenerates and sanctifies you, He also comes to dwell inside of you.
7. The Holy Spirit is separate and apart from the Word or the Holy Bible.
8. The Holy Spirit works closely with the Word to help you work through trials and spiritually grow.
9. The Word is actually the Holy Spirit's Sword that is used to fight and overcome evil. It is both offensive and defensive.
10. Your understanding of the Spirit's indwelling can be helped by considering it from a negative aspect. Romans 8 gives us an explanation of what those are like who "hath not the Spirit" (8:9b).

Personal Reflection

List three things that you learned or that were reinforced that helped you understand the Holy Spirit and his characteristics, his providential working or how he can be blasphemed.

1.

2.

3.

Indwelling and Work of the Holy Spirit

Chapter Thirteen

If you want to grow, you should let the Holy Spirit help you. His job is to help you grow and mature if you listen to his urgings. Scriptures state that he was given to you as a gift from God at baptism (Acts 2:28) and he stays within you, helping you become the spiritually mature person that God wants you to be. So, what does the Holy Spirit do that helps you? We are going to attempt to identify what the Bible says concerning the Holy Spirit and his workings. Several important areas will be briefly discussed.

- The Holy Spirit Regenerates and Sanctifies
- The Holy Spirit is a Gift
- The Indwelling of the Holy Spirit
- The Holy Spirit's Role in the Christian Life

The Holy Spirit Regenerates and Sanctifies

Scripture shows that the Holy Spirit is given to you at baptism (Acts 2:38). What is his primary role in baptism? As you are being baptized, the Holy Spirit regenerates you and changes you from being a vessel of darkness and sinfulness into a vessel that is meant for holiness. The Holy Spirit is the person who sanctifies and regenerates or changes you from darkness to light and holiness as you are washed in Christ's blood.

Saul, who changed his name to Paul, wrote to the Christians in Corinth. Paul tells us something interesting about the Holy Spirit in 1 Corinthians 6:11 he states,

"And such were some of you. But **you were washed,** you were sanctified, you were justified in the name of the Lord Jesus Christ and **by the Spirit of our God.**"

Titus also communicates the Holy Spirit's role in salvation. In Titus 3:5 he writes,

"He saved us, not because of works done by us in righteousness, but according to his own mercy, **by the washing of regeneration and renewal of the Holy Spirit**,"

So, the Holy Spirit is the agent that washes you in the blood of Jesus. It is by Him that you are regenerated and Sanctified. That's what you get when your sins are washed away. Baptism is often referred to as a washing in the New Testament. Your sins are forgiven, and you are made new and holy (See Crites, Grace and Salvation for a more detailed study on this).

You also need to ask, 'By what power does this washing forgive you or wash away your sins?' In 1 John 1:7 the answer to that last question becomes evident.

"But if we walk in the light, as he is in the light,
we have fellowship with one another,
and the blood of his Son cleanses us from all sin."

So, the Holy Spirit sanctifies you or makes you holy. It is through the blood of Jesus that you are cleansed as you are washed. When you are regenerated by the Holy Spirit you are also truly forgiven of your sins. Several Scriptures allude to this cleansing or forgiveness of sins. All of the New Testament writers do use the same words, but they all suggest that it is through Jesus' blood that you are saved. Let's look at some of these Scriptures to see what they say.

The Holy Spirit regenerates you, sanctifies you and makes you holy.

Holy Spirit, Salvation and Regeneration	
John 3:5	Jesus answered, "Truly, truly, I say to you, unless one is born of water **and the Spirit,** he cannot enter the kingdom of God."
Jamieson-Fausset-Brown Bible Commentary: "...the thing intended was no other than a thorough spiritual purification by the operation of the Holy Ghost. Indeed, element of water and operation of the Spirit are brought together in a glorious evangelical prediction of Ezekiel (Eze. 36:25-27)... it was soon to become the great visible door of entrance into "the kingdom of God," the reality being the sole work of the Holy Ghost (Titus 3:5).	
Titus 3:5	"He saved us, not because of works done by us in Righteousness, but according to his own mercy, by the **washing of regeneration and renewal of the Holy Spirit**."
Lipscomb (1964) "Moved by his own mercy, he saved us through the washing of regeneration and the renewing of the Holy Spirit.....Here the washing or bath of regeneration refers to baptism. It means the washing or bath connected with regeneration....Baptism is a part of God's way of making man righteous. So is a renewing of the Holy Spirit."	

Taken from Grace and Salvation by Crites (2022)

All Christians are sealed by the Holy Spirit when they respond in obedient faith to God's grace (Mark 16:16; Ephesians 1:13-14). Though all baptized believers possess the indwelling Holy Spirit, not all are spiritually mature. Many remain in an extremely carnal state, leading to a frustrating, self-defeated life (1 Corinthians 3:1). Yet the goal and ideal of the Christian life is to constantly be controlled by the Spirit. Just keep in mind that it is a process. Spiritual growth does not happen immediately.

The Holy Spirit is a Gift

God is a gift giver. In Romans 12:3-8 we are told that He gives us Spiritual gifts of Charismata (See Spiritual Gifts and Ministry by Crites, 2019). However, an even more important gift is the Gift of the Holy Spirit. Without this gift there is no salvation (See Grace and Salvation by Crites, 2022). Basically, God wills that the Holy

Spirit do something to you first. He regenerates you and Sanctifies you or makes you Holy (Titus 3:5). At the very moment you are Regenerated and Sanctified, the Holy Spirit is given to you by God as a gift. Let's look at some Scriptures that address this.

The Gift of the Holy Spirit	
Acts 2:38	And Peter said to them, "Repent and be baptized every one of you in the name of Jesus Christ for the forgiveness of your sins, **and you will receive the gift of the Holy Spirit.**
Acts 5:32	And we are witnesses to these things, and so is **the Holy Spirit, whom God has given to those who obey him**."
Ephesians 1:13	In him you also, when you heard the word of truth, the gospel of your salvation, and believed in him, **were sealed with the promised Holy Spirit,**
1 Corinthians 6:19-20	Or do you not know **that your body is a temple of the Holy Spirit within you,** whom you have from God? You are not your own, for you were bought with a price. **So glorify God in your body.**
Galatians 4:6	And because you are sons, **God has sent the Spirit of his Son into our hearts**, crying, "Abba! Father!"
Romans 5:5	and hope does not put us to shame, because God's love has been poured **into our hearts through the Holy Spirit who has been given to us.**
2 Timothy 1:14	By **the Holy Spirit who dwells within us**, guard the good deposit entrusted to you.
STS: Scriptures may be underlined in orange.	

The Indwelling of the Holy Spirit

Before you put on your New Life in Christ you were dead in your sins. You were walking with Satan (Ephesians 2:1-3). As a result, you were 'excluded from life with God' (Ephesians 4:18). The Scriptures tell us that God the Father and Christ the Son dwell within Christians (2 Corinthians 6:16; Colossians 1:27; 1 John 4:15). Does The Holy Spirit dwell within us also? The Scriptures tell us that when you became a child of God, you received the Holy Spirit (John 14:23-26). The

The Holy Spirit is a gift from God, and it is through the Holy Spirit that God and Christ abides in you!

Holy Spirit is a gift from God (Romans 5:5), and it is through the Holy Spirit that God and Christ abide in you (John 14:23-26). You can praise God for the fact that the presence of the Spirit in you is a seal of your sonship (you are an adopted child of God) and redemption (Ephesians 1:13; 4:30). The following Scriptures communicate that the Holy Spirit indwells every Christian.

Indwelling of the Holy Spirit	
Acts 2:38	And Peter said to them, "Repent and be baptized every one of you in the name of Jesus Christ for the forgiveness of your sins, and you will **receive the gift of the Holy Spirit.**
2 Corinthians 1:21-22	And it is God who establishes us with you in Christ, and has anointed us, and who has also **put his seal on us and given us his Spirit in our hearts** as a guarantee.
2 Corinthians 5:5	He who has prepared us for this very thing is God, who **has given us the Spirit as a guarantee.**
1 Corinthians 6:19	Or do you not know that your body is a **temple of the Holy Spirit within you, whom you have from God**? You are not your own,
Galatians 4:6	And because you are sons, **God has sent the Spirit of his Son into our hearts**, crying, "Abba! Father!"
2 Timothy 1:14	By **the Holy Spirit who dwells within us**, guard the good deposit entrusted to you.
STS: Scriptures may be underlined in orange.	

What You Get When the Holy Spirit Indwells

What does the Holy Spirit do for Christians? Does He protect you in some way? Does he speak to you personally and help you decide what to do? What do you get when you receive the Holy Spirit as a helper? Let's look at some ways the Holy Spirit helps you when you become a Christian. First, he gives you the use of his sword. In Hebrews 4:2 we are also told how the Holy Spirit's sword can help us.

"For the word of God is living and active,
sharper than any two-edged sword,
piercing to the division of soul and of spirit,
of joints and of marrow,
and discerning the thoughts and intentions of the heart."

The Holy Spirit also helps you by communicating what you must know about the Word, which is His sword, so that you can fight off temptation or attacks from spiritual forces of darkness. Ephesians 6:17 says,

"And take the helmet of salvation, and the
sword of the Spirit, which is the word of God."

What does this Scripture say about the sword? It should be obvious that the Sword of the Spirit is actually the word of God. It is the Scriptures that the Holy Spirit helped the writers pen when the New Testament was first being formed. All of the words, chapters, letters and books were inspired by the Holy Spirit. His sword is truly the inspired Word and when you use it to define biblical from non-biblical, fleshly from spiritual, evil from good, He is helping you as you use His word. This has been said before and will be said again. That is why you must know the word. You must know what it says. You must know how to use it against spiritual forces of darkness when they are sent against you to tempt you. They are wanting to damage your spiritual self and alienate you from God. Without the Holy Spirit's sword and the knowledge you need to use it, you would very easily fall to temptation. The book titled Comparative Doctrine (Crites, 2022) could help you see what Scriptures you need to know so that you can more deeply understand doctrines that are important to Christians. These Scriptures can then be used to overcome temptation. Obviously, they would be of great benefit when you are showing others what the Bible teaches about living a Christian life. So, knowing the Holy Spirit's Word is extremely important, but does he help Christians in any other way other than the written Word? Let's take a look.

The Holy Spirit's Role in the Christian Life

Living by the flesh is a dangerous thing even if you have become a Christian. The sad thing is that it can produce spiritual death. As a Christian you should want to be 'led' by the Holy Spirit. One of the purposes of this leading is for Him to help you deal with temptation and grow spiritually. You become less fleshly and more spiritual focused. In Romans 8:13-14 we are told,

"For if you live according to the flesh you will die,
but if by the Spirit you put to death the deeds of the body,
you will live. **For all who are led by the Spirit of God
are sons of God."**

Other than leading you through the use of the inspired Scriptures, how else can the Holy Spirit lead or help you? When writing about the Holy Spirit, Dr. Jack Cottrell stated that, "The leading that comes from his indwelling is not subjective enlightenment of the mind, but an inward empowerment of the will. He gives us the inner strength to be 'putting to death the deeds of the body,' as Romans 8:13 explains verse 14. He does this through an inward prodding of the conscience, encouraging our will to do what we already know is right based on the teaching of Scripture. The Spirit thus leads us by taking our hand and gently pulling us along the path of righteousness" (The Holy Spirit by Cottrell, 2006). He reminds you of God's will, tries to nudge you in the right direction but even then it is still your choice to obey God, or not.

In 1 Corinthians 10-13 Paul shares an important aspect of the Holy Spirit and how he leads us. He wrote,

"these things God has revealed to us through the Spirit. For the Spirit searches everything, even the depths of God. For who knows a person's thoughts except the spirit of that person, which is in him? So also no one comprehends the thoughts of God except the Spirit of God. Now we have received not the spirit of the world, but the Spirit who is from God, that we might understand the things freely given us by God. And we impart this in words not taught by human wisdom but **taught by the Spirit, interpreting spiritual truths to those who are spiritual**."

There is a lot to unpack from this Scripture but we want to focus on last sentence. He says, "We impart this in words not taught by human wisdom but taught by the Spirit, interpreting spiritual truths to those who are spiritual." So, the Holy Spirit helps you understand (he interprets) spiritual truth for those who are spiritual. He's talking about Christians. The point is that the Holy Spirit is attempting to help you learn Spiritual truths. That is one of his most important things to do as he seeks to help you grow and mature spiritually. The more you listen, the more He can teach you so that you can continue to grow.

Personal Reflection

List three things that you learned or that were reinforced that helped you understand the Holy Spirit's role in regeneration, what getting the gift of the Holy Spiri means and what you receive when he indwells you.

1.

2.

3.

The Holy Spirit and Spiritual Growth

Chapter Fourteen

The Spirit wants to help you grow and mature. We all should be thankful for the Spirits work in our lives even if at times it is uncomfortable. The Holy Spirit does several things for you that will help you live the Christian life. It's important to know that the Holy Spirit is constantly seeking to help you when you are tempted by darkness or your carnal nature. But how does He do this and in what ways does the Spirit seek to help you. Let's look at what the Bible says about how He works in your life.

- Being Filled with the Holy Spirit
- The Holy Spirit's Role in Spiritual Growth
- Getting Help from the Holy Spirit
- Being Tempted vs Being Tested
- The Holy Spirit, Testing and Spiritual Growth

Being Filled with the Holy Spirit

What does being filled with the Holy Spirit mean? People have varied opinions about the meaning of being filled with the Holy Spirit. Let's take a closer look at what the Bible says in hopes of making this clearer for you. In Ephesians 5:18 Paul states,

"And do not get drunk with wine, for that is debauchery,
but **be filled with the Spirit**,"

For many reasons we choose to interpret this as the ongoing sanctifying work of the Holy Spirit. However, there is also an ongoing responsibility that we all have as Christians to constantly seek to be holy. Why do we believe this? If you read the Scripture in the Greek language you would find that it uses a verb that is imperative when discussing the Holy Spirit and filling. Cottrell explains this. He states, "In Ephesians 5:18 the verb is imperative; we are commanded to be filled. We do not sit back and wait for it to happen; it is our responsibility. It requires our submission and cooperation. The verb is also a present imperative, signifying continuing, ongoing action. Thus 'to be filled with the Spirit' means to take full advantage of the already present and available power of the Spirit who resides within us." Basically, God wants to be in total control of your life. The more control you give God over every aspect of your life simply means that you are allowing the Holy Spirit to fully fill or lead you in your life. He has already filled you. He is not just partially there nor is just part of his power. His total power is ready to be unleashed to help you. You are what limits Him. The more spiritually mature you become, the more the Holy Spirit and his qualities can become evident in your daily life.

To become spiritually mature takes effort as you die to self and let God (Holy Spirit) control your life (Galatians 2:20). Initially, it's more difficult to listen to the Holy Spirit's urgings but in time we learn to listen better. We have shared this Scripture before but it helps communicate the necessity of Spiritual growth and how it is accomplished. In Hebrews 5: 13-14 it says,

"for everyone who lives on milk
is unskilled in the word of righteousness,
since he is a child. But solid food is for the mature,
for those who have **their powers of discernment trained**
by constant practice to distinguish good from evil."

What does the word discernment mean in context, what does constant practice mean and what is the author trying to imprint on those who have not yet grown Spiritually? What is the key element that he is attempting to teach them? To say the least, what is being communicated is extremely important for a Christian. To better understand this let's look at a few commentaries to see what they share.

Commentaries on Hebrews 5:
Barnes Notes on the Bible
It refers to the delicate taste which an experienced Christian has in regard to those doctrines which impart most light and consolation. Experience will thus enable one to discern what is suited to the soul of man; what elevates and purifies the affections, and what tends to draw the heart near to God. The meaning is, that by long experience Christians come to be able to understand the more elevated doctrines of Christianity; they see their beauty and value, and they are able carefully and accurately to distinguish them from error; compare the notes at John 7:17.
Pulpit Commentary
But solid food is for them that are of full age (τελείων, equivalent to "perfect;" but in the sense of maturity of age or growth, in contrast with νήπιοι; as in 1 Corinthians 14:20; cf. 1 Corinthians 2:6; Ephesians 4:13; Philippians 3:15), those who by reason of use have their senses exercised to discern good and evil...... So, in the spiritual sphere, the mental faculties, exercised at first on simple truths, should acquire by practice the power of apprehending and distinguishing' between higher and more recondite ones. It was because the Hebrew Christians had failed thus to bring out their faculties that they were open to the charge of being still in a state of infancy.
Robert Milligan Commentary on Hebrews
"As solid food belongs only to those who are of full age, who by reason of habitual exercise, have their senses so perfectly educated, as to be able to discern through them the physical properties of bodies; so also more profound and abstruse principles of the Christian Religion, such as the priesthood of Christ, his atonement, et., are suitable only for those, who from long study and experience in the school of Christ have their inward senses so trained as to be able to discriminate accurately between the right and the wrong, the good and the evil (Milligan, 1989)."

If we agree with the commentators shown above, it becomes increasingly obvious that through the process of study and experience we can gradually allow the Holy Spirit to lead you. Filling is simply described as how much you allow the Holy Spirit to lead you versus how much you choose to be in charge. He's already there; all of him. It's you, I and everyone else that needs to let him take control over our spiritual life; in all that we internalize, think, say and do.

What if we intentionally choose to not follow God by not letting the Holy Spirit guide us through the word and by his urgings? This is another way we can sin against the Holy Spirit. It's certainly not as serious as blasphemy but is does damage us spiritually. In Ephesians 4:30 Paul states,

"And **do not grieve the Holy Spirit** of God,
by whom you were sealed for the day of redemption."

So, how do you grieve the Holy Spirit? You grieve the Holy Spirit when you intentionally continue to sin. As a result, you minimize your spiritual growth because you are living life for you and not for God. The sanctified walk calls for you to die to self and to seek to be holy in all that you do. We can thank God that He understands that it is a process. As long as we are seeking to become holy He is a gracious father In 1 Peter 1: 15-16 we are told,

"But as he who called you is holy,
you also be holy in all your conduct,
since it is written, "You shall be holy, for I am holy."

The Holy Spirit's Role in Spiritual Growth

We must think spiritually. Why? Because it is through your connection with the Holy Spirit that you can begin to truly comprehend spiritual truths. You must employ spiritual means to reach spiritual ends. Your relationship with God's Spirit is the foundation for pleasing Him and bearing fruit. Even though you have already been delivered from sin, you must recognize that the Holy Spirit alone can grant you the strength required by your inner person. Any deception of self-pride, egotism or ignorance only grieves the Holy Spirit and yields continued immaturity. God considers your inner man all important. It is not terminal like your outer body. He especially cares for your inner man by providing growth-oriented circumstances that:

1. Reveal who is genuinely Lord.
2. Breaks each individual of self-reliant habits.
3. Causes us, whether sooner or later, to depend upon Him (the Holy Spirit) working through our inner man.

We should all desire to have a greater understanding of God's Word and in doing so have the opportunity to spiritually mature. In Luke 6:40 we are told that one of our primary objectives in life is to be like Christ. This is accomplished through the Holy Spirit. The Holy Spirit helps us mature as we follow God's guidelines so to speak.

Keep in mind that, we develop spiritual maturity in direct proportion to the degree we resist Satan who wants us to live based on our carnality (self-wants, needs, desires, etc.). The more we listen to the Holy Spirit and the Word, the more we mature. Often Christians feel that they can make use of all the power that is available from the Holy Spirit when they are newborn Christians. This is not so! We must realize that the maturing process comes through testing as we resist the temptations of Satan. What can we do to ensure that we can get all the help possible from the Holy Spirit? Let's look at some things you can do.

Getting Help from the Holy Spirit

What can you do to maximize help that can come from the Holy Spirit? Clearly the Bible talks about ways that you can connect more clearly with the Holy Spirit in your day-to-day walk. Let's look at some helpful ways that the Holy Spirit can help you in your daily walk. Cottrell (2006) suggested several things that we can do. The first and most obvious is that you need to understand what the Scriptures say about both sin and holiness. What should be in your life and what should not be in your life. How do you know if you are making the right choices? In Psalm 119:105 we are told that, 'God's Word is a lamp to our feet and a light to our path.' If you focus on looking at the Word, you have a much better chance of letting the Holy Spirit work in you and help you as you are tempted and as you seek to live the holy life. You also have a much better chance of determining if your thoughts, words or deeds are spiritual or fleshly.

You also need to develop a greater awareness that the Holy Spirit really is inside of you. He truly is there seeking the best for you, but he will not make your choices for you. He can nudge, guide or direct you if you simply listen and if you internalize God's word. This leads us back to the point that you must want to, or desire to put away sin and put on holiness. If you don't really want the Holy Spirit's help to lead you to holiness, your fleshly nature will make decisions for you. You will sin. In Hebrews 12:14 we are told to pursue sanctification. In 1 Peter 1:16 it says, "You shall be holy, for I am holy." You should desire and seek to be holy each day of your life.

How do you do that? Prayer is foundational in accomplishing this. It should be an ongoing part of your daily life. When you speak with God you are speaking through the Holy Spirit. He too hears what you pray. He actually communicates the deeper meanings of what you are trying to communicate to God. He is there for you in the moment you pray and when you are not praying. In Romans 8:26-27 Paul shares this,

"Likewise the **Spirit helps us in our weakness**.
For we do not know what to pray for as we ought,
but the Spirit himself intercedes for us
with groanings too deep for words. And he who searches hearts
knows what is the mind of the Spirit,
because the **Spirit intercedes for the saints**
according to the will of God."

So, as you seek to be holy and as you seek God and the Holy Spirit's help through prayer what else should you be doing? You cannot just acknowledge that you cannot live a Godly, sanctified life by your own strength and will. You must be willing to die to self (Galatians 2:20) and let the truth of the word and the guidance of the Spirit make all of your decisions.

You must also trust that God and the Holy Spirit will do exactly as they say they will do (Psalm 9:10). As you pray, and let the Holy Spirit help you make decisions and as you trust that they will make the best decision for what you must think, do, or say, there is one more thing that must happen.

Because we do have free will it is our choice to obey God's will by following his Word and listening to the urges of the Holy Spirit. However, we must obey. You must make the decision to obey and act as the Holy Spirit and his Word guides you. In Philippians 2:12-13 we are told,

"Therefore, my beloved, as you have always obeyed,
so now, not only as in my presence but much more in my absence,
work out your own salvation with fear and trembling,
for it is God who works in you,
both **to will and to work for his good pleasure**."

When you have accomplished this in your life, you will be following both God's will and the leading of the Holy Spirit instead of utilizing your own self-will, self-desire, etc. Your prayer should always contain a thought of thanksgiving for what God, Christ and the Holy Spirit have done for you (Philippians 4:6). You are a child of God, not just on the outside, but on the inside also.

Now that we can see how to open ourselves up so that the Holy Spirit can truly help us, let's take a closer look at how He can help us when we face temptation. So, who does the tempting and who does the testing and are they the same?

Being Tempted vs Being Testing

We want to make one thing perfectly clear. God does not tempt us to do wrong or sin. That comes from Satan and his varied spiritual forces of darkness. They are the ones that do the tempting. God does allow it, but as it happens, He turns it around and provides you a way to grow spiritually when you are faced with temptation and sin. It is called, testing. So, when we are tempted, God offers us an opportunity to grow spiritually. It truly is by testing that we can grow. That is God's plan. He turned what was negative into something that can be positive spiritually if we just listen to Him. Instead of focusing on being tempted, we need to acknowledge it and recognize that God has now provided us with an opportunity to grow spiritually. Feeling miserable, negative, blaming bad things on God is Satan's subtle way to pull you into his dark kingdom. God has a solution. It's called testing and all you have to do is follow the plan. He never said it would always be easy here on planet earth.

> *Instead of focusing on being tempted, we need to acknowledge it and recognize that God has now provided us with an opportunity to grow spiritually.*

We are constantly being tempted in multiple ways each day of our lives. Satan's spiritual forces are at work around us and really want to damage our relationship with God. We are tempted with food, sex, time, alcohol, drugs, work and so much more. Forces of darkness will use the smallest of things to gradually divert us from the Christian path. They are very deceptive. Just know that dark spiritual forces are constantly trying to find ways to temp us and ultimately cause us to distance from God. As odd as it sounds, you should want to be tested by God, for it is through that testing that you can grow and become more mature spiritually. Too many people stay comfortable in their Christianity. Often those people don't seem to be tempted much. They are already in danger and they just need to be nudged towards darkness by spiritual forces of darkness. All out war is not necessary. Such people often gradually disconnect from God if they don't accept the help that is available.

The Holy Spirit, Testing and Spiritual Growth

According to the NAS New Testament Greek Lexicon the Greek word translated as "test" in the New Testament is dokimazo. It means to test, examine, prove, scrutinize (to see whether a thing is genuine or not), as metals and to recognize as genuine after examination, to approve, deem worthy. This is what God does to help us spiritually grow. God does allow you to be tempted. He also allowed his Son to be tempted. Jesus obviously overcame, but because he faced it, He can identify with your anger, greed, fears and struggles as you deal with temptation. In Hebrews 4:15 we are told,

"For we do not have a high priest who is unable to sympathize with our weaknesses, but one who in every respect has been tempted as we are, yet without sin."

As frustrating as it can be for many, we have to attempt to understand why God allows us to be tempted by Satan's spiritual forces of darkness. God turns this situation into a testing that can help you grow. Your response literally determines whether you grow spiritually or if you gradually become frustrated, give in to darkness and ultimately step away from God. Let's take a look at one Scripture and see how it applies to this situation 2 Corinthians 1:3-5,

"Blessed be the God and Father of our Lord Jesus Christ, the Father of mercies and God of all comfort, who comforts us in all our affliction, so that we may be able to comfort those who are in any affliction, with the comfort with which **we ourselves are comforted by God.** For as we share abundantly in Christ's sufferings, so through Christ we share abundantly in comfort too."

So, one important aspect of being tempted is that God will comfort you. What does the verse above say? It says one of the reasons you are afflicted and comforted by God is so that you can turn around and comfort others. It's a learning process. As you help others you in turn help yourself. That's also called, Discipleship.

Personal Reflection

List three things that you learned or that were reinforced that helped you understand how the Holy Spirit works in your life or how He helps you when you are tempted.

1.

2.

3.

Works of the Spirit

Chapter Fifteen

We have been asked repeatedly, 'Does the Holy spirit work apart from the Word or is he limited to speaking to us through the Scriptures?' That is a really good question and deserves an answer. In previous chapters we have shown you Scriptures that support the fact that the Holy Spirit actually does work independent of the Word or Scriptures. However, let's dig into this a bit more. The phrase that best describes the Holy Spirit's work with man in this dispensation is called providential working. We have already looked at providential working in the last chapter but let's dig a little deeper. Let's look at what the Holy Spirit is responsible for in this dispensation.

- Miraculous Works or Not
- Specific Works of the Holy Spirit
- Providential Working of the Holy Spirit
- Holy Spirt, Prayer and Providential Working
- Working Behind the Scenes
- Providential Working and Spiritual Forces

Miraculous Works or Not

Christendom is split as to whether or not the Holy Spirit's miraculous or sign gifts, e.g., speaking in tongues, healings, and miracles are still active today. Charismatic Christians believe that they are active. Cessationists believe that those gifts were employed by those in the early church to prove or authenticate what God was accomplishing in building up the Kingdom. Cessationists believe that once the Kingdom was established, those gifts ceased to be needed. Their belief states that specific miraculous gifts ceased to be necessary shortly after the last apostle died. The also believe that some of those that were touched by one of the Apostles continued to exhibit various miraculous gifts. However, those men could not give others the right or ability to use those gifts, so they were not passed on to others. We believe that the Cessationists view is accurate, but with a bit of a twist. The miraculous or sign gifts that the Holy Spirit used through those men did cease. However, the Holy Spirit did not cease to work through the Word or providentially.

Specific Works of the Holy Spirit

What does the Holy Spirit do? Actually, he has several important responsibilities so to speak. He helps in the conversion of non-Christians (Acts 7:51-52). You can accept, resist or blaspheme the Holy Spirit (also Acts 7:51-52; 1 Timothy 1:18-20). At salvation he then regenerates and sanctifies or makes holy the newborn Christian (1 Corinthians 6:11; Titus3:5). At the same time, He indwells the newborn Christian so that he can be a helper (Acts 2:38; Acts 5:32). He assists as you learn the Scripture and how to utilize it to live the Christian life. When you become a Christian the Holy Spirit testifies to your sonship with God (Romans 8:16). He also makes intercession for you when you pray to God (Romans 8:26-27). Obviously, the Holy Spirit does or is responsible for many things in your life. All of the above can be seen as providential working of the Holy Spirit. In summary:

- He helps in the conversion of non-Christians.
- You can accept the Holy Spirit.
- You can resist the Holy Spirit.
- You can blaspheme the Holy Spirit.
- He regenerates you.
- He sanctifies you.
- He indwells you so that he can be a helper.
- He assists you through the Scriptures.
- He testifies to your sonship with God.
- He makes intercession for you when you pray to God.

Providential Working of the Holy Spirit

Does the Holy Spirit work outside using the Word to aid you, or does he have some kind of influence on you to help you in your Christian walk? There are many factions in the religious world that believe the Spirit works only through the Word, the Bible. If this were true, it would totally negate the providential working of the Spirit. For instance, why would God tell us to ask for wisdom through prayer (James 5:16). We are told that if we ask, we will receive an answer. It may not always be what we want but God knows what is best for us. This help is not from written pages in the Bible but by God and the Holy Spirit. However, knowing what the Bible teaches is also essential. You can't believe or internalize something if you don't know much about it. The Father works through the Holy Spirit to accomplish various providential works (Romans 8:2, 26-27).

It's good to know that we are never alone. It is God who works in you through and with His Holy Spirit to will and work for his good pleasure.

Holy Spirit, Prayer and Providential Working

One very important work the Holy Spirit is involved with is that He is connected to your prayer life. God willed this to be so and it's something that all Christians should be thankful for. Imagine for a moment what it would be like if the Holy Spirit did not intercede for us when we pray. He helps communicate what we are seeking to share with God in ways that are beyond our ability. With this in mind, His role in prayer is extremely important. In Romans 8:26-27 Paul tells us,

"Likewise **the [Holy] Spirit helps us in our weakness**.
For we do not know what to pray for as we ought, **but the Spirit himself intercedes for us with groanings too deep for words**.
And he who searches hearts knows what is the mind of the Spirit,
because **the Spirit intercedes for the saints**
according to the will of God."

H. Leo Boles (The Holy Spirit, 1942) takes it a step further and states that, "Hence each member of the Godhead is included in every acceptable prayer." He continues as he explains how the Holy Spirit communicates beyond our words. He stated that, "The 'groanings' are not the 'groanings' of the Holy Spirit; they are our groanings; they are inarticulate expression that the Holy Spirit makes for us. Words of the heart are oftentimes beyond the cogency [clarity] of language. The Holy Spirit is able to take the yearnings, longing, groaning of the soul and form them and direct them so as to make them express to God according to his will our true wants." The Holy Spirit in fact does much for us in prayer and in other ways according to Richard Rogers. He stated that, "The Spirit aids the saint's prayers when moments of grief, anxiety, or joy make words impossible and leads the soul-winner to the lost by His providential care and oversight. These are the relations that the Spirit of God sustains to the Word of God (Rogers, 2007). It's also interesting that your prayer is to GOD, through Jesus Christ and communicated to God by the Holy Spirit. That would mean that each person in the trinity is involved with every prayer you utter. This would support what Boles said on the previous page.

Your prayer is to GOD, through Jesus Christ and communicated to God by the Holy Spirit. That would mean that each person in the trinity is involved with every prayer you utter.

"In Acts 8, when the Lord wanted Phillip to go preach to the Eunuch, the Spirit led the preacher to the sinner. In Acts 16 the Spirit forbade Paul to preach in Asia and Bithynia and led him into Macedonia. Even so today God answers our prayers by leading us to where the lost are. The Holy Spirit of God has thus been active in our lives. The man who believes that God answers prayer must believe that the Holy Spirit works providentially" (Holy Spirt of God by Richard Rogers, 2007). If you deny the providential working of the Spirit then the only reason for prayer is because you are commanded to pray. You could not expect God to answer your prayers. Such a stance would be one of extreme legalism. If you are to believe the Bible, you must believe that the Spirit works in your life and that prayers are truly answered. To sum it up we might say that the Spirit gives revelation only through the Word today, but providential influence is exercised separate from, but consistent with the Word. The following Scriptures indicate God's providential working in our lives today.

Providential Working: General	
"And we know that for those who love God all things work together for good, for those who are called according to his purpose."	Romans 8:28
"Since God had provided something better for us, that apart from us they should not be made perfect."	Hebrews 11:40
Providential Working: Specific	
Therefore, confess your sins to one another and pray for one another, **that you may be healed. The prayer of a righteous person has great power as it is working.**	James 5:16
Beloved, never avenge yourselves, but leave it to the wrath of God, for it is written, **"Vengeance is mine, I will repay, says the Lord."**	Romans 12:19
And after you have suffered a little while, the God of all grace, who has called you to his eternal glory in Christ, **will himself restore, confirm, strengthen, and establish you.**	1 Peter 5:10
Therefore let anyone who thinks that he stands take heed lest he fall. No temptation has overtaken you that is not common to man. is God faithful, and **he will not let you be tempted beyond your ability, but with the temptation he will also provide the of way escape,** that you may be able to endure it.	1 Corinthians 10:12-13
For the Lord disciplines the one he loves, and chastises every son whom he receives."	Hebrews 12:6
But seek first the kingdom of God and his righteousness, and **all these things will be added to you.**	Matthew 6:33

Working Behind the Scenes

The Holy Spirit is constantly working behind the scenes to help you obey and follow God's commands and live a Godly life.

- You must trust that he will supply you with all you need.
- He is attempting to exhibit his fruit through you.
- He helps you obey the Word and live the life that God wants you to live.
- He helps you with your weaknesses.
- He intercedes and helps you in your prayer life.

First, you must also trust that His providence shall supply all things that are necessary to accomplish His will (Matthew 6.24–34; 2 Corinthians 9.8; Philippians 1.19, 20; 4.19; Genesis 22:8). Here are two examples.

"And my **God will supply every need of yours** according
to his riches in glory in Christ Jesus."
Philippians 4:19

"And God is able to make all grace abound to you,
so that **having all sufficiency in all things at all times**,
you may abound in every good work."
2 Corinthians 9:8

Second, God and the Holy Spirit works in a providential way that helps you internalize or become the nature of God, Christ and the Holy Spirit. It is very clear what some of those internal qualities are that lead to Godly behavior. In Galatians 5:22-23 Paul shares,

But the fruit of the Spirit is love, joy, peace, patience, kindness,
goodness, faithfulness, gentleness, self-control; against such
things there is no law.

Third, God and His Holy Spirit will help you obey or make right choices in how you act with brothers, sisters, the world and everywhere else if you let them. This has always been a desire of God. In the Old Testament it showed how God wanted to prepare his people for good works. The Prophet Ezekiel spoke about what God wants to do for his people in Ezekiel 36:25-27. He says,

"I will sprinkle clean water on you,
and you shall be clean from all your uncleannesses,
and from all your idols I will cleanse you.
And I will give you a new heart,
and a new spirit I will put within you.
And I will remove the heart of stone from your flesh
and give you a heart of flesh.
And I will put my Spirit within you,

and cause you to walk in my statutes
and be careful to obey my rules."

It's important to note that in the Old Testament as well as the New Testament you have been given help as you seek to live your life the way God wants you to live it. You will not have to do this work by yourself. As you internalize His qualities, God knows that you will face adversaries, both human and spiritual, who do not want you to live a Godly life. So, He gave the Holy Spirit a charge that He would help you when you are weak and struggling with following His will.

"For if you live according to the flesh you will die,
but if by the Spirit you put to death the deeds of the body,
you will live. For all who are led by the Spirit of God
are sons of God."
Romans 8:13-14

"If we live by the Spirit,
let us also keep in step with the Spirit.
Galatians 5:25

Fourth, the Holy Spirit helps you when you are weak. He strengthens and encourages you. When you feel weak, when you're tempted to sin, when you're not sure of the way to go or what to do is when you can access the help of the Holy Spirit. All you have to do is ask. Think about what God's will would be based on His Scriptures and ask the Holy Spirit to give you strength to do what is right. Paul tells us in Romans 8:26a,

"Likewise **the Spirit helps us
in our weakness.**"

Let's look at two commentaries to see how they explain this Scripture.

Commentaries on Romans 8:26a
Benson Commentary
"Besides the hope of future felicity and glory, which our holy profession administers to us for our support and comfort amid all the difficulties of our Christian course, we have moreover this important privilege, that the Holy Spirit of God helpeth our infirmities — The word αντιλαμβανεται, here rendered helpeth,

literally expresses the action of one who assists another to bear a burden, by taking hold of it on the opposite side, and bearing it with him, as persons do who assist one another in carrying heavy loads. Dr. Doddridge here interprets the clause, the Holy Spirit lendeth us his helping hand under all our burdens or infirmities. The word ασθενειαις, translated infirmities, signifies weaknesses and diseases, primarily of the body, but it is often transferred to the mind. Our understandings are weak, particularly in the things of God; our faith is weak…"

Matthew Henry's Concise Commentary

Though the infirmities of Christians are many and great, so that they would be overpowered if left to themselves, yet the Holy Spirit supports them.

Fifth, as previously discussed, we are told that the Holy Spirit will help us speak with God in a way that will help communicate our words, e.g., our adoration, confession, thanksgiving, supplication and more. He does it in ways that show what your heart is truly attempting to communicate. In Romans 8:26-27 Paul shares,

"Likewise the Spirit helps us in our weakness.
For we do not know what to pray for as we ought,
but **the Spirit himself intercedes for us with groanings too deep for words.** And he who searches hearts knows what is the mind of the Spirit,
because the Spirit intercedes for the saints
according to the will of God."

How the Holy Spirit Helps Us	
Scripture	**Summary**
Philippians 4:19 2 Corinthians 9:8	Supplies all things that are necessary to accomplish God's will,
Galatians 5:22-23	Helps you internalize or become the nature of God, Christ and the Holy Spirit.
Romans 8:13-14 Galatians 5:25	Helps you obey or make right choices in how you act.
Romans 8:26a Philippians 4:13	Helps, strengthens and encourages you when you feel weak; when you're tempted to sin,
Romans 8:26-27	Communicates the meaning and intent of our prayers to God
STS: Scriptures may be underlined in orange.	

Providential Working and Spiritual Forces

Why is it important that the Holy Spirit actually aid us providentially? Consider this. Does Satan and his minions attack us in a variety of ways? In Ephesians 6 we are told that we wrestle against the **rulers**, against the **authorities**, against the **cosmic powers** over this present darkness, and against **the spiritual forces of evil**. If you put thought to this, it should quickly become evident that there is a lot of darkness out there that is trying to damage you spiritually. It is intentional. Read that word again. INTENTIONAL! That means they choose to focus on you. They are specifically attempting to damage your spiritual relationship with God. IT IS INTENTIONAL and they are working hard to accomplish their task. They are attacking you every day in a variety of ways. You also must keep in mind that they are acting in ways to hurt you mentally, physically and spiritually via temptation. They tempt your carnal nature. They don't ask for permission. They aren't just out there in the spiritual world hoping you will give into your carnal nature. We are going to say it again. Their job is to tempt you and they are good at it. Consider the fact that these dark spiritual forces are thousands of years old and have had a lot of time to improve their tactics. They are good at what they do.

With the above in mind, we want you to really put thought into what we are about to communicate. Why are you told to put on the armor of God and learn to use the Sword of the Spirit to protect yourself? Are you putting on this armor or learning to use the sword simply because the Holy Spirit told us to do it, or is there an important purpose for following his instructions? In Ephesians 6:10-18 Paul writes,

"Finally, be strong in the Lord and in the strength of his might. Put on the whole armor of God, **that you may be able to stand against the schemes of the devil.** For we do not wrestle against flesh and blood, but **against the rulers, against the authorities, against the cosmic powers over this present darkness, against the spiritual forces of evil in the heavenly places**. Therefore take up the whole armor of God, that you may **be able to withstand in the evil day, and having done all, to stand firm**. Stand therefore, having fastened on the belt of truth, and having put on the breastplate of righteousness, and, as shoes for your feet, having put on the readiness given by the gospel of peace. In all circumstances take up the shield of faith, with which **you can**

extinguish all the flaming darts of the evil one; and take the
helmet of salvation, and the sword of the Spirit,
which is the word of God, **praying at all times in the Spirit,
with all prayer and supplication**.
To that end, **keep alert with all perseverance**,
making supplication for all the saints."

Satan has multiple types of dark, unholy spiritual forces that can attack our world and have done so since the beginning of planet earth. They have done their job well. Hate, pride, jealousy, envy, desire for power and so much more have led to evil permeating our world. The good news is that neither Satan nor any of his minions can force you to sin. His greatest tool to damage you spiritually is to tempt and deceive you instead. His lies are often subtle but effective. Every dart sent towards you is an attempt to damage you spiritually or ultimately cause your spiritual death. They send darts at you every day. Sometimes they sting or hurt even when you have your armor on. Sometimes you are damaged so subtly that you don't realize what's happening. They can encourage you to do something that appears to be right but in fact is simply taking you one step closer to darkness. They are deceptive and are committed to your downfall.

While Satan's minions are attacking you on a daily basis, the Holy Spirit who is inside of you can do nothing to help. He can't providentially act on his own. Is that right? That's absolutely not true! How could God allow Satanic forces to damage, throw darts at and tempt you and not let His Holy Spirit, who is inside of you, provide some protection? Obviously He doesn't allow you to stand alone and that's why the Holy Spirit can providentially work within you to help protect you from the wiles of Satanic forces. He can act and that is one of the reasons He is within each and every Christian. Do you really believe that the Holy Spirit within you sits back and chooses to not help you when you are tempted or tried by dark spiritual forces? What is the purpose of Ephesians 6:18?

"praying at all times in the Spirit, with all prayer
and supplication."

The darts of the evil one has often been described as temptations and we believe this interpretation is correct; it is through temptation that Satan can bring about spiritual injury and spiritual death.

Look at Ephesians 6:10-18 again. Is there a reason and purpose for following Paul's directions? Satan's minions are constantly attacking us. They are real. It is a fact that there are evil forces out there who are seeking to get into your head and tempt you to sin or question God and the Bible. They are real and they seek to pull you into darkness. Can any Christian believe that the Holy Spirit, who is inside of you, will not seek to help you in this battle? Would He not urge you to fight them off. We can't imagine that God would let Satanic forces impact you without allowing His Spirt to aid you. And why are you told to pray and make supplication? Are you to ask God to help you and His only answer is READ AND UNDERSTAND THE BOOK? Our God and His Spirit are greater than that. They can help in providential ways.

On the opposite side, are Satanic forces limited to using a book to cause you to change and go to the dark side? If so, what book are you reading that supports their agenda? Would you really want to read such a book? Most Christians would not want the Satanic Bible in their home let alone read it. Spiritual forces of darkness can obviously take action independent of any written work. They throw darts at you as often as they desire. C.S. Lewis wrote a book titled, The Screwtape Letters. This is a wonderful work on the deceptiveness of temptation and how Satan and his minions sometimes gently strike at all of us in order to gradually and deceptively pull us away from God. The fiery darts that spiritual forces of darkness send toward you are not always obvious. That's why Paul says in Ephesians 6:18,

> "To that end, keep alert with all perseverance..."

With this in mind, we cannot believe that the Holy Spirit does not work within you, urging you, nudging you towards light and holiness when darkness tempts you. That is one of His most important jobs.

When we read the Scriptures it tells us that that the Holy Spirit takes up residency within us when we are baptized (Acts 2:38). We are given the gift of the Holy Spirit and He does play a big role in our Christian walk. So, what does he do for you? He will help you through hard times. He will help you make better decisions regarding your daily holiness. He will help you grow and mature spiritually. In His own way he will nudge you in the right direction if you let Him. How does He do that? Let's look at Ephesians 6:17 again. God's word (New Testament) is described as the Sword of the Spirit. According to Thomas (1939) the Holy Spirit places that sword into the hands of the Christian so that he can battle evil forces. In other words, the Holy Spirit helps the Christian use His sword to defeat evil and to help protect himself.

The work of the Holy Spirit is extremely important so, let's summarize what we have written about the Holy spirit and how he works in your life. We believe that the Spirit works in two ways. First, he works in a way that can best be termed as 'revelation'. This is NOT extra Biblical revelation! It is an action by which the Spirit helps Christians better understand Scriptural truths (1 Corinthians 2:12-13). Have you ever read a Scripture for the third, fourth or fifth time and all of a sudden you get an insight. All of a sudden something makes more sense, or a realization of a deeper meaning occurs. Most of us have experienced this. This is one of the ways the Holy Spirit can reveal or help us finally 'get' what Scripture is communicating. This particular function is one of the most accepted works of the Spirit. This is where he functions through and with the Word. Second, the Holy Spirit works in a providential way. This means that God, through the Holy Spirit, works in your life and or affairs in ways that differ from the ordinary workings of natural law and in addition to the Bible. We know the Holy Spirit gives you strength and helps you when you are tempted. It's important to keep in mind that His workings support and agree with what is in the Bible. None of His 'revelations' or urgings will conflict with what you find in the Bible.

Personal Reflection

List three things that you learned or that were reinforced that helped you understand how the Holy Spirit works in your life in providential ways.

1.

2.

3.

Part Five: Balanced Christianity and Discipleship

As in all things balance is extremely important. So it is with Christianity. To put it simply, we need to have a horizontal relationship with brothers and sisters and also work with the unchurched. Our vertical relationship is also important. We need to be speaking to the father through prayer and listening to His Will by reading his word.

- Motivation and Balance is Key to Spiritual Growth
- Prayer
- Prayer and Fasting
- Meditation
- Knowing God's Word
- Outreach, Evangelism and Gifts
- Fellowship and One Anothering
- Fellowship and Worship
- Confession and Forgiveness in Relationships
- Fellowship, the World and Spiritual Warfare
- Judging, Reproving, Rebuking and Helping Fellow Christians

Motivation and Balance is Key to Spiritual Growth

Chapter Sixteen

You have learned much about God, Faith, Spiritual Growth, the Holy Spirit and how you live the Christian life. All the information that has been placed before you up to now is foundational in many ways as you seek to allow Christ to work in you. However, at this point, there are two more important points that you need to honestly consider. First, you need to understand that God has given you a specific motivation that can bring you joy and helps you function in His body the way He intended. He actually chose a Gift that He wants you to use for both your benefit and for the benefit of your brothers and sisters in Christ. That gift also becomes a natural way for you to reach out to the unchurched. Second, he wants you to have a proper balance spiritually. He wants you to, 1) have a progressive and growing hunger for the Word, 2) a consistent prayer life, 3) a consistent involvement in fellowship, and 4) a consistent outreach. We will cover the following in this chapter.

- The Underlying Motivation for Balance
- The Purpose of Your Motivational Gift
- Key Takeaways Regarding Our Gift
- Motivational Gifts
- The Proper Balance

The Underlying Motivation for Balance

To begin with, it is important for you to understand that you are given a Motivational Gift by God. To fail to know or understand your Gift is to minimize your ability to function in His body as He desires. It is with this in mind that you need to develop a better understanding of what your primary motivational Gift (Gift of Charismata) is so that you can use it to Glorify God and support the body. When utilized as God intended, your Gift can, help the body grow, give you a natural avenue to reach out to the unchurched or those who need a closer relationship with God and the body and provide you with joyful experience as you serve God. All of the motivational Gifts are essential for the local body to function efficiently. Each one is important in the body and all of us should be working together in harmony for the benefit of the whole body. We want to share something that is important but often overlooked. The local church is not an organization, it is an organism. It should be a functional, working body of Christ in this world and should be treated as such. It is supposed to be a body that functions in support of each part. That doesn't mean that the body shouldn't be organized. Actually, the gift of administration or organization is in a sense the brain of the body. It helps each part do their job as God intends. See the work titled, Spiritual Gifts and Ministry (Crites, 2019) for examples as to how the body as an organism is meant to work together. When you see how the gifts differ and how they support one another for the benefit of the whole body it all seems to make more sense. So, in summary, your Gift is given you for three specific reasons.

All of the motivational Gifts are essential for the local body to function efficiently. Each one is important in the body and all of us should be working together in harmony for the benefit of the whole body.

1. To benefit and help brothers and sisters grow and mature in Christ.
2. To help the unchurched see what a Christian life is like and ultimately be changed because of it. In other words, your Gift can become your natural outreach or evangelistic method.
3. To benefit you by giving you joy in service. This happens as you function in the body using your Gift as God intended.

The Purpose of Your Motivational Gift

Your gift is a God-given motivation for serving in the body of Christ to show glory and honor for God! It is a spiritual motivation to work for God in building up the body of Christ (1 Peter 4:10-11; Ephesians 4:11-12).

In 1 Peter 4:10-11 Peter states,

> "As each has received a Gift [Charisma], use it to serve one another, as good stewards of God's varied grace: whoever speaks, as one who speaks oracles of God; whoever serves, as one who serves by the strength that God supplies--in order that in everything God may be glorified through Jesus Christ. To him belong glory and dominion forever and ever, Amen."

Key Takeaways Regarding Your Gift

How do you get this motivational Gift? Is it something you develop by practice? Let's see what the Scripture says about how you obtain a motivational Gift. Read the Scriptures shown below and then look at our interpretation as to what it means. Are our statements correct or not?

Key Takeaways Regarding Our Gift	
1 Corinthians 1:7	God gives you a Gift that He wants you to have and use in the body.
1 Peter 4:10	The purpose of your Gift is for you to use it for the benefit the body.
1 Corinthians 12:12-26	God arranges the parts of the body as He wants them to be!
STS: Underline the Scriptures above in orange.	

So, yes, you have been given a Gift by God. You should know what it is, or at the very least want to learn what it is so that you can begin to find your place in the body. You should be functioning in the body using your Gift just as God intended. If you are, you will get more joy from service. If you don't use your Gift, you may feel off, weary or frustrated at times. It may be more like a chore when you serve and that is not what God wants for you. God gave you this specific motivational Gift (Charismata) for a purpose. He placed you in the body where He wants you to be so that you can best serve, uplift and benefit the body.

Motivational Gifts

Each motivational Gift has a purpose and aids the body in a specific way. The chart below shows how each Gift can positively impact the body and how it can be used to reach the unchurched or help those who are less involved. Read each one and try to determine which one is most like you. Most of all, which one seems to be enjoyable when you participate in it. The work titled, *Spiritual Gifts and Ministry* has a test in it that would help you better determine what your Gift is and how you might use it in ministry and as a possible outreach or in-reach method. It is also a detailed study of Gifts and Ministry.

Motivational Gift	**Biblical Manifestation**
Prophecy Romans 12:6	Preaching the Word of God by being motivated by God's Gift He gave you.
Service Romans 12:7	Acts of service toward others or the church that is motivated by God's Gift He gave you.
Teaching Romans 12:7	Searching for truth and Teaching God's word that is motivated by God's Gift He gave you.
Exhortation Romans 12:8	Counsel, consolation and exhortation to others motivated by God's Gift He gave you.
Giving Romans 12:8	Giving that is motivated by God's Gift He gave you.
Organization/ Administration Romans 12:8	Organizing or administrating parts of the body motivated by God's Gift He gave you. Seeing the body as an organism.
Mercy Romans 12:8	Acts of love motivated by God's Gift He gave you.

You should research these gifts to see which one seems to be the one that fits you best. As you have helped out in your local congregation in the past, which area were you drawn to the most? Which one seemed to produce the most joy in you when you were serving others?

The Proper Balance

We believe that there are four more key areas that stand out as being essential to spiritual growth and the discipling process. Yes, this book is about discipling. However, a disciple is much more effective if he has the needed tools and knowledge to help groups, fringe members and non-Christians. Hopefully this book will prepare you to be the best disciple you can be. The four areas are:

1. A progressive and growing hunger for the Word (2 Timothy 2:15). You should want to learn more about what the Bible teaches (See Comparative Doctrine for over fifty doctrinal beliefs that focus on what the Bible teaches.)
2. A consistent prayer life (John 14:13). Martin Luther is often quoted as saying, "I have so much to do that I shall spend the first three hours in prayer."
3. A consistent involvement in fellowship (1 John 1:7). God wants us to grow together. He wants us to build each other up using our Gift so that the local body of Christ can function at its peak level.
4. A consistent outreach (Matthew 28:18-20). God wants each of us to reach out to others and He has provided us multiple ways to accomplish this. Our God given gift is one of the best ways to reach out to others.

All of us should be making these areas a priority in our lives. God wants us to grow into all four areas in ways that make us Spiritual adults who can truly impact others. This fourfold concept best describes what a mature disciple should work for and hopefully ultimately possess. Let's break this down into two important parts. First, you need to realize that your vertical relationship with God is essential if you are to be spiritually healthy. That means you need to have both an ongoing prayer life and study of God's Word. Second, you need to have ongoing horizontal relationship with fellow Christians. You need to be spending time in relationship with your brothers and sisters in order to help build each other up and to recharge so to speak. You also need to consistently be reaching out in ways that are consistent with your God given gift. There are many ways to accomplish this, and they will be discussed in a later chapter. Your physical body functions best when rest, food, exercise, and revitalization are consistent in your life. The same thing applies to the Christian, but on a spiritual level. A true disciple must have or be growing into:

To road to spiritual maturity calls for you to be progressing in your time with God which is prayer, meditation and study of his word, and outreach and fellowship.

Spiritual Rest	=	Prayer (& Meditation)
Spiritual Food	=	Word
Spiritual Exercise	=	Outreach
Spiritual Revitalization	=	Fellowship

Remove any of the elements above and the road to Spiritual maturity becomes increasingly difficult.

You have seen the necessity of building a good foundation for your Christianity and how important preparation is in the Discipleship process. The next four chapters will provide a deeper look at each of these four areas listed above. They are all necessary for you to become a balanced disciple.

Personal Reflection

List three things that you learned or that were reinforced that helped you understand how your spiritual motivation and balance can bring you joy and helps you function in His body the way He intended.

1.

2.

3.

Prayer

Chapter Seventeen

Prayer is our direct communication with God. Unlike most people you know, God will take a call at any time. He's listening, waiting to hear from you. In Philippians 4:6 Paul states, "Do not be anxious about anything, but in everything by prayer and supplication with thanksgiving let your requests be made known to God." That sounds easy, but for some it is difficult. Just keep in mind that praying becomes more natural as you participate in it. As humans, we have a tendency to want to fix things for ourselves. The good news is that once we become a Christian, we can talk with God and He will help us. Just like a new found friend, the more we talk to our Father, the easier it will become to share our thoughts, needs, thanksgiving and more. The point is this. You just need to talk with God. It doesn't have to be formal. You don't have to use eloquent words. Simply share what's on your heart. There will be times for specific, deeper and much larger asks from God. There should also be times of adoration for God, thankfulness and much more. However, right now just consider how you could intentionally take moments in time and dedicate them to moments of prayer. With this in mind let's take a close look at prayer and what this simple act can do for you and how you can make it a part of your everyday life.

- The Purpose of Prayer
- The Conditions of Prayer
- Pray as the Master Would
- Your Prayer Life

- Different Kinds of Prayer
- Answered Prayer
- Some Keys to Prayer
- Prayer and Fasting

The Purpose of Prayer

When you met your closest friend some time ago what caused you to become and stay friends? Yes, there had to be some commonality. Yes, there needed to be some interest on both your part and the other person. But what kept it going? Not to over-simplify this, but you kept in touch. You talked. You shared good times and bad. You helped each other when things weren't going well and shared joy with each other when wonderful life events occurred. One of the greatest and often overlooked purposes of prayer is to be able to speak with the Father and to listen to Him so that you can grow in relationship. The good news is that He talks back to you through His Written Word and through the Holy Spirit. Even more important is that you should listen. Those talks are what help you develop a stronger relationship, a better connection. There are many Scriptures that communicate the purpose of prayer and indeed there are many reasons why it is important. Robert Milligan made what we believe is a powerful statement about prayer. He stated that, "It enables us to form a habit of close and intimate union, communion and fellowship with God (Milligan, 1868). If all of us could truly do that with prayer, would we ever want to let God down by not living the life He wants us to live. We think not. Habits can be good or bad. However, if we seek to develop a prayer life that habitually draws us closer to God, it would obviously be a good thing. That is one of the reasons we are told in 1 Thessalonians 5:16-18 that we are to "pray without ceasing." To us and many others that simply means that we should have a prayerful attitude at all times as we seek to become the nature of God. It also means that we should be constantly thankful for what God has done for us and so much more. When we keep those things in mind, it makes it both easier and desirable to take a moment and speak with God.

It enables us to form a habit of close and intimate union, communion and fellowship with God.

The Conditions of Prayer

Are there conditions for prayer? Does God have an expectation regarding how we pray, not just whether or not we actually pray? Milligan (1868) believed that prayer should be offered in the way and on the conditions which God has himself prescribed. Using both his words and some mild adaptation they are as follows:

1. Your prayers should be offered up in faith. In Hebrews 11:6 we are told, "And without faith it is impossible to please him, for whoever would draw near to God must believe that he exists and that he rewards those who seek him."
2. That it be offered in the spirit of obedience; or with an honest purpose and intention to do the will of God; to cease to do evil, and to learn to do well. In Psalm 66:18 it says, "If I had cherished iniquity in my heart, the Lord would not have listened." Proverbs 28:9 also communicates this message. "If one turns away his ear from hearing the law, even his prayer is an abomination." If our prayers are offered in a selfish way or if we live a life turned away from God we must question if we have the right motive in our prayer life.
3. Prayer should be offered in the spirit of profound reverence and humility. In James 4:6b we are told, "God opposes the proud but gives grace to the humble." We should come before God with a humble heart, showing our adoration and recognition of His ultimate greatness.
4. Our prayers should be offered in the spirit of forgiveness. We must have a forgiving heart and in turn show forgiving actions. How can we plead for forgiveness if we are not forgiving others. Matthew 6:15 Jesus said, "but if you do not forgive others their trespasses, neither will your Father forgive your trespasses." A life of forgiveness is both good for the forgiven and also healing for the one who forgives.
5. Prayer should be offered through Christ as the great and only mediator and great high priest of the New Covenant. In Hebrews 4:14-16 we are told, "Since then we have a great high priest who has passed through the heavens, Jesus, the Son of God, let us hold fast our confession. For we do not have a high priest who is unable to sympathize with our weaknesses, but one who in every respect has been tempted as we are, yet without sin. Let us then with confidence draw near to the throne of grace, that we may

receive mercy and find grace to help in time of need." Most Christians do pray to God the father in the name of Jesus the Christ. That is as it should be.

These five conditions for prayer appear to be important if we are to pray in a way that is both meaningful and opens the door for God to listen to you as one of his children. Are these the only conditions? No, they are not. Will God accept our prayers even if we don't fulfill all those conditions shown above? If you pray with a penitent and humble heart we are sure that God will hear your prayer. After all, one of the benefits of the Holy Spirit is that he will speak for you to the Father. That doesn't mean that we shouldn't seek to grow to the point that our prayers represent how we should respect and Glorify God. If so, you are on the right track. Look at the chart on the next page to see how you might improve your prayer life.

Conditions for Prayer	
Condition	**How am I doing?**
My prayers offered up in faith.	__Yes __Needs Work __No
My prayers offered up with the intention to do the will of God; to cease to do evil, and to learn to do well.	__Yes __Needs Work __No
My prayers are offered in the spirit of profound reverence and humility.	__Yes __Needs Work __No
My prayers are offered up with a forgiving heart and in turn show forgiving actions to others.	__Yes __Needs Work __No
My prayers are offered through Christ as the great and only mediator and great high priest of the New Covenant.	__Yes __Needs Work __No

Pray as the Master Would

Your Christian life is best planned and lived through earnest and fervent prayer. Through prayer, God can freely work in your heart and in your daily life. You need to consider that God can accomplish far more than you could ever plan or imagine. During Jesus time on earth he was able to share with others how to save the world, not for just the time he was here but for future generations. Jesus shared one of his greatest secrets that allowed him to accomplish so much. Simply stated, Jesus spent much of His time in prayer to His Father. We can't imagine that he didn't discuss how he would live, minister, worship, suffer and die on the cross with his Father. Because of the New Testament we can see the life of Jesus showing us real life lessons about how to pray to the father.

> *"If Jesus felt He needed to pray, how much more do we need to pray."*
> *Billy Graham*

If you want to have a powerful and beneficial prayer life, you may want to follow Jesus example regarding prayer. There are over twenty examples in the Gospels that specifically call attention to Jesus' practice of prayer. Let's take a look at these and see how prayer was important in His life.

Jesus' Prayers

Each of the Scriptures below address special times in Jesus' life. In most cases we can only imagine what was on his mind before these events occurred since he was in Prayer with His father before so many events.

Scripture	Basic Scripture Content
Luke 3:21	His baptism.
Mark 1:35	Healing the multitudes.
Luke 5:16	Before conflict with religious leaders.
Luke 6:12	Selection of the 12 Apostles.
Matthew 14:19	Feeding of the five thousand.
Mark 6:46	After sending away the five thousand.
Mark 7:34	Healing of the deaf mute.
Matthew 15:36	Feeding the four thousand.
Luke 9:10	The confession of His Messiahship.
Luke 9:29	On the Mount of Transfiguration.
Luke10:21-22	On hearing the disciples' reports on evangelism.
Luke 11:1	Teaching the disciples to pray.
Mark 10:16	Blessing little children.
John 12:27	In the discussion with the Greeks.
Luke 22:32	His loving concern for Peter.
John 17:6-19	His high priestly prayer before he goes to die.

Luke 22:39-46	In Gethsemane.
Matthew 26:27	The Last Supper.
Luke 13:46	On the Cross.
Luke 24:30	After His resurrection in Emmaus.

Even before Jesus' ministry began, we can't imagine that He wasn't praying to His Father. Considering the fact that He had been previously standing next to His father, helping with creation, talking to Him about what was to come and so much more, we can't imagine that He didn't want to take time to pray and talk to his father about his daily events. He knew what was to come, as did his father, yet He spoke to his Father over and over while on earth. He was giving his disciples and us an example of how prayer was important to a Christian. Each prayer was an example showing the necessity of having communication with the Father. Even though His disciples did not always understand the need for prayer, he was an example of living a prayer filled life. His goal was to teach them to pray in all things. Through his teaching they would grow to understand that they could not truly be mature disciples until they had learned to pray to God as Jesus prayed. This very principle applies to us today. To be a mature disciple of Christ calls for daily prayer.

Your Prayer Life

As a Christian you need to seek to be wise like Jesus and engage in prayers to God when decisions and choices need to be made in your life. You should talk to Him often. The Holy Spirit gives you all the assistance you need to pray (Romans 8:26). He will help when you cannot find the words to communicate what you want to say. You just have to initiate the conversation with God. In addition, as a forgiven sinner who is subject to temptation and sin, you must continue to pray and constantly seek to better know, do and internalize the will and nature of God (1 Thessalonians 5:17; Romans 12:12; Psalms 55:16-17). It's sad to say that many of our prayers are vague, indefinite collections of commonly stated requests. Our prayers should be filled with adoration to God for who He is and for what He has done for us and for our world. We should confess our weakness and sins to Him and ask for help and strength to become stronger and more mature. We should be offering out thanks for answered prayer and for all the good things that He has given us. And yes, we should lay our concerns, our hurts, our needs before him as well as the concerns, hurts or needs that our world or the people around us are experiencing. If your prayer is the same prayer every time you speak to God, you have to ask, 'Am I growing?' 'Am I learning how to really speak with the Father as Jesus did?' Many important blessings from God are missed by many Christians because they do not ask or fail to receive because they ask amiss (James 4:2-3).

We really want you to consider the following question. Though Christians recognize the facts that, 1) God assists us in our prayer, 2) prayer defeats sin, and 3) prayer gives direction, why do countless Christians continue to have a poor prayer life? If that is true about you, what do you need to do instead?

It's sad that many of our prayers are much like a child crying to be fed as the mother attempts to put food in his mouth. We pray, God seeks to answer our prayers, but due to our impatience or simply because we do not acknowledge the answer He gives us, we entirely miss out on His blessings. Believers must persevere or pray without ceasing. It is through prayer that we can more deeply understand the indwelling, working and help that the Holy Spirit can give. Even though our prayer may be weak in the beginning, due to spiritual immaturity, sin (Psalms 66:18), unbelief (Matthew 21:22; James 1:6-8), we can be sure that it will grow in strength and meaning as we mature in Christ and as we let the Holy Spirit work within us and for us.

No matter how beneficial prayer can be, it is sad to note that prayer is often on the bottom list of our daily priorities. It often gets left out because of all the daily demands and frustrations. That is one of the reasons why it is so important. Consider the following statement. We heard someone say this during our travels. Prayer is the most difficult work on earth, because the devil will find a thousand good things for you to do to keep you from praying. Is this true for you? If so, what should you do? If this is occurring in your life, your priorities are out of order. It is usually not just a question of having time to pray. It has more to do with what you hold important and whether or not you are self-disciplined in your Christian life (2 Peter 1:3-11). We obviously make time for those things in our life that we believe are important or that is urgent. We need to subjugate all that is earthly and instead make our spiritual life a priority or we may miss out on

> *Prayer is the most difficult work on earth, because the devil will find a thousand good things for you to do to keep you from praying.*

either seeing or benefiting from the positive results from our prayers.

In conclusion, we must consistently work on developing a stronger, healthier prayer life. Speaking with the Father is a powerful way to keep yourself on track. The more you speak to Him the closer you will feel to Him. Prayer can be difficult. Satan makes it so. Just remember that God is merciful, caring, and yearns to listen (Psalm 50:15; Psalm 81:10; Jeremiah 33:3). When all else fails, pray as the master would. One last thing you should consider is this. Rather than use my own words I'd like to take a quote from Andrew Murray. In his book, With Christ in the School of Prayer, he stated, "Reading a book about prayer, listening to lectures and talking about it is very good, but it won't teach you to pray. You get nothing without exercise, without practice. I might listen for a year to a professor of music playing the most beautiful music, but that won't teach me how to play an instrument." So, if you want to learn to pray the first thing you must do is take time to pray; often.

Different Kinds of Prayer

Several people have identified different ways to describe various aspects of prayer that should be considered in your prayer life. When you study the Bible, you will find that there are several different kinds of prayer. Obviously, there are different reasons why you talk to God. The information on the next page is meant to help you remember some of the primary reasons for prayer. We are going to use the word ACTS to help you remember the different reasons for prayer. The word ACTS stands for:

- **A**doration
- **C**onfession
- **T**hanksgiving
- **S**upplication

Reason	**Example**
A doration	Adore or revere God for His qualities. Read Psalms 145:1-8 and list some of His qualities. Review chapter one of this book for more reasons to adore or revere God.
C onfession	Confess you sins to God and ask for strength and help to overcome your weaknesses.

T hanksgiving	Thank God for what He has done in our lives. Think back over the week. List four things that He has done for you, then thank Him!
S upplication	Give supplication to God. Make requests for self and others. Think of two people who need your prayers or two needs that you know about. List them and read Ephesians 6:18.

ACTS is an easy way to remember specific types of prayer. However, there are other types of prayer that we want to briefly address. Petition is also a form of prayer. This is where you specifically ask God for something that you need. This is a form of Supplication. Another form of Supplication is intercession. This is when you ask for God's assistance for others, e.g., health, financial issues, struggles of any kind. Perseverance is also an important aspect of prayer. We should continue to ask God so that He can see that we are 'serious' about what we are asking for. However, we also want communicate we understand that that we must accept His will. You can break down prayer into many different forms for many different reasons. However, the most important thing about prayer is that the more you participate in it, the closer to God you should become.

Some of you may have noticed that asking for forgiveness of sins is not listed as a purpose of or type of prayer. Yes, it is good to acknowledge or confess your sins to God. That shows a contrite heart that God wants. Keep in mind that you should always have a penitent heart. However, you should also want to let Him know that you appreciate His forgiveness. With humility, you should constantly thank Him for the forgiveness that He gives you each day. Must we ask for forgiveness of sins to be forgiven? Good question!

One of the greatest aspects of Grace is that because of Christ's work on the cross we are forgiven even before we ask. Let me explain. Through Justification God declares that you are not guilty of any sin, past, present and future as long as you continue to be his child. Justification is the judicial or legal aspect of Grace. God also gives you Jesus' righteousness. Was Jesus sinless? Yes he was and will ever be that way. When you were baptized, you were covered by his blood that was shed on the cross. As a result, when God looks at you He chooses to see His Son's perfection, not our sins. God along with his Holy Spirit regenerated you, sanctified you and made you a holy vessel. As long as you live a holy life dedicated to Him, forgiveness is there for you from a loving father even before you ask. See Grace and Salvation (Crites) for a deep dive into this topic.

Answered Prayer

We have found that it can be very helpful and revealing when you keep track of God's answers to our Prayers. Too many times, in our weakness, we get frustrated because God doesn't seem to answer our prayers. What many of us fail to realize is that He is constantly answering prayers if we are asking. We all know we should be praying on a daily basis. We often ask for the return to health of a friend or loved one. We also ask for distant desires like good mates for our children when they grow up. Those are good things to speak to God about. However, because of our failure to see God's answers to prayer, many of us become doubting Thomas'. We require concrete evidence of God's working in our lives. All of us like to see or hear of answered prayer. It makes us feel good to see or hear that God is working in other people's lives. In the next few days or weeks write down a few of your requests in the spaces provided below. It may take time but watch to see how God answers your prayers.

Keeping track of God's answers to prayer can be a fulfilling way to see how God is working your life and the lives of others. A complimentary work titled, *Prayer Journal: Keeping Track of Answers to Prayer* (Crites, 2018) is a great tool to help you keep track of how God is working in your life and in the lives of those you pray for. Just keep in mind that a non-answer or an answer that you don't prefer doesn't mean that He isn't doing the best thing for you in the long run. Use the chart below as a model if you like.

Answered Prayer		
Date	Request	God's Answer

> *"When I pray coincidences happen, when I don't, they don't."*
> *William Temple*

A Challenge to You

There is nothing that will indicate a person's spiritual condition as quickly as his personal prayer life. For the next thirty days carefully listen to the context of 1) your own prayers, 2) the prayers of your friends, and 3) the congregational public prayers. Mentally take notice of which of the following three categories each prayer falls under. For instance:

- A general, thank you, Lord.
- Help us and others to overcome, Lord.
- Give 'things' to us and others, Lord (spiritual or material).

Now, ask yourself the following questions:

- Did the prayer reveal positive possession of what Christ has already give us through His Word.
- Did the prayer center more upon the words, 'I, me, our, we, us', OR on the words, 'thy, thou, you, your'? Where was the focus?
- Did the prayer generally express Christ's victory for us?
- Did you hear **A**doration, **C**onfession, **T**hanksgiving and **S**upplication?

Keep in mind that different prayers may need to include different aspects of ACTS. Sometimes, many of our prayers might be more meaningful if all four areas were part of the prayer as we speak to our God. We also need to be aware that we should be specific and persistent when there is a need. Just keep in mind that as Christians, we need to praise God in our prayers declaring that because we are in Christ we cannot fail or be defeated. The battle has been won by Christ and we need to acknowledge that often. Remember that the time lapse between our prayer request and the answer to our prayer is but our loving Father testing and purifying our faith which to Him is more precious than gold.

Biblical Prayer	
Scripture	**Concept Summarized**
Christ Teaches Us	
Luke 11:1	Only He can teach us to pray.
Prayer is Conditional On	
John 15:7	Must abide in Him.
John 15:16	Must be righteous, bearing abiding fruit.
Our Prayers Should	
John 4:23-24	Be offered up in spirit and truth.
Mark 11:22-24	Be in faith.
1 John 5:14-15	Be in boldness, knowing that they are in accordance with His will.
Mark 10:51	Be specific.
Luke 18:1-8	Be persevering.
1 Thessalonians 5:17	Be without ceasing.
Matthew 6:6	Be in secret.
Matthew 18:19-20	Be united.
God's Response	
Matthew 7:9-11	He will give to those who ask.
The Major Importance of Prayer	
John 14:13	So that the Father may be glorified.

Some Keys to Prayer

In summary, the following are some keys to prayer that we all should be considering as we seek to speak with God. Keep in mind that we are not all perfect, but we should seek to have a prayer life that truly shows our desire to speak with God while at the same time in humility we seek to be what God wants us to be.

- Your prayers should be offered up in faith, believing that Gode listens and will answer. It may not always be what we want or when we want it but he will answer.
- One of the greatest purposes of prayer is to maintain a 'dialogue' with God. You should be open to listening to him in the quietness that prayer offers.
- Prayer provides you with an opportunity to develop a spiritually healthy habit of maintaining a close relationship

with the Father. You build relationship by talking with your friends. You can do the same with God.

- Prayers should be offered in the spirit of obedience; or with an honest purpose and intention to do the will of God; to cease to do evil, and to learn to do well.
- Prayer should be offered in the spirit of profound reverence and humility.
- Your prayers should be offered in the spirit of forgiveness. You must have a forgiving heart and in turn show forgiving actions.
- Prayer should be offered through Christ as the great and only mediator and great high priest of the New Covenant.
- Know that the Holy Spirit communicates for us even when our thoughts and words aren't adequate.
- As a Christian you need to seek to be wise like Jesus and engage in prayers to God when decisions and choices need to be made in your life. You should also ask often.
- Adoration: Prayers should be specifically filled with adoration to God for who He is and for what he has done for you specifically and for the world.
- Confession: You should confess your weaknesses and sins to Him and ask for help and strength to become stronger and more mature.
- Thanksgiving: You should be offering your thanks for answered prayer and for all the good things that He has given you.
- Supplication: You should lay your concerns, your hurts, your needs before Him as well as other concerns, hurts or needs that this world or the people around you are experiencing.
- Your prayers should communicate a thankfulness to God for your forgiveness for He has already forgiven you (see Grace and Salvation by Crites 2022). However, that doesn't mean that you should never pray for forgiveness even if you are already forgiven. It shows a right heart when you do.

My son (Russ' Son) recently taught a bible class on Prayer. One of the statements he made caused me to rethink prayer and how often it should possibly occur for Christians today. He said, "I want us to become more comfortable going to Him for everything. Part of this is making time for him. I personally think a 3x a day prayer rhythm is an attainable goal. For those of us who barely pray now this seems extreme but if we want to be people who truly try to be like the early church (and isn't that our claim to fame) then this is what they did. Read through the book of Acts and see how many stories have a line [scripture] about going to a place of prayer or when it was time for prayer. Everything for our spiritual ancestors happened around the times of prayer. Ever wonder how all these people were able to gather so quickly for all of the amazing events that happened on random days in a time when there were no phones and no clocks. They were able to meet because they were already meeting. So, what does a 3x a day rhythm look like? That's up to you." How it happens for you might be different from everyone else. Regardless, we are asking you to consider this 3x a day for your prayer life. It's up to you.

There is so much more that could be said about prayer. We could review all of the books of the Bible and even church history to take a closer look at prayer. However, with what you have read in this chapter we hope that it is obvious that prayer should be at the center of the Christian life. As the theologian George Buttrick said "Prayer is more than a lighted candle, it is the contagion of health, it is the pulse of life." Our hope is that you will make prayer a daily constant that will aid in your Spiritual Growth and help you develop a stronger connection to God.

Personal Reflection

List three things that you learned or that might help you with your personal prayer life.

1.

2.

3.

Prayer and Fasting

Chapter Eighteen

Before we leave prayer, it is important that we take a moment and explain how fasting is often something God's people have done for thousands of years. Fasting has been practiced with and without prayer throughout history for both health and spiritual reasons. The Old Testament is filled with examples as is the New Testament. Moses, David, Esther, and many other Old Testament figures prayed and fasted for several reasons. Prayer and fasting can also be found in the New Testament with Jesus leading the way. If it was important to Him, we certainly should be considering the possibility that fasting is something that God wants us to do. Even though it does not appear to be a command for us to fulfill, the spiritual and physical benefits are significant. We will be covering the following in this chapter.

- Old Testament and Fasting
- New Testament and Fasting
- The Purpose of Fasting
- Physical Effects and Benefits of Fasting
- Spiritual Benefits of Prayer and Fasting

Old Testament and Fasting

In the Old Testament there are multiple times when fasting occurred. Most of the people in the Old Testament fasted in a crisis. However, prayer was often part of the fasting event. Here are some examples:

Fasting in the Old Testament	
Event	Scripture
Ezra fasted for protection. He declared a corporate fast and prayed for a safe journey for the Israelites as they made the nine-hundred-mile trek to Jerusalem from Babylon.	Ezra 8:21-28
Seeking God's Guidance. Nehemiah mourned, fasted, and prayed when he learned Jerusalem's walls had been broken down, leaving the Israelites vulnerable and disgraced.	Nehemiah 1:1-4
Jehoshaphat fasted in the time of the invasion of the confederated armies of Canaanites and Syrians.	2 Chronicles 20:3
David fasted and plead for his son's life.	2 Samuel 12:22-23
David humbled his soul.	Psalm 69:10
God called for the Israelites to return to Him with Fasting, weeping and mourning	Joel 2:12
Through Joel God called His people to fast and cry out to the lord because of their rebellion.	Joel 1:14
Moses fasted for 40 days.	Deuteronomy 9:18-10
Moses Fasted for 40 days.	Exodus 34:28
Esther fasted when faced with danger (Esther 4:16).	Esther 4:16
In repentance, the king of Nineveh covered himself with sackcloth, sat in the dust and ordered the people to fast and pray.	Jonah 3:10
Israelites cried out to God and fasted for help against the enemy.	Judges 20:26
Fasting is a way to humble self in the sight of God.	Psalm 35:13; Ezra 8:21

New Testament and Fasting

It is obviously important that we take a moment and explain how fasting is often connected to prayer in the New Testament. The act of fasting is documented multiple times in the New Testament. It was often done at specific times and events. Jesus and his disciples fasted when decisions were to be made. Sometimes it happened before events occurred and at other times it occurred after events. Even though He did not often discuss the importance of fasting in the New Testament, He certainly stated that should be a part of our lives. In fact, when Jesus taught about fasting, he did not say, if you fast. He said, when you fast, not if. Let's look at Matthew 6:16-18 and read the words of Jesus.

"And when you fast, do not look gloomy like the hypocrites,
for they disfigure their faces that their fasting may be seen by
others. Truly, I say to you, they have received their reward. But
when you fast, anoint your head and wash your face,

Jesus, his apostles and disciples lived a life of prayer connected to fasting. When they had issues that needed to be addressed they not only prayed but often fasted also. For instance:

Fasting in the New Testament	
Jesus fasted after His baptism.	Matthew 3:13
Jesus fasted to prepare himself for God's work on earth.	Matthew 4:1-17
Jesus told his Disciples that they would fast when He was gone.	Mark 2:20
Anna devoted her life to God and daily fasted and prayed.	Luke 2:36-37
Fasted to prepare others for ministry. Paul and Barnabas prayed and fasted for the elders of the churches before committing them to the Lord for His service.	Acts 14:23
Paul fasted for the safety of a ship and its crew.	Acts 27:9-10

The Didache

An early Christian teaching document, the Didache, which most people believe was dated near the end of the first century says this about the role of fasting in the New Testament Church of the day.

In Chapter 8 it says,

"But let not your fasts be with the hypocrites,
for they fast on the second and fifth day of the week.
Rather, fast on the fourth day and the Preparation (Friday).

Do not pray like the hypocrites,
but rather as the Lord commanded in his Gospel, like this:..."

So, the statement of a writer who may very well have known one of the Apostles stated that the church was fasting twice a week. Apparently, fasting was something everyone expected that they would do at that time. However, they were told to not be like the hypocrites when they fasted. Not IF they fasted! Again, that makes sense when you read Jesus' statement when he said, "When you fast" in Matthew 6:16-18.

The Purpose of Fasting

It certainly appears that this habit of fasting two days a week could be signified as a devotional practice among the Christians of the early New Testament church. You have to consider that when you fast you may have opportunity to connect with God at a deeper level, refocus on your calling to fulfil his will in your life and acknowledge that without Him you would have no real purpose.

It's also important that you consider that you aren't fasting so that you can get something from God, although you do get some amazing benefits. However, it certainly is an opportunity for you to give to God in prayer your body and mind as a living sacrifice to Him (Romans 12:1-2).

"Therefore, I urge you, brothers and sisters,
in view of God's mercy, to offer your bodies as a living sacrifice,
holy and pleasing to God—this is your true and proper worship.
Do not conform to the pattern of this world,
but be transformed by the renewing of your mind.
Then you will be able to test and approve what God's will is—
his good, pleasing and perfect will."

With the fact that God's people have fasted for many reasons both in the Old Testament and the New, it should cause you to pause and consider whether or not you should consider fasting as part of your spiritual life also.

Science is just beginning to prove that fasting is indeed healthy for your body in many ways. Let's look and see what has been found up to this point in time.

Two Types of Fasting

Keep in mind that in general there are two types of fasting. First, there is Intermittent fasting (IF). This is an eating pattern that cycles between periods of fasting and eating. It doesn't specify which foods you should eat but rather when you should eat them.

For instance, one common intermittent fasting method includes a 16-hour fast during the day. You can do this once a week, twice a week or several days in a week. It's up to you.

Fasting (PF or Periodic Fasting) occurs when you do not eat anything for a day, three days a week or longer. You should drink water when you fast but no food can be eaten. This is the kind of fast that you most often read about in the Bible. Biblical fasting is often combined with prayer.

Physical Effects and Benefits of Fasting

- Generally, fasting can produce metabolic health benefits. It can improve various risk factors and health markers (Dote-Montero, 2022).
- It can help you burn body fat and reduce weight (Welton, 2020).
- Intermittent and periodic fasting (IF and PF, respectively) are emerging as safe strategies to affect longevity and health span by acting on cellular aging and disease risk factors (Longo, 2021).
- Practicing intermittent fasting for 1 year was more effective at decreasing levels of inflammation and reducing certain risk factors for heart disease compared to a control group (Moro, 2021).
- Alternate-day fasting could reduce levels of total cholesterol and several risk factors for heart disease in people with overweight compared to a control group (Park, 2020).
- Alternate-day fasting could significantly decrease blood pressure, as well as levels of blood triglycerides, total cholesterol, and LDL (bad) cholesterol (Yuanshan, 2020).
- The American Cancer Society Journal notes that intermittent fasting may benefit the treatment and prevention of cancer in some situations. It may decrease

tumor growth and toxicity from chemotherapy in some people (Clifton, 2021).

- In animal studies data suggests that fasting may protect against and improve outcomes for conditions such as Alzheimer's disease (Nasaruddin, 2020) and Parkinson's (Ojha, 2023). Studies are continuing to see if in fact it also impacts humans but the research is encouraging.

There were another hundred or more studies that supported the above studies or looked at a variety of other benefits of fasting or intermittent fasting. Not to be redundant, but I want to be clear on this one thing. God knew all of this long before science began to figure it out. Barring some medical condition, fasting is good for the human condition.

Spiritual Benefits of Fasting and Prayer

Spiritual benefits of Fasting are often subjective and hard to prove. However, so is faith. Just because you can't prove it, doesn't mean something isn't happening. I choose to believe that fasting and prayer coupled is something that God wants and in some way it connects us in a different but good way. Our bodies/brains literally change when we fast. Many have suggested that in Spiritual terms there's a thinning of the veil between this world and the spiritual world.

You can decide for yourself if fasting with prayer enhances your communion with God. At the very least, it produces a healthier body and clears the mind of unwanted and hurtful thoughts.

What are some other potential benefits from fasting? In addition to the physical and spiritual benefits here are a few practical benefits that you may experience. Here are a few.

- Focus on how fasting can help you put thought to how thankful or grateful you are for what God has given you.
- As you learn to master your hunger, you can master any other issue you struggle with, e.g., anger, lust, pride. Give it to God in prayer as you fast.
- Learn to share important issues with God in Prayer.
- Learn to control your urges and be reminded that immediate gratification is not necessarily good for us.

Augustine said, "Fasting cleanses the soul, raises the mind, subjects one's flesh to the spirit, renders the heart contrite and humble, [and] scatters the clouds of concupiscence."

Warning: If you have a medical condition you should speak with your physician before you begin a fast. Those taking medication often need to eat a meal first. Some must take pills twice a day. If that's the case, you can still get benefit from intermittent fasting. Simply eat larger breakfast, skip lunch and eat a small meal later in the day.

Personal Reflection

List three things that you learned or that were reinforced that helped you better understand prayer and/or fasting and what these two acts can do for a Christian.

1.

2.

3.

Meditation

Chapter Nineteen

Prayer is talking to God with the Holy Spirit's help. Simply stated, meditation can simply be contemplating God's will for you and your life. Sometimes prayer can include adoration of God, thankfulness for who He is and what He does for us and so much more. In a sense prayer can also be meditative. Meditation can also be peaceful thoughts or thoughts that produce stillness. Anytime you focus your mind on something relaxing, peaceful, good, etc. you can call it meditation even if it is in the form of a prayer.

Prayer and meditation are actually important for everyone, so please read through this section. Bear with us for a moment. Let's pretend that God will not answer our prayers. He gives no response and provides no help at all. Let's pretend that there is no spiritual benefit of any kind from praying or meditating. We know that is not true but follow this line of thought for just a moment so you can see where we are going. What would be the benefit of prayer or meditation if God wasn't involved? Would there be any kind of benefit? Our question is, 'Could it be that God actually has a purpose for prayer and meditation that goes beyond the spiritual? A benefit that God planned, but did not explain in the Bible? Hopefully that has piqued your interest. Let's take a look at meditation and what it could do for a Christian.

- Old and New Testament View of Meditation
- Physical and Mental Benefits of Meditation
- What We Think is Important
- The Spiritual Side of Meditation
- Optimist and Health
- The Positive Side of What We Think About
- The Spiritual Side of Meditation
- What God Wants From Us
- Prayerful or Meditative Application

Old and New Testament View of Meditation

Both the Old Testament and the New Testament suggest that mediation is something God wants from us. Actually, "in the old testament, prayer was a state of meditation, which completed the circle of communication with God" (Lemmon 1978). The Old testament uses the word meditate in several scriptures (Psalm 119:15; Psalm 63:6; Psalm 119:148). The New Testament also includes several passages that calls for the follower of Christ to focus their mind (meditate) on God (Philippians 4:4-9; Colossians 3:1-3; Romans 8:5-7; Hebrews 3:1; Hebrews 12:2). God does ask us to meditate, be thoughtful or focus on specific spiritual things in our life. We also need to accept that at times prayer can produce a meditative state. Those who have prayed for longer periods of time may have experienced a peacefulness; a calmness that is refreshing. In our world today there is much research that shows several benefits of meditation. As a matter of fact, Dr. Herbert Benson who was a professor from Harvard, wrote a book called the Relaxation Response. His research has been backed up by more current research and some of the findings are amazing. He has continued to write other works explaining how meditation can help a person be healthier in several ways. Before we connect this to what God has asked us to do, let's look at what research has found that shows us how beneficial meditation can be. There are multiple Scriptures that tell us that meditation is a good thing for us to do. We will show those to you soon. Just keep in mind that we are told to meditate on the Lord. Let's take a brief look at the benefits of meditation.

Physical and Mental Benefits of Meditation

What happens when you go into a deep prayer state or meditative state which also produces a state of relaxation? Actually, what happens is astounding. God did make our bodies and He knew that if we meditated or prayed thankful or reverent types of prayers we could go into a relaxed state that would be healing for body, mind, and spirit. Benson found several benefits when he was doing his research. Let's take a look at some of the physiological changes that occur when you spend ten to twenty minutes in a 'meditative' state.

It's important to note that some of these benefits do not occur when you sleep. The only time there are significant changes in your body is when you meditate. God made us the way we are and He built within us mechanisms that helps us live a healthier life and have a healthier mental self. Let's look at some of the benefits.

Changes in the Body	Benefit to Body
Turns off Fight or Flight Response	Immediately reduces stress in the body.
Oxygen Consumption Reduced	Helps prevent dementia.
Respiratory Rate Reduced	Enhances cognition.
Heart Rate Reduced	Can help reduce pain.
Alpha Waves Increased	Emotions can be less overwhelming.
Blood Pressure Reduced	Reduces the risk of hardening of the arteries.
Decrease in Blood Lactate	Body relaxes, less anxious feelings

Our question is, since we know that God does exist, do you believe that He knew that when He made us that this 'relaxation response' would provide these benefits for man? Of course, He did. That is why He asked us to think or act in ways that sometimes doesn't always make sense to us. Why did He tell us to be still and know that He is God (Psalm 46:10)? It's because He made us to be a people who would make prayer and/or meditation part of our daily life so that we can be healthier mentally, physically and spiritually. Let's dig a bit more into what God knew when He made us and what research has found regarding meditation.

Research on the Physical Benefits of Meditation

The following is a list of some of the research that has been done on meditation and how it can impact the body.

- Meditation is associated with self-reports of greater engagement in valued behaviors and interests (Brown & Ryan, 2003) and of ability to engage in goal-directed behavior when emotionally upset (Baer et al., 2006).
- Meditation can improve the quality of life (Nyklíček, & Kuipers, 2008),
- Medication can improve behavioral regulation (Keng, Smoski, Robins, Ekblad, & Brantley, 2010).
- Meditation can enhance greater engagement in valued behaviors and interests (Brown & Ryan, 2003).
- Meditation can enhance the ability to engage in goal-directed behavior when emotionally upset (Baer et al., 2006).
- Meditation can lead to self-reported improved behavioral regulation (Robins et al., 2010).
- Meditation can reduce stress (Goyal, 2013).
- Meditation can reduce the inflammation response caused by stress (Melissa, 2013).
- Meditation may also improve symptoms of stress-related conditions, including irritable bowel syndrome (Shanman, 2017).
- Meditation may also improve symptoms of stress-related conditions, including fibromyalgia (Aman, 2018).
- Meditation may also reduce depression by decreasing levels of these inflammatory chemicals (Kasala, 2013).
- As we get older, our telomeres naturally shorten. Chronic stress can speed up this process, causing faster biological aging. Stress-relieving activities, like metta meditation, can ease this effect. A small 2013 study found that metta meditation is associated with longer telomere length. The researchers speculated that the practice could help improve longevity (Hoge, 2013).

NOTE: We will share more about Metta meditation shortly.

Research on the Mental Benefits of Meditation

In addition to experiencing several physical benefits, meditation can also provide some significant help with your mental or psychological sense of self. We would like to say that it can also impact your spiritual sense of self. The following is a list of some of the research that has been done on meditation and how it can impact your mental, psychological or spiritual self.

- Mindfulness [meditation] is positively associated with psychological health, and training in mindfulness may bring about positive psychological effects. These effects ranged from increased subjective well-being, reduced psychological symptoms and emotional reactivity, to improved regulation of behavior (Keng, 2011).
- Meditation has been shown to predict increases in sense of spirituality (Carmody, 2008).
- Meditation can produce positive states of mind (Bränström, 2010).
- Meditation can decrease rumination, i.e., repetitive thinking or dwelling on negative feelings and distress and their causes and consequences (Shapiro, 2007).
- Meditation can decrease perceived stress (Bränström, 2010; Shapiro, 2007).
- Meditation can reduce overall psychological distress (Carmody, 2008).
- Meditation can reduce cognitive reactivity, i.e., negative patterns of thinking can easily be reactivated through only minor triggers such as subtle changes in mood. (Raes, 2009).
- Meditation can reduce depressive symptoms (Shahar, 2010).
- Meditation may also improve symptoms of stress-related conditions, including post-traumatic stress disorder (Hilton, 2016).
- Meditation may decrease anxiety. Notably, this effect was strongest in those with the highest levels of anxiety (Ome-Johnson, 2014). It may also reduce generalized anxiety (Hoge, 2013).
- People who completed a meditation exercise experienced fewer negative thoughts in response to viewing negative images, compared with those in a control group (Kiken, 2014).

- Meditation improved attention and accuracy while completing a task, compared with those in a control group (Norris, 2018).
- Meditating for just 13 minutes daily enhanced attention and memory after 8 weeks (Basso, 2018).
- Multiple meditation styles can increase attention, memory, and mental quickness in older volunteers (Gard, 2014).

So, God did know what He was doing when He told us to meditate on Him and is Word. Science as once again proved that the Bible has truths in it that are still being discovered. Meditating on God or His word can give you the benefits shown above and for Christians it also provides spiritual benefits.

What We Think is Important

What we think literally defines our character and also determines our mental, physical and spiritual health. Before we jump more deeply into meditation, let's look at one more thing about how we think can impact us. What is optimism? Is it a Biblical concept. We think it is. Free Dictionary defines optimism as, "A tendency to expect the best possible outcome or dwell on the most hopeful aspects of a situation." Merriam Webster defines optimism as "a feeling or belief that good things will happen in the future." Dictionary.com defines optimism as "a disposition or tendency to look on the more favorable side of events or conditions and to expect the most favorable outcome." Regardless of who you look to for a definition they all focus on the idea that an optimist looks for favorable outcomes or believes that something good will happen in the future. All Christians should be optimistic simply because we know our future. The fact that God Justified us or declared us not guilty of all sin when we were saved tells us that He made a way for us to know that we are saved. That non guilty state never changes. Each minute of each day God declares us not guilty of all sin. We can be optimistic because of that great hope that God has given us.

There will be bumps in the road of life. However, the promise of a home prepared for us should cause all of us to become optimists. How does optimism or a lack thereof affect you as a person? Can pessimism cause health problems? Can optimism actually make you healthier or feel better? God knew the answer to those questions before anyone even thought to ask them. He told us how to live in a way that would produce more health mentally, physically and spiritually. Before we go any further let's look at research that has proven God right once again.

Optimism and Health

In a study done in 2009, Rasmussen found that optimism is a significant predictor of positive physical health outcomes. Additional research also suggests that optimism can have positive impact on your life. The results shown below are just a small sample of some of the research that shows how optimism has a positive influence on your health and life.

- In a study found in in Psychological Bulletin on April 17, 2012, researchers from the Harvard University School of Public Health found that a positive psychological outlook appears to reduce the risk of heart attacks, strokes and other cardiovascular events.
- In another study, reported in Archives of Internal Medicine (February 28, 2011), researchers found that individuals who were optimistic about their diagnosis, treatment and recovery were more likely to be alive after 15 years than individuals with lower expectations.
- In the November 2004 issue of The Archives of General Psychiatry a 10–year study was reported regarding optimism. They found that individuals who were most optimistic were 55 percent less likely than those who were most pessimistic to die from any cause during the study.

Pessimism and Health

We haven't found one Scripture that tells us that we should be negative or pessimistic. On the contrary, many Scriptures tell us to be positive, not someone prone to anxiety, depression, and anything else that promotes a negative response within us. In 1 Peter 5:7 tells us that you should be,

"casting all your anxieties on him,
because he cares for you."

God doesn't want you to experience anxiety, depression or any other negative thought or experience. He knows that you will have problems, so He gave you a way reduce or remove negative thoughts and feelings. You just need to let Him help. One of our favorite songs was written by David Slater and is based on

1 Peter 5:7. If you can find it, you may want to memorize it and sing to God when life gets you down. Here is the part that should speak to you.

"I cast all my cares upon you,
I lay all of my burdens down at your feet
And any time I don't know what to do
I will cast all my cares upon you."

Why should you let God help you with pessimism, negativity, etc.? Seligman, who wrote a national best seller titled Learned Optimism reviewed research that suggested that pessimism can cause sickness. A variety of studies he noted suggested that pessimists went to the doctor twice as much as optimists did, and also had twice as many infectious diseases. In another study women who had breast cancer and were optimistic survived longer than their pessimistic counterparts. More recent research supports this data. So, with this in mind there certainly appears to be a connection between pessimism and health. In summary, pessimists are more likely than optimists to suffer from several different health issues. If we listen to God and do what he asks it can have a positive impact on all aspects of our health. Memorize 1 Peter 5:7 and say it to yourself over and over when you are experiencing any negative feeling or sing the song shown above. Research has proved it; God knew it would work when He first created man.

"casting all your anxieties on him,
because he cares for you."

Characteristics of Optimists

We would be remis if we didn't share the basic characteristics of optimism. When you look at these characteristics you shouldn't be surprised that many of them can be found in people who are truly trying to live a Godly life. Here they are:

- Optimists are seldom surprised by trouble.
- Optimists look for partial solutions.
- Optimists believe they have control over their future.
- Optimists allow for regular renewal.
- Optimists interrupt their negative trains of thought.
- Optimists heighten their powers of appreciation.
- Optimists use their imaginations to rehearse success.
- Optimists are cheerful even when they can't be happy.

- Optimists believe they have an almost unlimited capacity for stretching.
- Optimists build lots of love into their lives.
- Optimists like to swap good news (not hurtful gossip).
- Optimists accept what cannot be changed.

With all of the above in mind, let's look at both the positive and negative sides of meditation. Obviously if you 'think a lot' about negative things whether you are in a meditative state or not, it can be damaging. That's what you don't want. One of the good things about meditation is that when you meditate your body responds in a beneficial way even more than when you sleep.

The Positive Side of What We Think About

Psalm 46:10a is a very interesting verse. It calls for us to be still. However, we are not always to just be still, we should be thinking of God; that He is God and that He wants the best for us.

"Be still, and know that I am God."

If you are still and meditate on God the relaxation response that Benson and so many others are now writing about, occurs and your body, mind and spiritual self benefits from it.

Did Paul understand this underlying concept when he penned the words in Philippians 4:8,

"Finally, brothers, whatever is **true**, whatever is **honorable,**
whatever is **just,** whatever is **pure**, whatever is **lovely,**
whatever is **commendable,** if there is any **excellence,**
if there is anything worthy of **praise,**
think about these things."

If you simply think of such things more often it would be very beneficial for your mind, body and spiritual health. If you mediated on such things, it has an even greater positive impact on you as shown in the research above. God knew what He was doing when he made man, and meditation is one of His blessings that all of us simply do not do enough.

What about the Negative

Guess what else He knew when He made us. He knew that if we focused on the negative in life, e.g., worry or anxiety, anger, revenge that it would corrupt our spiritual nature and damage us spiritually, mentally and physically. In Galatians 6:7 Paul states,

"Do not be deceived: God is not mocked,
for whatever one sows, that will he also reap.

That includes what we think, say and do. So, He told us to remove those things from our lives. He told us to not dwell or think about those things. In Colossians 3:1-2 Paul shares this.

"If then you have been raised with Christ,
seek the things that are above, where Christ is,
seated at the right hand of God.
**Set your minds on things that are above,
not on things that are on earth."**

Why? Because negative thoughts damage you mentally, physically and spiritually. On the other hand, if you INPUT or think about positive, Godly things (Set your minds on things that are above) that are peaceful, loving, positive, kind, honorable, etc. that is what you will become! Becoming is a spiritual process and God wants you to be constantly seeking to be more spiritually mature. The benefits are enormous.

The Spiritual Side of Meditation

Optimism, thinking positive thoughts, and prayer have positive benefits. So, even if prayer had no meaning other than it could send you into a relaxation response that could heal your body and mind it would still be a wonderful thing. However, prayer is real. It does have meaning. God does listen and He does answer prayer. He also wants you to meditate. What does God ask you to do regarding meditation? Let's see what some of the Scriptures say about what you could be meditating on.

Meditate on Gods Law: Psalm 1:2 says, "but his delight is in the law of the LORD, and on his law he meditates day and night."

Meditate on God's Word: In Joshua 1:8 we are told to "meditate on the word day and night."

Meditate on God's Ways: Psalm 119:15 "I will meditate on your precepts and fix my eyes on your ways."

Meditate on God: Psalm 63:6 "When I remember you upon my bed, and meditate on you in the watches of the night;"

Meditate on His Promises: Psalm 119:148 "My eyes are awake before the watches of the night, that I may meditate on your promise."

Meditate on his Wondrous Works: Psalm 145:5 "On the glorious splendor of your majesty, and on your wondrous works, I will meditate."

Meditate on His Wondrous Works: Psalm 119:27 "Make me understand the way of your precepts, and I will meditate on your wondrous works."

Meditate on all God has Done: Psalm 143:5 "I remember the days of old; I meditate on all that you have done; I ponder the work of your hands."

Think about God's creation, not just our world but the vastness of all that He created. You can also meditate and be thankful for what God and His Son has done for you. There are so many things that you could identify that would be worthy of your meditation. So, God does want all of us to meditate on Him or His ways and much more. It would be easy to focus on one Scripture for minutes. Meditation is not just something Psychology created. Meditation is something that God has wanted His people to do for thousands of years. What else does God want us to do that will help us be healthier mentally, physically and spiritually.

What God Wants from Us

Paul wrote a letter to the Philippian church that many believe was one of his favorite churches. Let's look at Philippians 4:8 again. He communicates an extremely important message when he says,

"Finally, brothers, whatever is true, whatever is honorable,
whatever is just, whatever is pure, whatever is lovely,
whatever is commendable, if there is any excellence,
if there is anything worthy of praise,
think about these things."

Ultimately, what you put in your mind determines what you will think, say and do. It defines your heart, who you are deeply inside.

Why think about those things? We will go back to a statement that we made earlier. The information you input into your mind defines you. If you meditate on it, the information becomes more deeply imbedded; more part of you. Ultimately, what you put in your mind determines what you will think, say and do. It defines your heart, who you are deeply inside. Why do you think that God wants you to read and understand the Bible? Why do you think He wants you to internalize not just the milk of the word, but the meatier messages that the Bible has within it? It's because what you internalize you become, and He wants you to grow spiritually and eventually become a mature Christian (Hebrews 5:11 through 6:1-3). He also wants you to focus on or think about things that will lift you up and make you healthier mentally, socially, physically and spiritually.

What God Doesn't Want From Us

He doesn't want you to focus on being anxious, angry, revengeful or any other negative feeling that destroys you from the inside out. God wants you to be at peace, unhurried, thankful for each moment that He has given you. In Philippians 4:6-7 Paul writes,

[Do not do this]
"Do not be anxious about anything,

[Do this]
but in everything by prayer and supplication with thanksgiving
let your requests be made known to God.

[If you follow His directions this will happen]
And the peace of God, which surpasses all understanding, will
guard your hearts and your minds in Christ Jesus."

We have said this several times, but it is important to remember. Please keep in mind that God knew what He was doing when He created man. He knows what is best for you and He has communicated in a variety of ways an important message. Think on positive or Godly things. Think on things above. Think about what He has in store for you. When you think, pray or meditate on such things, the body, mind and spiritual life that He gave you will be more fulfilling, happier and healthier. Now, how do you pray or meditate in way that produces such health in all three areas? We will discuss that next.

Prayerful or Meditative Application

With all of the above in mind it should be apparent that God intended you to meditate for two reasons. First, God wants you to meditate on who He is and what He has done for you. He also wants you to meditate on those things that are healthy, holy, and beneficial. Your prayers should also communicate your deep thankfulness for God and what He has done and express your adoration for Him. Second, God made you in a way that when you follow His will by experiencing deeply meaningful prayer and meditation your body can heal and become healthier. According to the research that Benson (The Relaxation Response) did, any relaxation that lasts over 9-11 minutes triggers your body to heal itself at a faster rate and much more. It's amazing to us that research has begun to understand how when we follow God's will, it can have a significant positive impact on our mental, physical and spiritual health. So, how should you meditate? What do you do so that meditation can provide the benefits that God intended for you to experience? Practically speaking, there are five basic elements that are important when you want to go into a meditative state.

1. A Quiet Environment.
2. An Object to Dwell Upon.
3. A Passive Attitude.
4. A Comfortable Position.
5. Avoid Distractions.

I remember when Rick and I and several people from the MEF team were lying out in a field late one night looking up at the stars. I was peaceful, yet in awe of what I was looking at. I was meditating on God's great creation. I was peaceful, relaxed and totally into what God had done for all of us. I have continued to do such things for years. When I do I feel peaceful, relaxed and connected to God. It's a wonderful feeling. So, what else could a Christian dwell on for meditative purposes? There are several options. Here are a few.

- Seek to be still and know God (Psalm 46:10). Think of one of His attributes
- Research shows that if a person simply states a spiritual saying like, 'The lord is my Shepherd' or 'God Loves me', over and over it will help him relax and become peaceful.
- Identify a scripture that you can quote over and over that helps you with a situation in your life.

Just remember that prayers or meditation that lasts longer than twelve minutes provide extra benefit according to research. Every minute beyond that produces greater benefit for you. So, my friends, pray without ceasing. Be still and know God. Set time aside where you can fix your mind on things above, not on earthly things (Colossians 3:2) and you will be healthier mentally, physically and yes spiritually. Dedicate twenty minutes a day to praying or mediating on God or his Word. Pray a simple prayer over and over showing your appreciation for your great God and what He has done for you. Not only will you receive the physical and mental benefits that God wants you to have, but He may very well answer your prayer. Imagine that.

Positive or Metta Meditation

In his book Relaxation Response, Benson determined after much research that the way you meditate does not determine the outcome. It is whether or not you meditate in some way. You just need to do it. Metta means positive energy and kindness toward others. From a Biblical point of view, it would be thinking the best for those around you. This would include thinking of happiness, comfort, love, peace, joy, good health and so much more for those around you and yourself. So, either meditating on God because of His love and greatness or simply thinking good thoughts for those around you and for yourself while in a peaceful state can be very beneficial for you and possibly for others. We will focus on statements that are beneficial for you.

In order to promote that peaceful state, you simply recite phrases that are meant to make you feel better. Here are some examples of Metta meditation:

- "I am peaceful."
- "I am happy."
- "I am loved by God."
- "I am loving."

You don't need any equipment to do this kind of meditation. All you need is a comfortable place where you can sit or lay down.

Another bonus is that you can do it anywhere you like — in a quiet corner of your home, outdoors in a yard, or even at your desk. Try to choose a spot where you're least likely to be distracted, then follow these steps:

Sit in a comfortable position. Close your eyes. Take a slow, deep breath in through your nose and continue breathing deeply. Focus on your breathing. Imagine your breath traveling through your body. Focus on the air going in out of your nose. That helps reduce unwanted thoughts.

When you feel you are in a relaxed state, choose a kind, positive phrase. Silently recite the phrase, directing it toward yourself. You can say, "I am happy. I am safe. I am peaceful. I am loved by God. Thank God I am saved. Thank you God for your Creation. A Scripture you like."

Slowly repeat the phrase (or Scripture). Acknowledge its meaning and how it makes you feel. If you get distracted, just return to the phrase and keep repeating it. As much as possible, don't let anything distract or disturb you.

Avoid Distractions

The last thing we said that you need to become good at if you are going to meditate or be quiet is to not let anything disturb or distract you. You will get better at this in time if you follow the instructions.

First, you need to get rid of any external distractions. Turn the phone off. Shut your computer down. Get in a room that is free from unwanted noise or potential distractions. White noise like an air purifier can mask unwanted noises. Some people use soft 'elevator' music that doesn't have a beat. Others turn on the sound of rain or the surf. Identify a scenario that works best for you.

Mental Distractions

You are usually distracted when your mind starts thinking about a task or something else that you forgot. You have probably had that happen when you have tried to pray at times. Such mental distractions keep attacking you and the benefits may be lost. There is an answer for mental distractions. Russ teaches a technique in therapy that helps people deal with this problem. He calls it the Refocus Strategy. Learn this and you should be able to have uninterrupted time to meditate or pray.

The Refocus Strategy

If a thought or image starts to creep into your mind when you are praying or meditating, **immediately** go back to focusing on your chosen object, word, Scripture or thought. However, **DO NOT** tell the intrusive thought or image to go away. **DO NOT** talk or reason with the image. **DO NOT** argue with or get disturbed by the thought or image. WHY? Because every time you talk to the thought or image you make it more powerful....more real. Here's an example. Have you ever started to get anxious about something? When you do, you have a tendency to think about what is making you anxious. When you think about it, you become more anxious. The more you think about it, the more anxious you become. It seems like you are in a negative spiral that causes your anxiety to get worse and worse. **ITS BECAUSE YOU ARE TALKING TO YOUR ANXIETY.... THINKING ABOUT YOUR ANXIETY..... FOCUSING ON YOUR ANXIETY.** When you think about it, or talk to it, your anxiety usually gets worse and becomes very difficult to manage. So, you ask, 'What do I do then?' When something starts to creep into your mind when you are praying or meditating simply refocus on your chosen object, word, Scripture or thought or what you were praying about. Refocus, refocus, refocus! Don't talk, don't think, don't focus on the unwanted thought, feeling, or distraction!!! REFOCUS!!!!! IMMEDIATELY!!!!! TAKE CHARGE BY REFOCUSING! (Adapted from the Foundations Workbook - 2016 by Crites).

Hundreds of people have benefited from using this easy-to-use technique that allows you to have quite time with self or God.

Personal Reflection

List three things that you learned or that were reinforced that helped you better understand meditation and how it can help you spiritually, physically, and/or mentally.

1.

2.

3.

Knowing God's Word

Chapter Twenty

God wants you to know His will. To do that you must read His message. You have to read it or hear it to understand it. The Bible should be your textbook for the hereafter, and you should want to be an "A' student when it comes to this text. We heard a funny, but accurate definition of what BIBLE means. It means, **B**asic **I**nstructions **B**efore **L**eaving **E**arth. That's a pretty accurate statement if you want to head down the right path. If you indeed want to head down the right and relatively narrow path with the narrow gate at the end of our journey, you need to know what the ultimate will of God is for your life. To do that you need to do a lot of study so that you can understand what God wants from and for you. In this chapter we will cover:

- Reasons to Study the Word
- A Proper Perspective of the Word
- Application of the Word
- Enjoying the Word

Reasons to Study the Word

There are four basic reasons that we should study God's Word. God in His infinite knowledge has placed much information in the Bible so that we can know what He wants of us and for us. First, we are commanded to know God's Word simply because we need to understand how to live the Christian life. In 2 Timothy 2:15, Paul tells us,

"Do your best to present yourself to God as one approved,
a workman who does not need to be ashamed
and **who correctly handles the word of truth**."

Keep in mind that the amount of knowledge a disciple has of God's Word, the understanding of the meaning behind the Scriptures and the level it is internalized and applied suggests the level of maturity a Disciple is currently experiencing.

Second, we are commanded to know God's word because spiritual growth is impossible apart from it. In 1 Peter 2:2 Peter states,

"like newborn babes, long for the pure milk of the word,
that by it **you may grow in respect to salvation**."

Third, we are commanded to know God's word because it is our offensive weapon in spiritual warfare. In Ephesians 6:17 we are told,

"Take the helmet of salvation and the **sword of the Spirit,
which is the word of God**."

Last, we are commanded to know the word of God because we are responsible for dealing with error when it arises. In Titus 1:9 we are told that we must,

"hold firmly to the trustworthy message as it has been taught,
so that we can **encourage others by sound doctrine** and
refute those who oppose it."

If we are not studying the Word, it's easy to become negatively impacted by the interpretations and teachings of the world. Nor can we help others who are being pulled away or damaged by inaccurate or false teaching.

The last command that explains our responsibility to refute or correct doctrinal error is a great message for us today. Many people have distorted God's Word for their own benefit or to promote their particular 'interpretation' of God's Word. You need to know what God truly wants you to believe. The only way to ensure that you know true doctrine or how to correct false doctrine is to study the Word and not just listen to those who want to tell you what it means (Comparative Doctrine, Crites). In 2 Peter 1:20 we are told,

"knowing this first of all, that no prophecy of Scripture comes
from someone's own interpretation."

In addition to being commanded to study the word, you are told that you must continue to study and apply it if you are to grow or mature in Christ. Continuing in it means making it part of who you are internally. You are letting it change you from the inside out. Knowledge of the word provides several important helps in your Christian Life.

1. Becoming a student of the Word enables you to become adequate to face life and the problems that come with it. In 2 Timothy 3:16-17 Paul states that, "All scripture is God-breathed and is useful for teaching, rebuking, correcting and training in righteousness, so that the man of God may be thoroughly equipped for every good work."
2. Becoming a student of the Word also gives you hope. In Romans 15:4 Paul tells us, "For everything that was written in the past was written to teach us, so that through endurance and the encouragement of the Scriptures we might have hope."
3. Knowing God's Word produces a greater spiritual and mental stability. In Ephesians 4:14 we are told, "Then we will no longer be infants, tossed back and forth by the waves, and blown here and there by every kind of teaching and by the cunning and craftiness of men in their deceitful scheming."
4. Becoming a student of the Word produces within you a wisdom that is from God. In Psalm 119:98-100 David states, "Your commands make me wiser than my enemies, for they are ever with me. I have more insight than all my teachers for I meditate on your statues. I have more understanding than the elders, for I obey your precepts."
5. Becoming a student of the Word also gives you peace. It Psalm 119:165 we are told that, "Great peace have they who love your law, and nothing can make them stumble."
6. Becoming a student of the Word helps you improve your ability to be victorious as you struggle with sin. In Psalm 119:11 David states, "I have hidden your word in my heart that I might not sin against you."

It is foundational that you study the Word, for without the knowledge the Word of God gives you it is impossible to mature in Christ. To be like Him, you must know both His will and His Father's will. Both are found in the Bible.

A Proper Perspective of The Word

Jesus wanted his disciples to put His teachings above all of the Old Testament commandments or laws, as well as the teachings and traditions of men. Putting heavenly authority above earthly authority and focusing on principles rather than basics. Jesus also told His disciples over and over that if they wanted to be part of his Kingdom, they had to have inward change, not just external correctness in following His teachings. They had to live a life that transcended that of the teachers of the Law (the Pharisees). To better understand this concept let's look at God's priorities for our Christian life in contrast to the priorities of the religious world in Christ's time. If we but look at the priorities of the Pharisees, we may sadly see in ourselves some of those very beliefs.

A Focus on Priorities: Who do We Listen To
Inner Circle = Christ Outer Circle = Pharisees

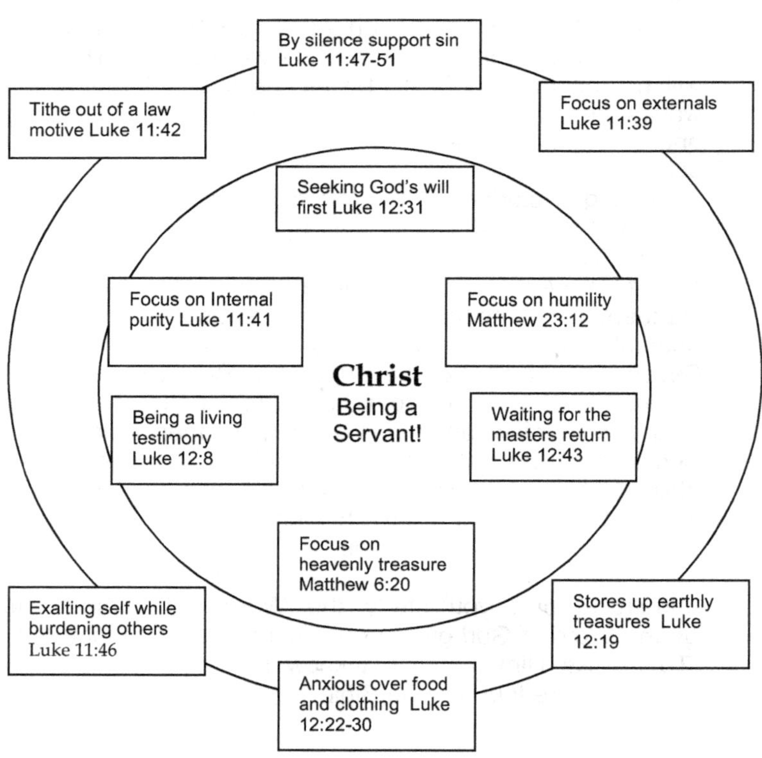

If needed, look back at the chart on the previous page again. The Pharisees focused on externals (looking good on the outside), tithed out of a law motive, supported sin by remaining silent, stored up earthly treasures, compromised Jesus as Lord, exalted self while burdening others, were anxious over food and clothing and were often engulfed in busywork. In contrast, Christ taught that Christians should focus on justice and love, be genuine, seek heavenly treasure, seek God's will first, wait for Christ's return, be a living testimony, be humble, and develop internal qualities such as purity and holiness. That is what God wants from you.

The goal of every maturing disciple is to have a proper perspective of God's will as it applies to his own life. Spiritual victory, blessings and growth will only arise when a Christian's priorities are patterned after Jesus' life and teachings (Matthew 5:48; John 13:34). Specifically, there are three things you must keep in mind. First, you must put Jesus' teaching above all the traditions of men. Second, you must put heavenly authority above earthly authority. Third, you must focus on principles that are supported by Biblical fact. As you focus on the wisdom of God it will aid you as you seek to consistently major in majors and minor in minors (1 Corinthians 2:5). God wants you to focus on His priorities, not the priorities taught by man.

Seeing what God doesn't want and what He does want from and for you is easy to see. However, sometimes it becomes hard to do. When that occurs, we are usually short sighted. That simply means that we are thinking of the here and now instead of eternity. That's difficult for many, but God wants us to know that when we follow His ways He will take care of us. It may not be in our timing, but it will happen. Our responsibility to Him is to do the best we can to become more like Jesus. That is what our focus should be every day.

Application of the Word

You too must apply the word to your daily life, in thought, word and action, so that you might obtain victory.

Now that we have a basic understanding of what God wants us to focus on in our life, we need to develop a deeper understanding of His word so that we can apply it in our lives. That's your job. All throughout God's Scriptures He makes it clear that you should be applying the word daily in your life as you deal with specific life situations. He meant for the word to be helpful not a hindrance to you. Just as Jesus daily applied the word or the will of God to specific problems, you too must apply the word to your daily life, in thought, word and action, so that you might obtain victory. The Word can be applied as you focus on Christ and His will. You can also apply the word by using it as a standard for your behavior.

Christ Like Thinking

In Robert Coleman's book titled, Master Plan of Evangelism, he writes, "His [Jesus'] life was ordered by His objective, everything He did and said was a part of the whole pattern. It had significance because it contributed to the ultimate purpose of His life in redeeming the world for God. This was the motivation vision governing His behavior. His steps were ordered by it. Mark it well. Not for one moment did Jesus lose sight of His goal." You too as a Christian must also:

- Understand this Principle.
- Internalize and put this principle into practice, so that you can develop into the mature spiritual man you are capable of becoming.

We define spiritual thinking as the process of relating everything in our lives to our ultimate goal or purpose, which is glorifying God. Carnal thinking is defined as a selfish (fleshly) process by which our activities, knowledge and concerns are objectives and ends in themselves. The majority of us have been conditioned to think in terms of immediate results rather than long-term spiritual growth. Our failure to think on a spiritual plane has caused minimal growth, stagnation and poor spiritual application in our daily lives. Many of us have failed to let our spiritual self function anywhere near its potential. The result of this failure to focus on Christ and the Word can be evidenced by a person's failure to bear fruit, and the fact that their life is not a true indicator of what he says he believes.

We define spiritual thinking as the process of relating everything in our lives to our ultimate goal or purpose, which is glorifying God.

The man who is motivated by ultimate Biblical principles is daily thinking spiritually. If you are truly thinking on a spiritual plane, you have purpose. As you look into your inner being, ask yourself what your primary purpose or ultimate goal is in this life. The Bible teaches that your primary purpose in life is to glorify God (Isaiah 43:7). There are three questions that you should ask yourself whenever you must make a decision or when you are facing an attack from one of Satan's dark forces.

1. Is what I'm doing or about to do going to glorify God?
2. Could I do this in a way that would bring more glory to God?
3. Could I do something different that would glorify God more?

To answer those questions, you must know God's Word.

Christ Like Actions

One of the greatest purposes of the Word of God is not to just increase your knowledge, but to guide you in your daily walk. The Bible must be practical, not just theoretical or theological. You must be able to internalize it and apply it in your life. It must become part of your daily life, or it has no true meaning for you. There are four simple steps you can take if you want to make the Word active and real in your life. Every time you deal with a sin or potential sin you should:

- Find a passage that deals with that issue and determine what it specifically says to you personally.
- Ask yourself how that sin is specifically affecting your life. Give yourself specific examples.
- Determine what you should do based on the Word.
- Memorize the Scripture that specifically deals with the problematic sin and then quote the Scripture to yourself as you have to deal with that specific sin in your life. You may also want to think about it each morning and each night before you go to bed. Here is a form you can use.

This four-step approach to applying the word to cut sin out of your life (Hebrews 4:12) can also be used as part of your daily Bible study. The worksheet on the next page gives you several examples of sin and scriptures that could be used.

Personal Sin and Scripture
Worksheet

Key Scripture: 1 John 1:9
"If we confess our sins, he is faithful and just to forgive us our sins and to cleanse us from all unrighteousness."

Instructions:

1. Identify the sin and place it in the left-hand column.
2. Identify a Scripture you will memorize and place it in the righthand column.
3. Every time you start to struggle or fail to deal with sin, repeat the Scripture to yourself at least five times.
4. If you need help, seek out your brothers and sisters and confess your sins so that they can help you.

Your Identified Sin	Scripture that Counters It
Pride	James 4:6b Therefore it says, "God opposes the proud but gives grace to the humble."
Putting self-first – Selfish	1 Corinthians 10:24 Let no one seek his own good, but the good of his neighbor.
Anger	James 1:19 Know this, my beloved brothers: let every person be quick to hear, slow to speak, slow to anger;
Lying	Proverbs 12:22 Lying lips are an abomination to the Lord, but those who act faithfully are his delight.
Gossiping or hurtful talk	Ephesians 4:29 Let no corrupting talk come out of your mouths, but only such as is good for building up, as fits the occasion, that it may give grace to those who hear.
Sexual Sin	1 Corinthians 6:18-20 Flee from sexual immorality. Every other sin a person commits is outside the body, but the sexually immoral person sins against his own body. Or do you not know that your body is a temple of the Holy Spirit within you, whom you have from God? You are not your own, for you were bought with a price. So glorify God in your body.

The worksheet shown on the previous page can be found in the appendices. You can copy it for your personal use.

Enjoying the Word

Why do many Christians not enjoy their Bible study or feel that reading their Bible is more of a duty than a pleasure? Christians too often do not understand the Bible and therefore cannot experience the joy of personal discovery (Acts 8:30). The truth is that if you understand what you are reading, you should enjoy reading the Bible. The Bible is a spiritual book and requires spiritual discernment to understand it. This power of discernment grows as a result of constant practice to distinguish good from evil in your day-to-day life (Hebrews 5:14). Therefore, before deeper spiritual insights can be attained you must be willing to intentionally attempt to discern good from evil each day. The Holy Spirit will help you develop a deeper understanding of what the Scriptures are communicating. As you mature spiritually those deeper meanings will become more evident. That's an important goal for all Christians.

Let's look at some scriptural truths that God uses to motivate you to hunger after righteousness. Feel free to read each Scripture in your Bible also.

Spiritual Truths that Motivate Us to Study	
Psalm 1:1-3	Blessed is the man who walks not in the counsel of the wicked, nor stands in the way of sinners, nor sits in the seat of scoffers; But his delight is in the law of the Lord, and on his law he meditates day and night. He is like a tree planted by streams of water that yields its fruit in its season, and its leaf does not wither. In all that he does, he prospers.
Proverbs 2:1-5	My son, if you receive my words and treasure up my commandments with you, making your ear attentive to wisdom and inclining your heart to understanding; yes, if you call out for insight and raise your voice for understanding, if you seek it like silver and search for it as for hidden treasures, then you will understand the fear of the Lord and find the knowledge of God.

Jeremiah 29:13	You will seek me and find me, when you seek me with all your heart.
Matthew 7:7	"Ask, and it will be given to you; seek, and you will find; knock, and it will be opened to you.
John 15:11	These things I have spoken to you, that my joy may be in you, and that your joy may be full.

How can you learn to love the Scriptures? You learn by reading and studying them. As a result, you not only learn, but you also see how the Scriptures can make you a more God-like person. According to R. A. Torrey, "It must be remembered, however, that the Bible contains gold, and almost anyone is willing to dig for gold, especially if it is certain that he will find it. It is certain that one will find gold in the Bible, if he digs." Let's start digging.

Personal Reflection

List three things that you learned or that were reinforced that will help you know, appreciate and develop a better understanding of God's Word verses laws or values of men.

1.

2.

3.

Outreach, Evangelism and Gifts

Chapter Twenty-One

To many Christians the relationship and balance between evangelism and discipleship has been little understood. They actually work together in many ways. Both are necessary and both were intended to be part of the great commission that Jesus gave. He didn't just want people to be saved. He wanted them to be saved and live the life of a Disciple. We will cover the following in this chapter:

- Evangelism and Disciple Making
- Evangelism of Jesus Christ
- Evangelism of the Early Church
- Three Basic Stages to Evangelism
- Methods of Evangelism
- Developing Your Testimony
- The Gospel Message and Doctrine

Evangelism and Disciple Making

Evangelism is the process of gathering valuable souls into Christ's church and disciple building is the process of teaching Christ's commandments, faithful obedience and the faithful training of others to do the same. These two aspects of the Great Commission must be perceived once again as one task. A return to New Testament methods of evangelism and to the New Testament balance and integration of evangelism with disciple building would produce the Christlike lifestyles needed to reawaken the restoration of New Testament Christianity in this century. Consider the following two statements:

1. Are those who have been saved reaching others? Are those we convert bearing fruit? Are we just adding more babies to Christ's body, or are we nurturing and training leaders who can reproduce themselves?
2. Is it wiser to instruct, nurture and train a few, who can train a few, who can train a few than it is to spend a whole life preserving a congregational outreach program?

Just what is our focus? Don't just read this and go on. What do you see happening? If it's not what God intends, what could you do?

Evangelism of Jesus Christ

If we are to ever become effective in evangelism, it will be because we have examined and then patterned our own evangelistic approach to that of the Master's. The ultimate goal of Jesus for His disciples was to reproduce His life in them so that they would know how to do the same to others. To accomplish this, Jesus used three forms of evangelism. Each form teaches converts to contribute to the process of disciple building in others. These three forms are:

1. Personal one and one evangelism.
2. Small group evangelism.
3. Mass evangelism.

The one thing consistent with Jesus evangelism is communicated in 2 Timothy 4:5. Regarding evangelism Paul simply states, "As for you, always be sober-minded, endure suffering, **do the work of an evangelist**, fulfill your ministry." This may be the most important little phrase in the Bible. What is the basic work of evangelism? It is to speak about Jesus. Who is supposed to do it? Every Christian is the answer. Jesus spoke to people everywhere he went. What if we did the same? What if we made it a point to bring up Jesus in our conversations where ever we were. Consider making it a point to find a way to bring up how Jesus has made you life better. Insert his name into the conversation. It certainly would be a good start.

Evangelistic Principles Jesus Displayed

In the ministry of Christ, personal evangelism was a method Jesus employed a great deal. Nicodemus (John 3:1-15), the rich young ruler (Mark 10:17-22), Simon the Pharisee (Luke 7:36-50), the adulterous woman (John 8:1-11) and the Samaritan woman (John 4:1-27). His disciples learned how to deal with people personally by watching Him. John 4:1-29 reveals six principles Jesus displayed when evangelizing the Samaritan woman. Look at each of these principles after reading the corresponding Scripture.

Scripture	Principle
John 4:	He was sensitive to her needs. He created out of His need an opportunity to meet her spiritual needs.
John 4:	He established rapport. He offered her a gift, aroused her curiosity, and got her to expose her need.
John 4:	He addressed the deeper need. He asked probing questions and avoided peripheral issues.
John 4:	He patiently accepted her rebuffs. He separated the sin from the sinner by recognizing the value of her soul.
John 4:	He bore significant witness to Himself. This is evidenced by her progressive responses. First, she calls Jesus a Jew, next sire, then a prophet, finally the Christ.
John 4:	He made Himself known to others through her. She ended up desiring salvation and proclaiming it.

Jesus frequently made home or small group visits of those interested in Him. He had personal contact with non-believers in the homes of Matthew (Matthew 9:10), the Pharisee (Luke 7:36), and Martha and Mary (John 12:1-3). On many occasions His disciples accompanied Him and carried on this method of evangelism while with Him. In Acts the homes of Jason (Acts 17:5-9), Justus (Acts 18:7), Phillip (Acts 21:8), and the mother of Mark (Acts 12:12) were used for prayer meetings, instruction of new converts, fellowship, communion service, impromptu gatherings or a planned event to witness to curious seekers. The home promoted communication enabled difficulties to be sorted out, easily allowed for maturing body life to act and serve, and simply facilitated meaningful fellowship.

Mass evangelism allows the presentation of the good news to large numbers of people at once. Think about tent meetings, weeklong evangelistic meetings, and other such like events. Excitement can be generated in a way that cannot be accomplished in either personal or home evangelism. Jesus preached on the mountainsides of Galilee (Matthew 5:1), in the synagogues (Mark 1:21), on the shores of Capernaum (Luke 5:3), in the Jerusalem temple (Luke 19:47), and near Aenon by the Jordan river (John 3:22-23). Masses came to hear Him and He touched many a soul. Such mass evangelism can win new converts today just as it did in the days of Jesus. Keep in mind that each of the evangelism types support the others. There is a place for every type of evangelism. Why? It's because people are different. Plus, if a person utilizes his or her own gift it might alter what that evangelistic method might look like. In addition, different people, based on their gifts, may be drawn to more than just one of the three. The most important thing is that your focus on evangelism should be based on what works best for you.

Personal Thought

Using Jesus' encounter with the Samaritan woman as an example, give a current day example of how you could lead someone to Him. Put some thought into it. On a separate piece of paper, write down what you might do and who you might speak to. Also, do you prefer to plant, water or reap the harvest when you talk to others. We are about to discuss that concept on the next page. Just keep all three in mind, because all three are important.

Evangelism of the Early Church

God has and is calling out from the world a people for Himself, and then sending them back into the world for:

1. The expansion of His kingdom.
2. The building up of Christ's body.
3. The glory of His name.

The early church made evangelism their number one priority. It would be very wise for us to admit that we have a good deal to learn from early church strategy, tactics, methods and approaches.

There are three basic stages to evangelism, that when followed usually produces disciples of Christ.

Three Basic Stages to Evangelism

Each stage is important and each of us should be willing to do all three. However, most of us will be better at one of the three stages. The first has to do with planting the seed. It may not seem to be as important as reaping the fruit or converting someone. However, if no one ever planted the seed the person may have never been open to discussing Christianity. Each stage is extremely important.

1. **Plant the seed.** By your words or actions, you may simply plant a seed when a person is not willing to have a deep conversation about God. You may need to simply let your life be an example of what Christianity is like. If no seed is planted, it makes it more difficult to help a person learn about Christ. However, some people are very open and when you plant the seed they immediately want to know more. You just have to be aware. If you plant the seed and they don't respond yet, go to the next step.
2. **Water the seed.** When possible, do something kind with no expectation of return. You may also want to periodically share how Christ has made your life better and how becoming a Christian can make life more joyful. Don't hide your pain. They also need to see how you deal with pain and hardship and the kind of support you get from your brothers and sisters.
3. **Reap the fruit.** At some point that person may become ready to listen and as a result may be open to becoming a Christian. You may not have been the person who planted the seed, but if they are willing to listen, you now have an opportunity to share the good news.

It's important to keep in mind that there may be a different individual who does each of these stages in a person's life. You may be the one to plant the seed, or water the seed. You may even be the one the person is ready to talk to about Jesus and become a Christian. Just remember all three are important. You don't always have to do all three. If you do one well, you can have a tremendous impact on many lives for Christ, even if you don't see the end results.

Methods of Evangelism

Regardless of if you agree with the contents of this book, if you are a Christian you should want to share what God has done for us. Once shared and as a Christian matures, we also need to teach the deeper, meatier doctrines of Adoption, Justification, Righteousness, Sanctification and Holiness, Glorification, Forgivness and many other important doctrines that help define what God wants us to believe and share with others. In the work by this author titled, Comparative Doctrine, many of those other doctrines and their supportive Scriptures are identified.

However, the question many people ask is, "How do I do that?" How do I share the Gospel? What method should I use? Throughout the years there have been a multitude of evangelistic methods promoted by different people. We actually don't have a problem with any of them if they are accomplishing the intent, saving souls. However, we do believe that we have often overlooked three methods that can be very effective. All three incorporate relationship building as a critical aspect to outreach or discipling and that fact is extremely important to keep in mind. In our opinion they are also the easiest and most effective ways to contact and teach others about Christ. Let's look at these three outreach methods.

- Relational Outreach
- Using Your Gift for Outreach
- The Discipleship Family or small home group

Relational Outreach

This method is similar to Friendship Evangelism, Lifestyle Evangelism and Service Evangelism. Actually, we believe that Relational Outreach is a natural way to place yourself into situations where others might be willing to talk to you about Christ. As Christians we don't want to spend 'fellowship' time with non-believers that might negatively impact us spiritually. However, we do need to spend time with them with the purpose of getting to know them. We might serve them when we see a need. We might invite them to small get togethers with other Christians for food and fun. We might invite them to a small group that includes both fellowship and some Bible study. There are many options.

The point is, if you can put yourself in a position where you can show the person that you are a compassionate, loving, concerned person they might confide in you. They might be open to discussing religion, the 'church' you go to, Christ, etc. You have to know them well enough for them to want to speak with you.

Studies have indicated that approximately 90% of all converts have some existing relationship with a current church member. With this in mind, it is obvious that a major thrust for outreach should be aimed at those we currently know in one way or another. How many non-Christians do you know right now? Think about who you know that does not attend church anywhere or who attends only sporadically. There appear to be three major categories by which you can list the unchurched people you know. They are, 1) family or relatives, 2) friends, and 3) associates. Obviously, if you know the person it makes it much easier to connect with them regarding the assembly or knowing more about Christ. In 1982 Win Arn wrote a book about Discipleship that incorporated the concept of 'friendship evangelism'. It was widely accepted and used as a method of outreach and discipleship in many churches. A book titled, The Master's Plan for Making Disciples described this method in detail and their training program provided videos of how they applied the discipleship concept in their church.

Years ago, a study was reported in Church Growth: American Magazine, that there was a significant importance regarding friendship in helping others become disciples of Christ (Church Growth American January/February, 1981). 94% of those who were converted by a church member who shared the message as a friend were still active in church. No other method came close to the same percentages.

HINT: Friendship or Relational Evangelism is one of the easiest ways to share Christ with others. All you have to do is talk to them about life. What are their joys, pains, problems, etc. What do they enjoy doing for fun? Do they like to eat out or do they like back yard barbecues? Talk with them about their life. Ask them to dinner or a cookout. Listen to what they have to say. Find ways to spend time with them and as you do show them by your words and life what it's like to be a Christian.

Using Your Gift for Outreach

This may be the most important information about evangelism you have read up to this point. Now that you have seen how important evangelism is to the church and ways in which it can occur, we are going to take a step back and show you how you can make evangelism unique to you. Basically, there is one evangelistic method that will work best for you, and we believe that it is based on the Motivational Gift that God has given you. Being in the ministry of Jesus Christ means that He has bestowed spiritual Gifts upon you as a Christian for the preservation and growth of His Kingdom (Ephesians 4:7; 1 Peter 4:10). Further study revealing the relationship between evangelism and Gifts will provide greater understanding and motivation to you as you labor for the advancement of God's Kingdom. Once again evangelism is a call for the work of reaching out to others in your daily life. As you come into contact with others you can communicate God's message in a multitude of ways. Many of these ways are simply natural ministry possibilities that you may have that can lead to helping others learn about Jesus and His will for them. Just keep in mind that if you build some kind of relationship with the people you are sharing with, they are much more apt to respond to you and the message. With this in mind here are some brief examples of how you could use your gift to share the Gospel.

Gift of Prophecy: If you have the gift of prophecy you are motivated to reveal God's truth to all people. You will want to call attention to sin and wrong attitudes, while showing characteristics that lead others to a closer relationship with God.

Examples:

- Advertise a community meet up where you can speak God's word to others.
- Small Group Bible Study that you do in your home.

Gift of Service: if you have the gift of Service, you probably are good with your hands. You may enjoy working on projects, fixing things, creating things, etc. If you see a neighbor who is struggling with something you could offer to help him with mowing his lawn, fixing a fence, etc. The time spent doing good, will impact that person and in most cases, it will open a door for you to share your story about God and what He means to you.

Examples:

- Lawn service for who are older, who are sick or even your neighbor.
- Technology helps those who are less knowledgeable.

Gift of Teaching: Searching for truth and Teaching God's word that is motivated by God's Gift He gave you.

Examples:

- Bilingual class that could be taught at home/church/etc.
- Teach a Bible class, lead a discussion group, teach in a Discipleship Family group, etc. where the non-churched or non-active Christians are invited.

Gift of Exhortation: Counsel, consolation and exhortation to others motivated by God's Gift He gave you. Romans 12:8

Examples:

- Find someone who needs more information about the Bible. Show them how to live and how to solve problems or to carry out God's work based on what the Bible says.
- Develop a support group where others could be encouraged to put their spiritual growth plan to work.

Gift of Giving: Giving that is motivated by God's Gift He gave you. Romans 12:8

Examples:

- Bible Purchases and give to others.
- Find a way to give to others who are in need through your business or through your family.

Gift of Organization or Administration: Organizing or administrating parts of the body motivated by God's Gift He gave you. Seeing the body as an organism. Romans 12:8

Examples:

- Be in charge of a specific Meal Train.
- Be in charge of a specific Mens/Womens Night Out.
- Be in charge or help with Ministry Fairs.

Gift of Mercy: Acts of love motivated by God's Gift He gave you. Romans 12:8

Examples:

- Shut in Buddy: Spend time with those who can't get out.
- Foster and Adoption Class.

So, you can see that when you use your gift as you seek to meet people you can evangelize, it becomes more natural for you. It seems to be easier, more enjoyable. It's up to you to make sure that you know what your gift is and then you must use it to build the body up, reach out to others and to experience motivation and joy in your own Christianity. When you share using your gift, in addition to building relationship, it is a very powerful method of touching others for Christ.

Responding to Why

Regardless, if you are using the relational approach to soul winning or using your gifts you will often cause people to wonder why you are doing 'nice' things. When you do anything nice or considerate using your gift, some people are going to wonder, 'Why are you doing that for me?' An example of this is when you identify something the person needs or may like, e.g., mow the lawn, take cookies to them, or spontaneously help them as you see a need. If and when they finally ask why you are being nice, you have an opening. You don't have to pull out your Bible and start looking at Scriptures. Simply plant a seed. You might say,

> Option One: "I've learned in life that if you treat people the way you want to be treated it not only helps them but it makes you feel more connected to God."
>
> Option Two: "I have to admit that it's something I learned to do when I read my Bible. It teaches us to be kind and considerate and I actually enjoy doing things for people."

Obviously there several other statements that could be made that suggest you are who you are because of God. Think about it. What would you say? Write it down on a piece of paper. Memorize it and then put yourself in a position where you will have the opportunity to respond to the 'Why?' question.

The goal is to get them to ask you why you are doing those kinds of things. It opens the door to discussing the Gospel and what it could mean for him or her. If they are open to learning more, you may now have an opportunity to do a Bible study. Start with your Testimony or your personal experience with God, share the Gospel Message, teach necessary doctrine and lead them to salvation. If they are not yet open, you have watered the seed. Keep doing what you can and hopefully they will eventually respond.

The Discipleship Family

Small groups are often one of the most effective ways to help members learn about Scripture, build each other up and also to bring new individuals into the local body. Whether it be called a Discipleship Family, a Community Group, a Life Group, a Bible Study Group, or any other name, these groups often have many similar goals. Your group could take place in someone's home, a building where the church meets, or any other place where Christians are gathered. Those present will have common goals. They will seek to learn more about the Bible and God, build Christian relationships through fellowship, pray together, build ministry, and utilize their group as a means of in-reach and outreach.

There are two key purposes for the Discipleship Family group. First, it is intended to be a method to support fellow brothers and sisters. It helps those in the group build relationships with one another. This type of group also provides both the younger and more spiritually mature Christians an opportunity to learn how to use their God given gift in a smaller setting. People are given opportunity to teach, pray, serve, organize, take on a role in the group, provide food, provide a location, and much more. Such cooperation helps each individual learn their importance in the body as they participate in their small group. This fosters growth in Christians. Second, those in the group are encouraged to seek out and invite others to come to dinner, enjoy some fellowship and have an opportunity to see how Christians can support and love one another. It also provides a time where they can learn about

> *They will seek to learning more about the Bible and God, build Christian relationships through fellowship, pray together, build ministry, and utilizing their group as a means of in-reach and outreach.*

God, Christ and the Bible. There is no pressure. No one needs to stay for the sharing or Bible study. The goal is to pique their interest and then you can share more about the Bible as a group or one person in the group could answer questions or teach them privately if the newcomers desire. This can also be used to help the non- involved church members become more connected and involved. They could be invited to group meetings and people in the group could attempt to build relationships and get them involved. This is important for leadership, especially elders, since they are responsible for the whole body and that's a hard task without some form of assistance.

Developing Your Testimony

To be effective with any of the above methods you need to be able to share your personal message about what Christ has done for you. Basically, your message is your story about how you came to know Christ, what it means to you and how becoming a Christian changed your life. Let's look at Paul as an example (Acts 26:1-23). When Paul spoke with King Agripa, the first thing he did was give his personal testimony (vs 1-18). Immediately following, he spoke about the plan of salvation (vs 19-23). Using this model, we all need to be able to share Christ in a personal way. As previously discussed, you can accomplish this using the Relational Model, using your Gift as a medium for outreach, or by using a small group. If you know of another method that you are comfortable with, use it. You decide what works best for you. Here are five things you can include in your testimony or message. We have encouraged people to write out what they would share so that they can clarify it for themselves. Once completed you can read it over and over. Doing so will not only validate your decision to become a Christian but will also clarify how you will communicate it to others when you have opportunity.

1. To develop your testimony or message, think back to what your life was like before you were a Christian? If you became a Christian early in life you may not have information to share. You could share what it has meant to you to be a Christian.
2. Share the Gospel about Christ, e.g., His birth, life, teachings, death, resurrection and what it means to all mankind.

3. Why did you become a Christian, e.g., you want to go to heaven, have purpose, want to help others become a Christian?
4. How did you become a Christian, e.g., what did you do, where did it happen?
5. What has Jesus done for you since you've become a Christian, e.g., change in attitude, desires, bad habits, behavior, thoughts?

The Gospel Message and Doctrine

The Gospel literally means Good News about Jesus Christ. Simply stated it includes the birth, life, death, resurrection and the post resurrection appearances of our Lord and Savior. For you to be able to share the good News it would be beneficial if you could identify the Scriptures that discuss these things. Hopefully, by sharing the Gospel message the person will want to become a Christ follower or Christian. So, ultimately, you will need to be able to share how that occurs also. Let's take a closer look at these important elements.

The Gospel: A Step-by-Step Guide

Why it's Needed.

1. Since the first man's sin, mankind has been under the condemnation of God (Romans 5:12).
2. Because everyone breaks God's perfect law by committing sin, everyone is guilty (Romans 3:23).
3. The punishment for the crime of sin is physical death (Romans 6:23) and then an eternity spent in a place of punishment (Revelation 20:15; Matthew 25:46).
4. This eternal separation from God is also called the "second death" (Revelation 20:14–15).

What the Message Is

The word gospel means "good news," so the gospel of Christ is the good news of His coming to provide forgiveness of sins for all who choose to become a Christian (Colossians 1:14; Romans 10:9).

God, because of His love for the world, has made a way for man to be forgiven of their sins (John 3:16).

He sent His Son, Jesus Christ, to take the sins of mankind on Himself through death on a cross (1 Peter 2:24).

In placing our sin on Christ, God ensured that all who will believe in the name of Jesus will be forgiven (Acts 10:43).

Jesus' resurrection guarantees the justification of all who believe (Romans 4:25).

Prophecy

Some people may or may not be interested in prophecy. If they are and it is helpful to see that Jesus fulfilled many prophecies you could share this with them. There were many prophesies about the coming of Jesus and what would happen to Him. Prophecies included His birth, life, death and more. Here are just a few prophecies that support the fact that Jesus truly did walk this earth.

In Isaiah 7:14 there is a prophecy that a virgin woman will give birth to God's son and he will be called Immanuel. This was written over seven hundred years before Christ was born.

Prophesy Fulfilled: Matthew 1:20-23 and Matthew 2:14-15

In Isaiah 9:6 it is prophesied that Jesus Christ will come as a baby; Jesus is described by several names.

Prophecy Fulfilled: Matthew 2:1

In Micah 5:2 it is prophesied that Jesus would be born in Bethlehem.

Prophesy Fulfilled: Matthew 2:1 and Luke 2:4-6

Isaiah 53 has numerous verses that speak about Jesus and what would happen to him. Verse 5: "But he was pierced for our transgressions, he was crushed for our iniquities; the punishment that brought us peace was on him, and by his wounds we are healed."

Prophesy Fulfilled: John 20:25-27 and Luke 23:35

Verse 6: I offered my back to those who beat me, my cheeks to those who pulled out my beard; I did not hide my face from mocking and spitting.

Prophecy Fulfilled: Matthew 26:67

Verse 7: "He was oppressed and afflicted, yet he did not open his mouth; he was led like a lamb to the slaughter, and as a sheep before its shearers is silent, so he did not open his mouth."

Prophesy Fulfilled: Mark 15:4-5

Verse 9: "He was assigned a grave with the wicked, and with the rich in his death, though he had done no violence, nor was any deceit in his mouth."

Prophesy Fulfilled: Matthew 27:57-60

In Zechariah 12:10 it was prophesied that Jesus would be pierced.

Prophecy fulfilled: John 19:33-34 and John 20:25-27

Prophecy and history tell us that Jesus was to and did come to this earth in the form of a child and became the Messiah for all who would follow him.

His Life

He lived a perfect life showing all who listened that there was a new way of living. A life that would allow us to become part of God's family. His teachings show us the plan for redemption and salvation. This plan includes belief, faith, repentance, confessing his name, baptism and living a life where you have died to self and are seeking to put on His very nature each and every day of your life.

His Death and Resurrection

His death was not a defeat. It was the greatest victory that man has known since the beginning of time. Let's read 1 Corinthians 15:1-6.

"Now I would remind you, brothers, of the gospel I preached to you, which you received, in which you stand, and by which you are being saved, if you hold fast to the word I preached to you—unless you believed in vain. For I delivered to you as of first importance what I also received: that Christ died for our sins in accordance with the Scriptures, that he was buried, that he was raised on the third day in accordance with the Scriptures, and that he appeared to Cephas, then to the twelve. Then he appeared to more than five hundred brothers at one time, most of whom are still alive, though some have fallen asleep."

Paul emphasizes the importance of the Gospel in teaching others how to become a Christ follower or a Christian. The two key facts in this Scripture are:

- Christ's death is proved by His burial.
- His resurrection is proved by the eyewitnesses.

The Result

Because of Jesus' death, burial and resurrection God has provided the way for all men to be freed from the penalty of sin (John 14:6; Romans 6:23). It is because of His message, His death and resurrection that you can be placed in His family, forgiven of sins and promised a home with Him if you live a Godly life. Every one of us will eventually die a physical death. However, those who believe in Jesus Christ and follow His plan are promised a physical resurrection unto eternal life (John 11:23–26). It is through Jesus alone that Salvation can be found (Acts 4:12).

The What Must I Do Question

The simple response to this question is that there are several aspects to becoming a Christian. This is also where Christendom is divided. Some believe that you are saved once you accept Christ by faith. Others believe that you must have faith and also be baptized. We want to share what the Bible says and you can determine for yourself what makes sense. If you read all the conversion examples in the Bible and did everything that those converts did it should be evident that you followed God's will for being converted. That makes sense to us. So, it would be wise to follow the conversion examples in the New Testament where the Apostles share the good news and people were converted. We will take that stance and just share what that looked like. We believe that that there are several things that need to occur if someone is going to follow the New Testament method of becoming a Chirstian

(See the appendices for a Conversion Chart that shows ten specific conversion examples and what was done in each example). The following were identified in at least one conversion example.

Hear: Obviously you must hear the message or you can't respond to it.
Believe: You must believe in God and what Jesus did for you.
Faith: You must have faith. Without faith it is impossible to become a child of God.
Repent: You must repent and make a radical turn from a sinful life to a life goal directed toward God.
Confess: You must confess that Jesus is lord of your life and that you want to serve him and only him.
Be Baptized: You choose to be baptized in the name of the Father, the Son and of the Holy Spirit so that, 1) you can receive remission of all of your sins and 2) so that you can receive the gift of the Holy Spirit who will come to live within you and seek to help you live the holy life.

In the Conversion Chart it shows specific Scriptures that simply say what happened when each new Christian chose to accept Jesus as Lord. Not all aspects of conversion were identified in each of those examples except for one. You look. You decide. The book titled, Grace and Salvation addresses the salvation process in much greater detail if you want more information. It can be used to help a possible convert understand God's grace and what is needed to become a Christian. It uses Scriptures, not opinion, to explain the salvation process.

Those who Reject or Fail to become a Christian

This is not something you want to share unless the person asks what the Bible says about not being a Christian. In Revelation 20:13-14 it states that those who reject Christ will not only die physically but will undergo a second death and will be sent to an eternal lake of fire. That is not what God wants. He wants all men to be saved and we should too. Give them time. Becoming a Christian out of a fear motive is not usually a good method. It should be based on what you receive when you become part of God's family.

Doctrinal Questions

We don't want to get too complicated here. The Gospel and the beliefs that are taught are pretty straight forward for most. However, many people you meet already have some beliefs about specific Biblical Doctrine. Many have learned doctrine that has been promoted by man, not God. The problem is that they have listened to what their 'teachers' have taught and not really studied what the Bible actually teaches. We often tell people that Doctrine or Biblical truths should be based on Scripture and never opinion. In addition, traditions are not Biblical truth. Biblical truth is truth that can only be found in the Bible. It is never found in any other work. It might help if you memorize the statement shown in the box. It is one of the greatest truths for those who are seeking how to become a Christian and how to live the Christian life. As a result, you may need to have an awareness of some of the basic Doctrinal truths found in the Bible. You may have to discuss such an issue and if you are not prepared, you may lose your opportunity to share with them. Once you are prepared to address those issues you are less likely to be faced with a question that you can't answer. Doctrine should be based on the Bible only and never a result of any other document or the words of any other man regardless of who he is. The Bible has the last word for all doctrine.

> *Doctrine or Biblical truths should be based on Scripture and never opinion. In addition, traditions are not Biblical truth. Biblical truth is truth that can only be found in the Bible.*

Personal Reflection

List three things that you learned or that were reinforced that helped you better understand how outreach or evangelism and gifts work together the way God intended to reach the lost.

1.

2.

3.

Fellowship and One Anothering

Chapter Twenty-Two

The third major area in this process of disciple building is fellowship. Whether you look at Jerusalem or Antioch or read between the lines of the Epistles to the Philippians or Thessalonians, or look at most any other letter written in the New Testament, you will see the importance of Christian fellowship.

We can only imagine how fellowship in the early stages of Christianity must have been. The success of their fellowship was evident as they grew in love and as they utilized their God given gifts to support each other and to share the good news of Christ. The church must realize the importance of this responsibility and when it is fully incorporated into the body many will become or remain dedicated disciples. We will discuss the following in this chapter:

- Benefits of Fellowship
- Fellowship and Spiritual Health
- Christian Relationships
- Fellowshipping with One Another

Benefits of Fellowship

Fellowship among believers provides an opportunity to share blessings and burdens with each other. It is one of the most important aspects of fellowship. There are several other benefits that occur when we fellowship, as we have been commanded. Look at the following Scriptures and see what benefits are available.

Benefits of Fellowship	
Fellowship with God and Jesus	
1 Corinthians 1:9	God is faithful, by whom you were called into the fellowship of his Son, Jesus Christ our Lord.
1 John 1:3	that which we have seen and heard we proclaim also to you, so that you too may have fellowship with us; and indeed our fellowship is with the Father and with his Son Jesus Christ.
Fellowship with One Another	
1 John 1:6-9	If we say we have fellowship with him while we walk in darkness, we lie and do not practice the truth. But if we walk in the light, as he is in the light, we have fellowship with one another, and the blood of Jesus his Son cleanses us from all sin. If we say we have no sin, we deceive ourselves, and the truth is not in us. If we confess our sins, he is faithful and just to forgive us our sins and to cleanse us from all unrighteousness.
James 5:16	Therefore, confess your sins to one another and pray for one another, that you may be healed. The prayer of a righteous person has great power as it is working.
Galatians 6:2	Bear one another's burdens, and so fulfill the law of Christ.
Mutual Ministry	
Romans 12:5	So we, though many, are one body in Christ, and individually members one of another.
Romans 12:10	Love one another with brotherly affection. Outdo one another in showing honor.

Romans 15:5-6	May the God of endurance and encouragement grant you to live in such harmony with one another, in accord with Christ Jesus, that together you may with one voice glorify the God and Father of our Lord Jesus Christ.
1 Corinthians 12:25-26	that there may be no division in the body, but that the members may have the same care for one another. If one member suffers, all suffer together; if one member is honored, all rejoice together.
Philippians 2:1-4	So, if there is any encouragement in Christ, any comfort from love, any participation in the Spirit, any affection and sympathy, complete my joy by being of the same mind, having the same love, being in full accord and of one mind. Do nothing from selfish ambition or conceit, but in humility count others more significant than yourselves. Let each of you look not only to his own interests, but also to the interests of others.
STS: You may underline the above Scriptures in Yellow.	

As we continue our study, we will begin to see how important fellowship is to Christians. We need to have meaningful and consistent fellowship with others. One of our major goals should be to create the kind of environment and conditions that will help us grow organically (we are a body, not an organization) in order to reach our individual and whole-body spiritual potential.

Fellowship and Spiritual Health

Psychologically, people need to be cared for. They must perceive that others do care and love them. Fellowship is one of the most important elements in developing and maintaining the mental health of the disciple. Without positive peer interaction and acceptance, mental illness will often ensue. People are drawn to organizations, groups, religions, etc., primarily due to this need for positive interaction. However, some people hurt so deeply that any interaction, even negative or indifferent, is readily accepted. This is better than none at all which produces the insidious horror of loneliness. This should never happen among those in Christ!

Spatial proximity does not guarantee integration. Basically, this means that just because you sit next to others or are around them does not mean that you are connected or benefiting from being close to them. If this happens with church members, it's not what God wants or expects. Each week we sit next to many people, yet many of us are guilty of not really fellowshipping or even really attempting to get to know our brothers and sisters. In 1 John 1:7 we are told, "But if we walk in the light, as he is in the light, we have fellowship with one another, and the blood of Jesus his Son cleanses us from all sin." Think about it for a moment. What does that mean to you and every other Christian. What is the practical application that comes from that Scripture? We should be talking and spending time with each other.

Remember this next time you go to the assembly. Don't neglect your brother or sister. Simply ask how their week has been. Without relationships (fellowship) you cannot truly continue to be a part of God's body, for a body has many parts and not one part can be alone. It is the church's responsibility to help build relationships within the body so that each person may grow into a mature disciple. It is also the church's responsibility to make sure that each member of the body is fellowshipping in a way that is conducive to proper spiritual growth and mental health. The church must realize the urgency of this responsibility, for by the realization of this need and resultant application, many will become or remain true disciples.

Christian Relationships

John well understood the need for Biblical fellowship (1 John 1:3). He stressed the fact that the source of their fellowship was their personal relationship with the Father and Son. Our fellowship then, must be both vertical and horizontal. Vertically we share in the life of God (See 'Knowing God: Mans Response). Horizontally we must share the life of God with others. Let's take a few minutes and see what God says about our relationships with one another and the world.

Basic Relationships

In Acts we find that each new community was based upon a very important relationship. What was this relationship?

1 Corinthians 1: 9 states,

"God is faithful, by whom you were called
into the fellowship of his Son, Jesus Christ our Lord."

What four things were these Christians devoting themselves to?

Acts 2:42

- Teaching
- Fellowship
- Breaking of Bread
- Prayer

What happened as a result of this devotion they had for one another? Acts 2:43-47 tell us what happened and what can happen for us today!

- Were together and had all things in common.
- Were selling their possessions and belongings and distributing the proceeds to all, as any had need.
- Day by day, were attending the temple together.
- Breaking bread in their homes, they received their food with glad and generous hearts,
- Praising God and having favor with all the people.

The Result: The Lord added to their number daily those who were being saved!

Fellowshipping with One Another

Let's take the next few minutes and look at what the Bible says about how we should be relating to one another. Read each of the Scriptures below.

Scriptures Concerning One-Another	
Scripture	Application
John 13:34-35	A new commandment I give to you, that you love one another: just as I have loved you, you also are to love one another. By this all people will know that you are my disciples, if you have love for one another."

Romans 12:10	Love one another with brotherly affection. Outdo one another in showing honor.
Romans 13:8	Owe no one anything, except to love each other, for the one who loves another has fulfilled the law.
Romans 14:13	Let not the one who eats despise the one who abstains, and let not the one who abstains pass judgment on the one who eats, for God has welcomed him.
Romans 14:19	So then let us pursue what makes for peace and for mutual upbuilding.
Romans 15:7	Therefore welcome one another as Christ has welcomed you, for the glory of God.
Romans 15:14	I myself am satisfied about you, my brothers, that you yourselves are full of goodness, filled with all knowledge and able to instruct one another.
Galatians 5:13	For you were called to freedom, brothers. Only do not use your freedom as an opportunity for the flesh, but through love serve one another.
Galatians 6:2	Bear one another's burdens, and so fulfill the law of Christ.
Ephesians 4:2	with all humility and gentleness, with patience, bearing with one another in love,
Ephesians 4:25	Therefore, having put away falsehood, let each one of you speak the truth with his neighbor, for we are members one of another.
Ephesians 4:32	Be kind to one another, tenderhearted, forgiving one another, as God in Christ forgave you.
Colossians 3:13	bearing with one another and, if one has a complaint against another, forgiving each other; as the Lord has forgiven you, so you also must forgive.
Hebrews 10:24	And let us consider how to stir up one another to love and good works,
James 5:16	Therefore, confess your sins to one another and pray for one another, that you may be healed. The prayer of a righteous person has great power as it is working.

1 Peter 4:9	Show hospitality to one another without grumbling.
1 Peter 5:5	Likewise, you who are younger, be subject to the elders. Clothe yourselves, all of you, with humility toward one another, for "God opposes the proud but gives grace to the humble."
1 John 1:7	Likewise, you who are younger, be subject to the elders. Clothe yourselves, all of you, with humility toward one another, for "God opposes the proud but gives grace to the humble."
Galatians 5:26	DON'T: Let us not become conceited, provoking one another, envying one another.
Colossians 3:9	DON'T: Do not lie to one another, seeing that you have put off the old self with its practices.
James 4:11	DON'T: Do not speak evil against one another, brothers. The one who speaks against a brother or judges his brother, speaks evil against the law and judges the law. But if you judge the law, you are not a doer of the law but a judge.
STS: You may underline the Scriptures above in yellow.	

Personal Reflection

List three things that you learned or that were reinforced that helped you better understand the benefits of fellowship and one anothering for Christians.

1.

2.

3.

Fellowship and Worship

Chapter Twenty-Three

How are fellowship and worship connected? Does it require a consistent place? Where are we supposed to worship? Those are all good questions and the answers, varied as they are, often shape what many churches look like. The perception of 'where we worship' also plays a large role in how we perceive worship is experienced. This chapter will discuss how fellowship and worship connect. It also addresses where we worship and the importance of the building or place where God wants us to worship Him.

- Fellowship in the Worship Experience
- The Worship Experience
- The Holy Church Building

Fellowship in the Worship Experience

One of the most misunderstood and misused words in the religious world today is 'worship'. Too many religious people today believe that worship is 'going to church' on Sunday morning, evening and for some Wednesday nights. This concept has permeated the religio-cultural world bringing about devastating results to all religious movements and the individuals within. Christ's church has not been immune to this obvious ploy by dark spiritual forces. First of all, you don't go to church. The church is the people of God. Christians are the church of God, Christ's church or the church of Christ that you read about in the Bible. All of us should be assembling with the church at our local congregation whether it be a building or someone's home (a house church). Most early New Testament Christians worshiped together in Temples, homes and schools (Acts.2:46; Acts 19:9; Romans 16:5; 1 Corinthians 16:19; Philemon 2). That was the norm all those years ago.

Another important aspect of assembling together is that we should truly be there to worship God, fellowship with one another and build one another up. Worship does suggest a mutual, communal event. In other words, when we assemble as a church we participate in worship together. The problem we often face is that proximity does not guarantee integration. We wrote that statement before, but it is a terrible truth. In other words, just because we are in the same room with people doesn't mean that we are connected. We may sing together, but not be connected. We may listen to a sermon, but not be connected. We may even speak to those around us, but not be connected. God wants us to be connected. To be connected takes effort. You must spend time with those who are in the body of Christ where you worship. We are the body of Christ and we should know and care for each other. The Scripture below suggests what this should look like for all Christians.

> Proximity does not guarantee integration!

"Let the word of Christ dwell in you richly,
teaching and admonishing one another in all wisdom,
singing psalms and hymns and spiritual songs,
with thankfulness in your hearts to God.
And whatever you do, in word or deed,
do everything in the name of the Lord Jesus,
giving thanks to God the Father through him."
Colossians 3:16-17

A good worship experience obviously should at the very least include what is taught in the Scripture above.

The Worship Experience

Yes, you should be connected when you worship together with your brothers and sisters. However, worship should actually be a part of your everyday life. Let's take a look at the Scriptures that define worship for all of us.

Worship and the Christian Life	
Romans 12:1-2	I appeal to you therefore, brothers, by the mercies of God, **to present your bodies as a living sacrifice, holy and acceptable to God, which is your spiritual worship.** Do not be conformed to this world, but be transformed by the renewal of your mind, that by testing you may discern what is the will of God, what is good and acceptable and perfect.
John 4:20-24	Our fathers worshiped on this mountain, but you say that in Jerusalem is the place where people ought to worship." Jesus said to her, "Woman, believe me, the hour is coming when neither on this mountain nor in Jerusalem will you worship the Father. You worship what you do not know; we worship what we know, for salvation is from the Jews. But the hour is coming, and is now here, when the **true worshipers will worship the Father in spirit and truth, for the Father is seeking such people to worship him. God is spirit, and those who worship him must worship in spirit and truth."**
Hebrews 13:15-16	**Through him then let us continually offer up a sacrifice of praise to God,** that is, the fruit of lips that acknowledge his name. Do not neglect to do good and to share what you have, for such sacrifices are pleasing to God.
1 Peter 2:5	**you yourselves like living stones are being built up as a spiritual house,** to be a holy priesthood, **to offer spiritual sacrifices acceptable to God through Jesus Christ.**

All of these Scriptures indicate that your whole life, second by second, is a worship to God. It's not just a place. A place, whether is be a building, home, etc., is a convenience and a blessing. So, other than a convenience or blessing what is the purpose of a building? You don't have to go to a building to worship (John 4:20-24). Obviously, you can worship anywhere. It's certainly nice to be able to worship together in a comfortable building.

However, when people believe that fulfilling their worship duty is to show up on Sunday morning, but don't develop and maintain a connection with the body of Christ, they are missing out on being part of a church, the body. When you understand the concept of worship you can see how the assembly is sometimes not what it should be. You see people coming to sing, pray, study the Bible and listen to people speak. Many of these people are fulfilling their 'worship duty' for the week. Such people find it easy to be distant and separate, yet somewhat friendly. They know what they must 'do' to fulfill their 'worship' experience when they assemble with the brethren. When individuals function at this level they are not truly connected to the body. We must be members of one another, helping each other grow spiritually, working as a body to further the great commission. On the other hand, if we just go to 'church' we are not connected and not really fulfilling God's will for His Kingdom here on earth. If the local church is failing to produce a body mentality or it focuses on numbers rather than relational Christianity and a discipleship mentality, it can have a negative effect. Congregations with this problem often:

1. Settle into a traditional rut in worship.
2. Have a few Christians who are living a life of worship.
3. Have uninspiring services.
4. Have difficulty getting visitors to return.
5. Lose many members.
6. Fail to utilize their building in a variety of ways to reach the lost or hurting masses.

The Holy Church Building

There are many well-known churches that have built huge edifices that are meant to be holy places of worship. Their meeting rooms are only used for prayer or worship. We have heard many say, "No one can use our church building except for us." Others have said, "We certainly can't have a Bible class in our church building. It's not Biblical. We are only here to worship God." "We can't have a kitchen or a fellowship hall. That's not Biblical." We can't have anyone speak in our church building about non-biblical topics, even if they would be of benefit to many people and even if it was a time when the building is normally locked up and not being used." "We can't have Christian daycare." "We can't have a Christian school." "We can't have a homeless program or a program where food or clothes are given to the needy." We can't.... we can't.... we can't because our church building is a holy edifice that has one purpose only..... to worship God.

All those that feel this way have missed the point. If you are a Christian you worship God daily with your life. You worship with your brothers and sisters whenever you meet with one another. You worship with your brothers and sisters wherever you meet on Sunday morning. Would it be okay to meet in a school building? Would it be okay to meet outdoors in a tent on someone else's property? Would it be okay to sit around a large campfire on a Sunday morning and praise God and worship him as a group of believers?

Yes....Yes.... and Yes again! It's okay and it has been done. Our worship is not a place. It's in your heart and you can share that experience with your brothers and sisters when you have opportunity to be with them. Obviously, you can meet together on Sunday mornings which is what most Christians do on every week. However, worship is not meant to be confined to a specific holy building or time. If you have a building, it should be used by the body of Christ to meet for multiple reasons, Sunday morning included. It should be a tool or an aid to help build up the whole body of Christ in a multitude of ways and it should be used as a tool to reach out to the unchurched. Why would you spend that much money to build a building that is not used every single day to reach out to the lost and hurting people in your community. That is what buildings should be used for. The building is not the church. However, our buildings should be a helpful tool in building up each other and in bringing others to Christ in a variety of ways.

Our buildings should be a helpful tool in building up each other and in bringing others to Christ in a variety of ways.

We want you to answer these questions. What is your church like and does it utilize its building daily to serve members and the community? Is it accessible to Christians and non-Christians alike every day during the week? Are at least parts of it open for people to come in and visit or learn, talk to someone or simply to relax? What would people think if leadership wanted their building to be visited by outsiders and church members every day simply for relationship purposes?' Leadership that has done this have opened up opportunities to share God with others, maybe while sipping on coffee or eating a donut. They have opened the doors for relationship building on a more consistent basis. The point is the building should be used as a tool to bring in the lost and to help brothers and sisters connect. If you don't have that, what should be done? Maybe your voice and opinion would matter.

Personal Reflection

List three things that you learned or that were reinforced that might enhance your worship and Christian relationships? What might be the benefit of opening up a church building to be used by members and the community and what might that look like?

1.

2.

3.

Confession and Forgiveness in Relationships

Chapter Twenty-Four

Fellowshipping or one anothering to enjoy relationship and in general to build one another up is extremely important as shown in the previous chapter. There were simply too many aspects to Fellowship to put into one chapter. With this in mind, there are other specific areas of fellowship that Christians need to make a part of their lives. Each of these areas can take on a specific role to help you with spiritual issues and maturational growth. Sometimes it is to protect you. Other times it is meant to help others. In this chapter we are going to focus on:

- Confession and Christian Relationships
- The Godlike Trait of Forgiveness
- Forgiving Others
- Forgiving Self

Confession and Christian Relationship

Confession is often hard for most people to participate in. It calls for you to be vulnerable. You have to be willing to put your sin or your burdens in front of others so that you can be helped in a multitude of ways. For Christians, confession is word that has two meanings. Before you became a Christian it was imperative that you confess that you believe that Jesus is the Christ and that you want Him to be Lord of your life. That is something that all Christians must do. However, after we become a Christian one of our greatest sources for help as we struggle with life and sin is when we confess our sins to one another.

The Catholic church teaches, promotes, and encourages its members to confess their sins to their priests. They do not believe that you are truly justified (Declared Not Guilty by God) and are given Christ's perfect righteousness. As a result, all Catholics must consistently confess to be forgiven and it must be done by a Priest. They have confessionals in all their church buildings. Priests are there most days to take confession. It's the way a Catholic gets forgiveness for sins committed. We have known some Priests who stay pretty busy each and every day. The members come to give confession of their sins. The Priest tells them what penance they must do. The person completes his penance and is now forgiven of his or her sins.

We agree that confession is a wonderful tool that can help a Christian stay on track and it also allows the individual to obtain prayers and assistance from others. Unlike Catholics who need to confess to a priest to be forgiven, as New Testament Christians we can know we are forgiven even before we sin (See Grace and Salvation by Crites). If the person has a burden or a need and wants help from the church he can get it if he asks. However, if his sin is hurting the body, the church, it becomes increasingly important that he confess his sin publicly. Why? Because it is through Christian relationships that he can gain help and strength to overcome sin in his life. So, how can people help if a person confesses in front of the church? Let's look at this for a moment.

Ways of Helping when Someone Confesses

First, Christians cannot be judgmental or self-righteous. It's easy to do. What's your first response when someone confesses a sin? Do you shake your head in disgust? Do you question how they could fall so low? Do you wonder what is causing them to be so weak? Those thoughts are not what God would expect from us. In John 8:7 we are told that we all sin. So as Jesus said, 'How can you cast the first stone at a brother or sister who sins when you too are sinful?' Because we are all sinners we should want to help each other. We should seek how we can help the person instead of condemning him (Luke 6:37-38).

Second, we cannot 'use' the information for gossip forums which in turn distances and damages the person even more. That too is actually a sin. We cannot look down on him and tell others how we just don't understand how he could be so weak spiritually, share it with others and then avoid him. God frowns on such behavior. There are Scriptures that strongly speak out against gossip (Proverbs 11:13; Ephesians 4:31; Romans 1:29; 2 Corinthians 12:20). These Scriptures condemn such behavior. In 1 Timothy 5:13 and 2 Thessalonians 3:11 busybodies are condemned when they speak about things not proper to mention and for speaking down about a brother or sister who is confessing, no matter how serious the sin is to God. We are to help and support, not hurt or condemn our brothers and sisters.

Third, we should pray for and with those who are struggling with sin. In James 5:16 we are told that we should, "confess our sins to one another, that you may be healed." Since that is God's plan, we should pray without ceasing when someone is struggling. Again, we should also be supportive in any way that would be helpful.

Fourth, we should not stop helping after the confession event. The person just opened up about a weakness; a sin he is struggling with. We should seek to communicate with him and let him know that we are praying for them. Not just in the moment of confession. Be supportive at other times. Give him a call. Share phone numbers. Have coffee. Be there for the person. Make sure he realizes you are there for him. God wants us to build one another up. We must be accountable to each other. We all sin and should support one another. Let's look at a few scriptures that communicate this important aspect of relating in the church.

Confession, Forgiveness and the Christian Life	
James 5:16	Therefore, confess your sins to one another and pray for one another, that you may be healed. The prayer of a righteous person has great power as it is working.
1 John 1:9	If we confess our sins, he is faithful and just to forgive us our sins and to cleanse us from all unrighteousness.

Luke 6:37-38	"Judge not, and you will not be judged; condemn not, and you will not be condemned; forgive, and you will be forgiven; give, and it will be given to you. Good measure, pressed down, shaken together, running over, will be put into your lap. For with the measure you use it will be measured back to you."
Romans 14:19	So then let us pursue what makes for peace and for mutual upbuilding.
1 Thessalonians 5:11	Therefore encourage one another and build one another up, just as you are doing.
Old Testament and the Need for Confession	
Psalm 32:3	For when I kept silent, my bones wasted away through my groaning all day long.
Proverbs 28:13	Whoever conceals his transgressions will not prosper, but he who confesses and forsakes them will obtain mercy.
When We Help One Another	
Proverbs 27:17	Iron sharpens iron, and one man sharpens another.

The Godlike Trait of Forgiveness

Does a belief that God truly forgives you of your shortcomings have a positive effect on your life? Actually, the importance of truly accepting God's forgiveness in your life cannot be overstated. It can make every day brighter. It can enhance your physical, spiritual, emotional, mental health and more.

It's interesting to note that there is research that shows a benefit of believing that God forgives you. Actually, there are several. Let's look at two of them. In a study done by Fincham, he reported that divine forgiveness was positively associated with all psychosocial well-being outcomes. He also found that divine forgiveness had a negative impact on depression and anxiety symptoms. In other words, depression and anxiety were reduced. As a result, he stated that forgiveness may be understood as being good by itself, but that it may also lead to better psychosocial well-being and mental health (Fincham, 2022). In another study specific to older adults, those who had high beliefs in God-mediated control over the study period received stronger health benefits of divine forgiveness. Forgiveness by God also had a stronger relationship with health compared to forgiveness of self and others. The findings underscore the importance of subjective beliefs about God (Upenieks, 2021).

> *Those who had high beliefs in God-mediated control... received stronger health benefits of divine forgiveness. Forgiveness by God also had a stronger relationship with health compared to forgiveness of self and others.*

So, in addition to the obvious spiritual benefits, just believing that God does forgive you produces physical and emotional benefits. Isn't that interesting? Remember, God made you and science is finding out how much God does have to do with your mental, emotional, physical and spiritual health. So, when the Bible tells us that we should not worry about being forgiven of our sins, we should listen and accept His ongoing forgiveness (Romans 8:30). Keep in mind that we are justified or legally declared to be not guilty by God because of Christ's sacrifice. However, that doesn't mean that we can sin all the more so that Grace will abound. We need to daily seek to be holy as He is holy and forgiveness is there before we even ask for it.

Scriptures on God's Forgiveness	
Matthew 6:14	For if you forgive others their trespasses, your heavenly Father will also forgive you
Mark 11:25	And whenever you stand praying, forgive, if you have anything against anyone, so that your Father also who is in heaven may forgive you your trespasses.
Ephesians 1:7	In him we have redemption through his blood, the forgiveness of our trespasses, according to the riches of his grace,
1 John 1:9	If we confess our sins, he is faithful and just to forgive us our sins and to cleanse us from all unrighteousness.

Forgiving Others

Damage occurs in every relationship simply because we are imperfect people. We make mistakes. Sometimes mistakes are intentional and sometimes they are unintentional. Both happen in relationships because we are all imperfect people. Being able to forgive allows you to move on in a healthy way. It also creates a healthier relationship regardless of the kind of relationship it is. Forgive for your own sake. If you don't forgive, bitterness, anger and other unhealthy emotions can take root and cause problems for you (Hebrews 12:14-15). Forgiveness is obviously also good for the person being forgiven. Making it a point to forgive is one of the best ways of maintaining healthy relationships. The Bible does tell us to forgive. Here are a few Scriptures that address this issue.

Scriptures on Forgiving Others	
Matthew 6:14-15	For if you **forgive others** their trespasses, your heavenly Father will also forgive you, but if you do not forgive others their trespasses, neither will your Father forgive your trespasses.
Matthew 18:21-22	Then Peter came up and said to him, "Lord, how often will my brother sin against me, and I **forgive** him? As many as seven times?" Jesus said to him, "I do not say to you seven times, but seventy-seven times.
Mark 11:25	And whenever you stand praying, **forgive**, if you have anything against anyone, so that your Father also who is in heaven may forgive you your trespasses."
Luke 6:37	"Judge not, and you will not be judged; condemn not, and you will not be condemned; **forgive**, and you will be forgiven;
Luke 17:3-4	Pay attention to yourselves! If your brother sins, rebuke him, and if he repents, **forgive him**, and if he sins against you seven times in the day, and turns to you seven times, saying, 'I repent,' **you must forgive him."**
Ephesians 4:32	"Be kind to one another, tenderhearted, **forgiving one another**, as God in Christ forgave you."

Colossians 3:13	bearing with one another and, if one has a complaint against another, **forgiving each other;** as the Lord has forgiven you, so you also must forgive.

We know that both Jesus and God want you to forgive others. Obviously, it is the Godly or Christian way to deal with hurts, offenses, etc. If you look closely, it is not really an option if you are a Christian. Forgiveness must be something you do, period. We will discuss how you handle things if you forgive and the person does not seek reconciliation later in this chapter. However, an important question is, 'Did God have another reason why we should forgive?' The answer is, 'Yes, He did.' Let's take a look at what research has identified regarding what forgiveness does for anyone who practices it.

Multiple studies have shown that stress and psychological turmoil can cause heart attacks, raise cholesterol levels, cause sleep problems, cause pain, produce high blood pressure, and levels of anxiety, and depression. You don't want stress or psychological problems that trigger these physical issues. It's just not good for you. God knew that could happen. As we have said over and over, God did create man and certainly knows what is good and bad for his mind and body. What does this have to do with forgiveness? To understand this, we need to look at more research regarding forgiveness. It's interesting to note that the simple act of forgiveness, not just words but really forgive and let it go, will reduce stress and psychological turmoil. In one study among the subset of volunteers who scored high on measures of forgiveness, high lifetime stress didn't predict poor mental health (Journal of Health Psychology, 2016). Toussaint stated that, "We thought forgiveness would knock something off the relationship [between forgiveness and stress or psychological distress], but we didn't expect it to zero it out." What did he say? Again, those who forgave liberally, even when they had lots of stress and psychological turmoil did not have the negative physical effects usually associated with them. Interesting!

Toussaint did another study where they followed participants for five weeks and measured how their levels of forgiveness ebbed and flowed. It was extremely interesting that they found that when forgiveness rose, the levels of stress in that person went down. As seen in other studies, the more stress was reduced, the greater the decrease in mental health symptoms occurred (Annals of Behavioral Medicine, 2016).

Forgiveness was so important to Jesus that he instructed his disciples to pray and forgive. Maybe the two working together enhances both spiritual, physical and mental health. So, if you are a Christian, you should forgive others over and over again. Sometimes this can be frustrating, but just remember forgiveness is for your benefit as much as it is for the other person.

The Offender

If someone offends, hurts you or does something inappropriate you must forgive every time no matter what. However, what does the offense do to your relationship? It can be damaging if not properly dealt with. Sometimes it damages the relationship so much that you don't want to be around the person. If a person offends, hurts, etc. and you forgive, possibly over and over, what do you do? What are your options? What does the offending party need to do? The answer is that they need to make recompense in order to rebuild trust in the relationship. You still forgive, but your ability to trust is diminished unless the person changes and makes things right. Trust must be rebuilt.

Recompense

There is an important word that sits between forgiveness and reconciliation that can either cause a relationship to grow or be purified or be damaged and positive feelings for each other can begin to be consumed. What does recompense mean? Basically, it means to give something to someone by way of compensation for damage, harm, hurt, etc. In other words, you attempt to make up for the offense. Merriam Webster defines recompense as, "To give something to by way of compensation (as for a service rendered or damage incurred)."

How are you reconciled? Obviously, something had to happen. It may be as simple as an apology. It is difficult to reconcile when recompense is not part of the healing process. Yes, the offended can forgive. Yes, the offender should say, 'I'm sorry'. However, if the sorrow doesn't produce a change in behavior and in many cases if something isn't done to compensate for the hurt, pain or loss, trust is damaged in the relationship.

What does recompense look like?

- Sometimes it can simply be a heartfelt I'm sorry, if in fact that is all the offended person needs.
- Sometimes something needs to be done. "I'm sorry, what can I do to fix this?"
- It may be something needed to repair an emotional hurt.
- It may be something that needs to be done to replace or fix physical damage of some kind.

Consider the story of a man who is rebuilding an antique car. He tediously searched for original parts. The cost and time spent was great but it was worth it for the man. He lovingly began putting the car together that he had wanted to own for years and years. As he was working on it a friend came by and was also excited about the car. He was told when the car was finished, he could take it for a drive. The man was excited. One day he was walking down the sidewalk and saw his friend's car in the driveway. It was finally finished. He was excited and yelled out but his friend didn't answer. He thought to himself, 'He told me I could take it for a drive. Surely, he won't mind.' He hopped into the car, turned it on and drove around the block. Just before he was back to his friend's driveway he hit a huge hole in the street. He lost control and ran into a telephone pole doing significant damage to the car. The man hurried over to his friend's house only to see his friend stepping out the door and started running towards him and the damaged car.

"What happened? What did you do to my car?", the owner of the car asked with fluctuating emotions racing through his mind.

"You told me I could drive it when you were finished. I saw it in your driveway and thought you wouldn't mind if I drove it around the block……

> **Option One Response:** "I'm really…..really sorry that your car got damaged. I know you are probably very upset. I would be too after all that work. Please forgive me…. and I hope you won't hold it against me." As he turned and walked away he said, "I hope you can fix it."

How would you feel if you were the man whose car was wrecked? Was it resolved in a way that was good for their relationship? What probably was going to happen? Even if you forgave him, which you should, how much would you trust him in the future? What kind of damage has occurred in the relationship?

> **Option Two Response:** "I am so sorry. I was just so excited to see that the car was finished. I should have asked first. I want you to know that I will pay for whatever it takes to fix this and I will spend my weekends with you as much as I can to help get it back together. I also promise to never drive it again unless you are with me and hand me the keys. I would totally understand if you never let me get behind the wheel again. Please forgive me my friend." Recompense must be realistic, adequate and acceptable to the offended so that trust can be healed.

Which response will promote and produce healing and rebuild trust? Obviously, the second response. The obvious question is then why is it better? It is simply because the offending person was more concerned about his friend than he was about himself. He was being selfless and wanted to heal the relationship. That is exactly what needs to happen when either person hurts the other in some way. That's what Christians should do for each other; every time there is damage done in a relationship. Option two shows an unselfish desire to make recompense in order to help heal the situation. That's the kind of response that would lead to reconciliation. Just keep in mind that just because you forgive, it doesn't mean that there will be a reconciliation. Reconciliation usually requires recompense and a desire on the other person's part to satisfactorily 'fix' the issue that caused the problem.

Reconciliation

Let's assume that you have forgiven someone for an offense and the other person has made recompense that was acceptable. What does it mean to reconcile? What is obvious is that God intends for you to fix the problem and reconcile when there are difficult situations in your relationship. Let's read Matthew 5:21-24 again,

"So if you are offering your gift at the altar
and there remember that your brother has something against you,
leave your gift there before the altar and go.
First be reconciled to your brother,
and then come and offer your gift."

Let's assume, which I believe is correct, that this Scripture addresses any Christian who has offended another Christian. Obviously, that means you have offended one of your brothers and sisters in Christ. There is an implied assumption that someone has something against you, so you must go speak with the person. It also says be reconciled before you offer your gift to God. What must you do to be reconciled? Do you just talk about the problem? Or do you do the 'right thing' to 'fix' (make recompense) the problem so that you can truly be reconciled. This reconciliation is so evident that you can take your offering to God who knows exactly whether or not you provided proper recompense regarding the issue. If you have offended someone and did not directly address it, you may not have reconciled.

Now let me say this in another way. The offender is only forgiven when there is genuine repentance which should include whatever it takes to make it right for the offense. Regardless, just as God forgave us, we should be extending forgiveness whether repentance is present of not.

Forgiveness is one thing; restoration and reconciliation is another. Forgiveness is mandatory, reconciliation is dependent on repentance.

Things to Keep in Mind

- People say, "Forgive and forget." We rarely forget.
- No matter what, we should always forgive.
- Sincerely say, 'I'm sorry' and be sensitive to their hurt.
- What does sorry mean? I won't do that again. Hopefully that means you have learned a lesson.
- If damage occurs, you must reconcile. To reconcile you must offer acceptable recompense.
- Making recompense does not mean we can immediately go back to our happy state. It is often a process.
- Depending on the offence, it may take time as you work on rebuilding trust in the relationship.
- Forgiveness recompense and reconciliation are all important and work together to heal relationships.

What if one person doesn't want to forgive or make recompense if needed. Consider getting help from, a Christian Therapist, Elders of the church, or people in your close circle that you trust.

Forgiving Self

God also wants us to forgive ourselves. A lack of forgiveness causes anxiety, anger and many more unwanted feelings that can be destructive spiritually, mentally and physically. In 1 Peter 5:7 we are told that we should be,

> "casting all your anxieties on him,
> because he cares for you."

In Psalm 55:22 we are told to,

> "Cast your burden on the Lord, and he will sustain you;
> he will never permit the righteous to be moved."

No matter what the cause is for your cares and anxiety, God wants you to cast your cares on him. Whatever you are going through, no matter how bad it is, no matter who has hurt you, it is not too much for God to bear. You just need to give your cares to him and know that it will be okay. Keep in mind that the more you think about your anxiety or problems the worse you will feel. You have to learn to do what you can about the situation, then give it to God and let it go. We want to address the psychological side of this one more time. It is so interesting to note that research is finding out so many things that support what the Bible says.

Current research shows that self-forgiveness is strongly associated with greater psychosocial well-being and lower psychological distress. To a lesser extent believing that God forgives was also associated with higher levels of psychological well-being and lower psychological distress (Long, 2020). It is amazing that research is finding out why specific Christian teachings are actually extremely healthy for the human condition. It we listen and follow his Word it really can make a big difference in our life beyond the spiritual.

Jesus' sacrifice of His own life on the cross for the sins of the world once and for all eliminated the need for people to bring sacrifices or take religious actions to try to make themselves right with God. God wants you to know Him, accept His forgiveness and then live out reconciliation and forgiveness with those around you. Religious activities or doing good deeds are important, but not as important as loving others in this way.

Personal Reflection

List three things that you learned or that were reinforced that could help you address confession, forgiveness, recompense or reconciliation in your life for self or others.

1.

2.

3.

Fellowship, the World and Spiritual Warfare

Chapter Twenty-Five

How do these three impact each other? Fellowshipping with one another is both beneficial for you and those you spend time with. If it is brothers and sisters the time you spend should be supportive. We should be helping each other grow and yes can we can have enjoyable time together. Your God given gift can positively impact your relationships. This includes relationships with those who are not Christians. In this chapter we will discuss how gifts have a positive impact on Christian relationships. We will also discuss what kind of relationships are acceptable with non-Christians and how we can help each other when we are attached by spiritual forces of darkness.

- Fellowship and Your Gift
- Fellowship with the World
- Fellowship and Spiritual Warfare

Fellowship and Your Gift

Just as with Evangelism, the use of gifts can be extremely beneficial in fellowshipping. Let's look at some brief examples about how you can utilize your gift in relationships. This is based on the Romans 8 motivational gifts of Charismata. These gifts were given to us by God so that we can serve and build up others.

Gift of Prophecy: If you have the gift of prophecy you are motivated to reveal God's truth to all people. You will want to call attention to sin and wrong attitudes, while showing characteristics that lead others to a closer relationship with God. In doing so, you would be helping brothers and sisters have an opportunity to grow spiritually.

Gift of Service: if you have the gift of Service you probably are good with your hands. You may enjoy working on projects, fixing things, creating things, etc. If you see a neighbor who is struggling with something you could offer to know about a brother or sister who is struggling with mowing his lawn, fixing a fence, etc. Time spent with brothers and sisters providing such service does build them up and makes them feel connected to the body.

Gift of Teaching: Searching for truth and Teaching God's word that is motivated by God's Gift He gave you. Being in teaching environment helps both the teacher and the learners build life together. Russ has always loved teaching and it is one of his ways to help the body grow. Youi too can teach others new truths so that they can better understand Biblical teaching and in turn grow spiritually. This can be accomplished in a Bible class, a small group or in any one-on-one situation.

Gift of Exhortation: Counsel, consolation and exhortation to others motivated by God's Gift He gave you. Helping others draws them to you and helps you build relationship with them. People are often struggling with life, have questions they can't answer and generally just need some support. You can help by simply spending time with them, listening, discussing potential solutions and by exhorting them to live the Christian life.

Gift of Giving: Giving that is motivated by God's Gift He gave you. You can be an example to others and may even be able to help them learn more about giving. Both of you benefit when you give. You can help people figure out how to get out of financial struggles. Using wisdom, you may even be able to help them financially.

Gift of Organization or Administration: Organizing or administrating parts of the body motivated by God's Gift He gave you. Seeing the body as an organism. Helping others find their place in the body can be exhilarating. It also provides opportunities for relationship building. At every opportunity you could be helping brothers and sisters find their place in the body where they can serve and be effective in building others up. That is the Administrator's greatest task. It is not to teach, or to do missions or anything else. Their task is to help make sure that every member of the body is connected, knows their gift and finds a place of service. In a sense the 'administrator' is the coordinator for the whole body.

Gift of Mercy: Acts of love motivated by God's Gift He gave you. When people are hurt and in pain it is an opportunity to help, get into their lives and see how God can work to help others. Seeing pain and problems that brothers and sisters are experiencing and then connecting with them in a loving way is how you show the gift of mercy. A loving touch. Sitting with a brother or sister who is sick. Being there in the time of grief are just a few ways the gift of mercy can be seen.

Do the Scriptures tell us that we should take care of one another and build one another up? Actually, there are several. The Ephesian verses are very clear that some of your building up is connected to your gift that is God given. We have provided four Scriptures for you to consider below.

Building One Another Up	
1 Thessalonians 5:11	Therefore encourage one another and **build one another up**, just as you are doing.
1 Corinthians 12:24b-25	But God has so composed the body, giving greater honor to the part that lacked it, that there may be no division in the body, but that the **members may have the same care for one another.**
Ephesians 4:11-14	11 And he gave the apostles, the prophets, the evangelists, the shepherds and teachers, to equip the saints for the work of ministry, **for building up the body of Christ,** until we all attain to the unity of the faith and of the knowledge of the Son of God, to mature manhood, to the measure of the stature of the fullness of Christ, so that we may no longer be children, tossed to and fro by the waves and carried about by every wind of doctrine, by human cunning, by craftiness in deceitful schemes.

Ephesians 4:15-16	Rather, speaking the truth in love, we are to grow up in every way into him who is the head, into Christ, from whom the whole body, joined and held together by every joint with which it is equipped, when each part is working properly, **makes the body grow so that it builds itself up in love.**

As Christians, we should all want to build up each other. Which of the gifts shown on the previous pages appear to be the gift that is most true for you? The point is, once you can identify what you believe your gift is, you need to determine how you can use it to encourage, help, build up your brothers and sisters in Christ. That is one of the important aspects of your 'job' as a Christian. Just keep in mind that these same gifts are also important in reaching out to non-Christians. Think about it for a moment. If in fact you believe you know what your gift is, how could you use the gift you have selected when you are assembling at the church's building with fellow believers? How could you use your gift in smaller social or fellowship settings? Chances are if you participate in fellowship using your gift, it will become more meaningful and will actually help your brothers and sisters in Christ grow and mature. That was God's intent.

So, you can see that when you use your gift as you seek to build up or support your brothers and sisters in Christ, it becomes more natural for you. It seems to be easier, more enjoyable. It's up to you to make sure that you know what your gift is and then you must use it to build the body up and support your fellow Christians. If you use your gift to do so, you will experience motivation and joy in your own Christianity. That is what God intended for you. The manual titled, Spiritual Gifts and Ministry (Crites, 2019) addresses this issue in detail. There is a test that helps you better determine what gift you have been blessed with by God.

Fellowship and the World

This issue has been a difficult for many Christians over the years, but it is an important part of relationship that needs to be addressed. Just what kind of relationship should Christians have with the world. One Scripture gives us an answer but is has been interpreted many ways. Let's see if we can clear this up for you. In 2 Corinthians 6:14-15 Paul states,

"Do not be unequally yoked with unbelievers.
For what partnership has righteousness with lawlessness?
Or what fellowship has light with darkness?
What accord has Christ with Belial?
Or what portion does a believer share with an unbeliever?"

The question you have to answer is what kind of relationship you should have with non-Christians? The best way to determine what type of relationship you should have with the world is to look to the Bible to see how Jesus related to those in the world. Consider the following examples:

Jesus and the World Around Him	
Scripture	**Jesus' Example: He spend time with**
Matthew 9:9-23	Tax Collectors
John 4:1-27	Woman at the Well
John 3:1-15	Nicodemus
Luke 7:36-50	Simon

You may want to read each of these Scriptures and see how Jesus related to the person in each situation. Should we seek to act as He did? You would think so. Luke reports in 5:29-31,

"And Levi made him [Jesus] a great feast in his house,
and there was a large company of tax collectors and others
reclining at table with them. And the Pharisees and their scribes
grumbled at his disciples, saying, "Why do you eat and drink with
tax collectors and sinners?" And Jesus answered them, "Those
who are well have no need of a physician,
but those who are sick."

When we combine the Scripture just quoted with the others above, it is obvious that we are to seek out some type of relationship with those in the world. It would be difficult to convert those in the world if you were not to spend any time with them. So, what type of relationship can we have based on 2 Corinthians 6:14-15? It appears that the key to answering this issue has to do with the phrase *'Do not be unequally yoked with unbelievers' (vs 14)*.

Obviously, it is important to understand what unequally yoked with unbelievers actually means. Let's define this phrase using other resources to help us. David Lipscomb (1963) described what yoked or bound meant. "To be unequally yoked would be to be so connected with the unbeliever that the believer would be controlled by the unbeliever." Warden (2019), quoted George Eldon Lad who "saw this as a warning...against close ties that link Christians with unbelievers in pagan ways of thought and action."

If we do not accept such definitions of yoked, then the limitations that are imposed on our relationship with the world make outreach extremely difficult and it certainly seems to go against what Jesus actually did as he lived with, ate with and spoke to others.

On the other hand, if you accept this definition, it suggests that you can have relationships with unbelievers, but you must be careful about how closely you intwine your life with theirs. You want to impact their life with changes that may eventually bring about salvation. If you start giving in to your fleshly nature by following their lead and doing things that are against Biblical teachings, you become unequally yoked and you may have lost the opportunity to help them understand Christianity. Your goal in spending time with non-Christians should be to be an example of the Christian life to them. In doing so, they can see the blessings that Christianity can give, and a door may very well open for you to share the Christ story. Here are some principles that will assist you in relationship development with the world.

> *"To be unequally yoked would be to be so connected with the unbeliever that the believer would be controlled by the unbeliever."*

1. We are in the world, but not of the world.
2. Healing from healthy relationships comes from fellow Christians.
3. The time spent with non-Christians should ultimately be directed toward conversion.
4. If you get no positive response shake the dust off your feet, continue to be a friend and example, but focus on someone else who may be more responsive to the Word. You may have planted a seed or watered it. Someone else may actually convert them.
5. All of our time cannot be spent with non-Christians. We must have fellowship with believers for our own spiritual health. We are built up and energized by spending time in worship and fellowship with fellow Christians. Keep a balance!

Fellowship	
Scripture	**Concept**
In Christ	
1 Corinthians 1:9	First with Jesus.
With the Holy Spirit	
2 Corinthians 13:14	Fellowship with the Holy Spirit.
Responsibilities	
Galatians 6:2	Bear one another's burdens.
Romans 12:10	Be devoted to one another in love.
Romans 12:13	Contribute to needs, practice hospitality.
Romans 12:15	Rejoice with those who rejoice, weep with those who weep.
Ephesians 4:16	Build each other up in love.
1 Corinthians 12:25	Have the same care for one another.
1 Corinthians 12:26	Suffer with one another, rejoice with one another.
1 Peter 4:13	Share in sufferings.
2 Corinthians 1:3-7	Comfort one another.
Hebrews 3:13	Encourage one another daily.
The Blessing of	
1 John 1:7	Fellowship with one another and Christ's blood cleanses us.

If you look in the Bible you will find dozens of 'One Another' passages that help us understand how we should be treating and caring for each other. The above is a good sampling of what God wants from and for us.

Remember, you are in the world,
but not of the world!

Fellowship and Spiritual Warfare

As a Christian you indeed must be in the world so that you can help those who are still of the world. The problem is that being in the world creates a ripe opportunity for forces of darkness to attack you. They are devious and constantly seek to find a weakness within you. That is another reason why it is important to fellowship with brothers and sisters. You know that old saying, 'Too close to the forest to see the trees'. Well sometimes when you are close to sin while doing God's will, darkness can sneak in and start causing damage and you may be so busy attempting to do Godly things that you don't see spiritual forces of darkness gently pulling you towards them. When that occurs fellowship can be very helpful. We can help each other see if we are ever so slightly crossing a line. All of us must be talking to each other, especially when we are seeking to help those in darkness.

Fellowship is essential when you are facing forces of darkness. It's been stated previously but in your battle with forces of evil your brothers and sisters can have your back if you let them. They can help you and you can help them. It is through fellowship and Christian support that we can aid one another in this ongoing battle against spiritual forces of darkness. It will be very difficult to wage this war without your brothers and sisters in Christ. You should never face spiritual forces of darkness without your brothers and sisters by your side. When you sense an attack, reach out. Call someone. Be open to having the elders pray over you. Don't let your pride get in the way of asking for help. It's one Satan's greatest manipulations that he uses against mankind. To do so, is to set you up for pain and potential failure. When we work together, talk about our outreach and preferably bring other people into our outreach methods it become increasingly more difficult for Satan's spiritual forces to damage us.

Personal Reflection

List three things that you learned or that were reinforced regarding gifts and building each other up, how we should fellowship with the world or how we should protect ourselves from the world when we are seeking to help others.

1.

2.

3.

Judging, Reproving, Rebuking and Helping Fellow Christians

Chapter Twenty-Six

This is a hard chapter to write and also hard for many to be part of when you are trying to help wayward brothers or sisters. Yet, it is also one of the most important aspects of Christianity that must be dealt with. When it is not properly handled people can lose their relationship with God and eternal salvation. No one wants that to happen to a fellow Christian. To better understand this issue, we have broken this chapter into the following specific areas.

- To Judge or Not to Judge
- Righteous Judgment
- Reproving or Rebuking One Another
- Disfellowshipping
- Help for the Unwilling
- Return of the Fallen

To Judge or Not to Judge

If we are to rebuke or correct someone we would have to judge that they did something wrong. Aren't we told to not judge each other? Is that completely true? In Matthew 7:1-5 Jesus states,

"Judge not, that you be not judged.
For with the judgment you pronounce
you will be judged,
and with the measure you use it
will be measured to you.
Why do you see the speck that is in your brother's eye,
but do not notice the log that is in your own eye?
Or how can you say to your brother,
'Let me take the speck out of your eye,'
when there is the log in your own eye?
You hypocrite, first take the log out of your own eye,
and then you will see clearly
to take the speck out of your brother's eye."

It sounds like we shouldn't judge each other. However, the third line above in that Scripture gives us a hint. It says the way we judge could be used against us. What if the way or measure is specific Scripture, biblical truth, specific doctrinal teachings that are clear in the Bible? We are told to rebuke a brother or sister if they are exhibiting sin. To determine if rebuking is needed there must be a standard and a judgment must be made.

Righteous Judgment

Let's make this clear. What standard do we judge others by? It is by using righteous judgment. What is righteous judgement? It is simply this. You use the words in the Bible to determine if a person is sinning and is in need of correction reproof or rebuke. Judgment based on Scriptures and Scriptures only is what you would call righteous judgment. Righteous judgment is identifying God's will in regard to behavior that we see in fellow brothers and sisters. His will is found in the Bible along with specific acts that a man can commit that are unacceptable to God. Such unacceptable actions or behaviors are identified throughout the Bible. They should also be unacceptable to us as fellow Christians. So, who are we to judge then? Paul says it very clearly. In 1 Corinthians 5: 12b he writes, "Is it not those inside the church whom you are to judge?" That was clear and to the point. We should be judging, but it must be done in the right way. Here are some possible responses when you seek to reprove or rebuke a brother or sister:

1. You share how the person's sin goes against the written will of God and they acknowledge it and make corrections.

2. You share how the person's sin goes against the written will of God and they ignore your teaching and do not make corrections. That can ultimately damage their relationship with God.
3. Their sin is grievous, hurtful or damaging to others. It is hurting both him and the local body of Christ. In love you communicate how the sin is seen as unacceptable to God using his holy Word. He might accept your input, seek to confess his sin and desire to get help to overcome.
4. Their sin is grievous, hurtful or damaging to others. It is hurting both him and the body of Christ. In love you communicate how the sin is seen as unacceptable to God using his holy Word. He refuses to acknowledge or accept your input and continues in his grievous sin. After repeated discussions with more than one person helping and no change occurs, the person is disfellowshipped.

So, when a brother or sister exhibits a damaging sin, God calls for us to recognize it and do something to help that brother or sister to remove that sin from his or her life.

Jesus vs Paul: Conflict or Not

Does there appear to be a conflict between what Jesus and Paul teaches about judging? Let's look at it for a moment.

In Matthew 7:1-5 Jesus states, "**Judge not**, that you be not judged."

However, Paul states in 2 Timothy 3:16, "All Scripture is breathed out by God and profitable for teaching, **for reproof, for correction**, and for training in righteousness,"

Is Paul in conflict with Jesus regarding judging or not? Let's see what two different commentaries communicate regarding judgment.

Barnes' Notes on the Bible
In the New Testament the word is used to express a judgment of what is wrong or contrary to one's will, and hence, to admonish or reprove. It implies our conviction that there is something evil, or some fault in him who is rebuked.

Commentary on the New Testament Epistles, by David Lipscomb
"For reproof - For reproving mistakes and wrongs to ourselves and others. For correction – **The Scripture is perceived as the rule of faith, convicting of error and guiding to truth."**

The key statement seen in these commentaries is that we are not personally placing judgment on the sinner. We are simply sharing how their sin runs against the will and law of God. Specifically, that sin is something addressed in the New Testament as being unacceptable. This truly is Righteous or Godly Judgment. Righteous Judgment is simply identifying what the Bible says about a sin and sharing it with the sinner with love.

What is the difference between Jesus' statement and Paul's? Jesus is stating that we cannot judge based on our own laws, beliefs, etc. Paul is saying that judgment must be made using God's standards in order to help correct and train a brother or sister. So, we should never judge a brother or sister using our own standards or beliefs. We can only judge by using Righteous Judgment.

So, when you reprove and rebuke it must be based on Righteous Judgment, not any belief, standard, rule, tradition that we have come to accept of believe. It must be based on Biblical truth or Scriptures that specifically define Godly from ungodly.

What if you utilize righteous judgment and the fellow Christian refuses to respond by working on or stopping his sinful activity? Let's see what the Bible says about that. There is a process that is found in the Bible that we should be utilizing.

Reproving, or Rebuking One Another

How long has there been a need for reproving or rebuking fellow Christians? Apparently, the church had that problem in the very beginning.

"I solemnly charge you in the presence of God
and of Christ Jesus, who is to judge the living and the dead,
and by His appearing and His kingdom: preach the word;
be ready in season and out of season; **reprove, rebuke, exhort,
with great patience and instruction.**

[WHY?]

For the time will come when they will not endure sound doctrine;
but wanting to have their ears tickled,
they will accumulate for themselves teachers
in accordance to their own desires,
and will turn away their ears from the truth
and will turn aside to myths."
2 Timothy 4:1-2

What do you think? Is this happening today or just when Paul wrote to Timothy? Why do you think there are so many religious institutions that claim to be teaching God's will but somehow many 'new' beliefs that are not found in the Bible are not being just taught but are foundational in those religions? It's simply because many men have not endured sound doctrine. Instead, they wanted to find doctrine that supports their own beliefs. We used to call that smorgasbord Christianity. Pick the doctrines you like and find a church that teaches them. That problem occurred then and it is occurring now. That is why we must reprove, rebuke and exhort one another. We must make sure that we teach the Bible and only the Bible and judge each other by its contents not by our own standards or beliefs.

It's important to note that you don't want to reprove, rebuke or correct non-Christians as your inroads to teaching them. You may just drive them away. That doesn't mean that you should not teach them right from wrong. However, non-Christians should be treated with care just like you would a baby or a child. You gently show them the path. It's different when you see a brother or sister who is exhibiting obvious sin. So, what do you do in that case? This is an area of Christian relationship that is often not discussed. People prefer to not deal with it at all because it seems to be negative, confrontive, hurtful and judgmental. We have to consider that just maybe one of the reasons this is rarely discussed or utilized in a church is that we all believe we are sinners and we shouldn't call someone out for their sin simply because, they could turn around and do the same thing to us. We just discussed the proper, Biblical reason to judge so we won't do that again. God wants us to reprove or rebuke each other when we err.

It's important to note that you don't want to rebuke or correct non-Christians as your inroads to teaching them.

Reproof

First, let's look at the definition of reproof in the Greek language. The Greek elegcho (ελεγχω), means confute, admonish, refute, or expose. It is elsewhere translated 'tell a fault' (Matthew 18:15), 'convict' (John 8:9), and 'convince' (John 8:46). It means to show people their wrong ways and to convince them of the right way of God's Word. The Greek verb elenchō (ἐλέγχω) is also used as a word for reproof in the Bible. In this case, Vines states that reproof is translated as "Convicted; the real meaning here is 'exposed' (Luke 3:19, John 16:8, 1 Corinthians14:24 and Ephesians 5:11-13).

Barnes' Notes on the Bible

"Reprove - Or "convince;" The meaning is that he was to use such arguments as would "convince" men of the truth of religion, and of their own need of it..... The word in this verse rendered "reprove," does not imply this, but merely that one may be in error, and needs to have arguments presented to convince him of the truth. That word also implies no superior authority in him who does it. He presents "reasons, or argues" the case, for the purpose of convincing."

Reproving seems to call for you to reprimand or correct someone's behavior or actions. Reproof seems to be done in a gentler, kinder way. Think of gently directing a child away from an unwanted behavior. You reprove a fellow Christian:

- In a spirit of kindness.
- In a way that is meant to be helpful.
- Calmly providing information that contradicts beliefs or actions.
- With brotherly love you expose or prove them to be wrong using Scriptures.

Rebuke

Now, let's look at what the definition of rebuke is in the Greek language. Elegchó is the Greek word used for rebuke. Mounce's Complete Expository Dictionary of Old and New Testament words describes rebuke or Elegchó as follows. "Rebuking can take on a number of forms, such as making someone aware of a sin (Matthew 18:15), exposing sin (John 3:20), and/or convincing someone of guilt (John 8:26). It can also refer to the refutation of false doctrine (Titus 1:9)." It is a stronger stance than what is taken with reproof. Sometimes it must be a lovingly clear disapproval or criticism of someone because of their behavior or actions. When you look at both reproof and rebuke it certainly appears that rebuke takes on a more negative connotation and is more directive in nature. It may be because of false doctrine that is being taught or believed. It could be because of an obvious sin that is causing others to be uncomfortable. Let's look and see what one commentary says about rebuke.

Barnes' Notes on the Bible

Rebuke - Rebuke offenders; Titus 2:15; see the use of the word in Matthew 8:26; Matthew 12:16, (rendered "charged"); Matthew 16:22; Matthew 17:18; Matthew 19:13; Matthew 20:31; Luke 4:35, Luke 4:39; Luke 17:13; Luke 18:15; Jude 1:9. In the New Testament the word is used to express a judgment of what is wrong or contrary to one's will, and hence, to admonish..... The word here rendered rebuke, implies authority or superiority, and means merely that we may say that a thing is wrong, and administer a rebuke for it, as if there were no doubt that it was wrong. The propriety of the rebuke rests on our authority for doing it, not on the arguments which we present. This is based on the presumption that men often know that they are doing wrong, and need no arguments to convince them of it. The idea is, that the minister is not merely to reason about sin, and convince men that it is wrong, but he may solemnly admonish them not to do it, and warn them of the consequences."

The person may need to be convinced of their guilt and admonished not to continue in it. It would be a strong stance showing disapproval as you rebuke a fellow Christian. You would do this:

- In brotherly love.
- To reprehend severely, chide, admonish.
- To call to account, show one his fault, demand an explanation. The use of Scriptures is important.
- To clearly correct false doctrine. Show Scriptures.
- To warn them of consequences.

Mounce also states that "the Bible commands rebuke (which entails judgment as an act of love)." God is our example as seen in Hebrews 12:5-6.

"And have you completely forgotten this word
of encouragement that addresses you
as a father addresses his son?
It says, "My son, do not make light of the Lord's discipline,
and do not lose heart when he rebukes you,
(New International Version)

Basically, rebuking is meant to help turn a brother or sister who is sinning back to the path of righteousness. As we have stated, it must be done in love. In 2 Timothy 4:2 Paul tells us to, "preach the word; be ready in season and out of season; **reprove, rebuke, and exhort, with complete patience and teaching."**

When we reprove or rebuke a brother or sister, it must be done in love, never with anger or with a superior attitude. We are all sinners and simply need to help each other on the journey.

Disfellowshipping

It sounds harsh but when done properly disfellowshipping is a way by which errant Christians can be returned to God. That makes it important. In Matthew 18:15-17 Jesus teaches that, if a person who claims to be a believer will not repent of specific sin after several confrontations, that person should be treated as an unbeliever.

"If your brother sins against you, go and tell him his fault,
between you and him alone. If he listens to you,
you have gained your brother. But if he does not listen,
take one or two others along with you, that every charge may be
established by the evidence of two or three witnesses.
If he refuses to listen to them, tell it to the church.
And if he refuses to listen even to the church,
let him be to you as a Gentile and a tax collector."

Paul also addresses this touchy subject regarding church discipline: In 1 Corinthians 5:9-13 he writes,

"I wrote to you in my letter not to associate with
sexually immoral people— not at all meaning the sexually immoral
of this world, or the greedy and swindlers, or idolaters,
since then you would need to go out of the world.
**But now I am writing to you not to associate with anyone
who bears the name of brother
if he is guilty of sexual immorality or greed, or is an idolater,
reviler, drunkard, or swindler—
not even to eat with such a one.
For what have I to do with judging outsiders?
Is it not those inside the church whom you are to judge?
God judges those outside.**
"Purge the evil person from among you."

So, unrepentant sinners within the church are to be removed from the local body. This is practically accomplished when the faithful members of the church withdraw their fellowship from the unrepentant sinner. It is this action on their part that forms the withdrawing of fellowship. That does not mean that you have no interactions with the person like some people suggest. Paul reminds the church in 2 Corinthians 2:7–8 to restore and forgive a repentant brother. The ultimate goal of excommunication or disfellowshipping is repentance and the restoration of fellowship.

God gives the church the authority to disfellowship a member who is habitually committing sin or is a danger to the congregation (Matthew 18:17; Romans 16:17-18; I Corinthians 5:1-5, 9-13; II Thessalonians 3:6, 14; Titus 3:10-11). Let's look at four specific Scriptures.

"But we command you, brethren, in the name of our Lord Jesus Christ, that you **withdraw from every brother who walks disorderly and not according to the tradition which he received from us."**
2 Thessalonians 3:6

"But now I am writing to you **not to associate with anyone** who bears the name of brother if he is guilty of sexual immorality or greed, or is an idolater, reviler, drunkard, or swindler—not even to eat with such a one."
1 Corinthians 5:11

"It is actually reported that there is sexual immorality among you,
and of a kind that is not tolerated even among pagans,
for a man has his father's wife. And you are arrogant!
Ought you not rather to mourn? Let him who has done this be
removed from among you. For though absent in body,
I am present in spirit; and as if present, **I have already
pronounced judgment on the one who did such a thing.**
When you are assembled in the name of the Lord Jesus
and my spirit is present, with the power of our Lord Jesus,
you are to deliver this man to Satan
for the destruction of the flesh,
so that his spirit may be saved
in the day of the Lord."
1 Corinthians 5:1-5

"**Now I urge you, brethren, note those who cause divisions and offenses, contrary to the doctrine which you learned, and avoid them.** For those who are such do not serve our Lord Jesus Christ, but their own belly, and by smooth words and flattering speech deceive the hearts of the simple."
Romans 16:17-18

Obviously, if we read these Scriptures it becomes apparent that we must withdraw fellowship if a brother or sister who refuses to discontinue a sin. It certainly suggests that we are to discontinue all types of interaction with the sinner. This includes social interactions. In I Corinthians 5:11, Paul tells us how to handle this situation. "But now I am writing to you not to associate with anyone who bears the name of brother if he is guilty of sexual immorality or greed, or is an idolater, reviler, drunkard, or swindler—not even to eat with such a one." Paul speaks generally when he says: "not associate with." He also gets very specific when he says, "not even to eat with such a one." Social interaction is not acceptable to Paul. The person must understand that in his present condition the saints of God cannot have any social association with him.

There is one exception to this teaching. You can spend time with the person in order to admonish him in love to repent and come back to proper fellowship (2 Thess. 3:15). If you are experiencing this and are not sure how to handle it, you should speak to your church leaders. They should be equipped to help you do what is best in that specific situation.

Just be aware that your leadership may handle this sensitive issue differently depending on the situation. However, it is important that the believer who has been disfellowshipped understands the gravity of his sin in hopes that he will return to God. Continue to communicate with gentleness and show him love as you seek to help him return to fellowship.

Help for the Unwilling

But what about those who sin and are not asking for forgiveness. Those who are seeking out specific sin in their life. There are a multitude of Scriptures that talk about how we should help one another. One key thing we can do is pray for the sinful one who is unwilling to change, even when prayers aren't wanted. As brothers and sisters, we should be on the lookout for anyone who might be oppressed and pray for them. In doing so, we constantly remind ourselves to be wary of the schemes of Satan and spiritual forces of darkness that seek to damage us spiritually. It also helps us stay alert and thoughtful about what God wants us to be and do. Consider this! Pray the Hedge of Thorns prayer. Let's explain this.

In Hosea 2:6-7 it gives an example of dealing with a person who is sinning. The well-known title for this issue is called, Hedge of Thorns. If someone is struggling with sin and doesn't want to stop, we can pray the Hedge of Thorns prayer. In this case it is a woman who is pursuing lovers but it certainly could be adapted for other situations.

Therefore, I will hedge up her way with thorns,
and I will build a wall against her, so that she cannot find her paths.
She shall pursue her lovers but not overtake them,
and she shall seek them but shall not find them.
Then she shall say, 'I will go and return to my first husband,
for it was better for me then than now.'

You may learn of a person who is experiencing sin that is damaging to self or others. Often such individuals don't have the wisdom to understand the destructive path that they are on. If they do, sometimes they are so invested in the sin that they aren't willing to let it go. When this happens, you can pray the Hedge of Thorns prayer. You would be asking God to separate or make it difficult for the person to find or participate in destructive influences or people who are luring them into evil ways.

You can adapt the Hedge of Thorns prayer to any situation. It doesn't have to be a long prayer. Let it be specific and heartfelt. Through the Holy Spirit, God will hear and understand what you are communicating and the urgency of your message. Consider how it could be applied to drugs, alcohol or any other dangerous unhealthy behavior. Love the sinner and pray that their sin will become more difficult or impossible to participate in. The applications are numerous and the potential benefit cannot be described by words. Here is an example that could be used for unfaithfulness.

Sample Hedge of Thorns Prayer

Father, God, I ask you to build a hedge of thorns around [insert name]. I ask you to separate my loved one [brother or sister] from darkness. I pray that those who are having a negative influence will lose interest. Not only that, but I also pray that they will become disinterested and that my loved one will lose interest in them as well. I fervently pray that you would put a hedge of thorns around [insert name] that will defend him/her against any contact with those who are leading him/her down a path of darkness. It's in your blessed son Jesus Christ that I pray. Amen.

Return of the Fallen

When a brother or sister falls into temptation and is ultimately disfellowshipped the most important task of the church is not to withdraw from him. It is to restore him. How do you do that if you are not supposed to spend time with him? You can spend time with him. The time spent is a time of love and gentleness as you seek to help him deal with his sin; not to have dinner and talk about trivia, social events or anything else. Show your concern as you seek to lead them to repentance. In doing so you may have saved a soul. Let's look at two important Scriptures that address this.

"Brothers, if anyone is caught in any transgression,
you who are spiritual should **restore him in a spirit of gentleness.** Keep watch on yourself, lest you too be tempted."
Galatians 6:1

Note that the concern is twofold in Galatians 6:1. First, there is a concern for the fallen who need to be restored. However, there is a warning. If the person is living a sinful life and continues to do so in front of you, then you should be careful lest you be tempted and fall to sin also while you are attempting to help him. Read what James has to say about this.

"My brothers, if anyone among you wanders from the truth and someone brings him back, let him know that whoever brings back a sinner from his wandering will save his soul from death and will cover a multitude of sins."
James 5:19-20

Basically, James is stating that when someone is brought back to a relationship with God all of his sins will be covered again and his soul will be saved from eternal death. Benson stated this in his Commentary. "From the false doctrine and bad practice to which he had turned aside, shall produce a much happier effect than any miraculous cure of the body; for he shall save a precious immortal soul from spiritual and eternal death, and shall hide a multitude of sins — Namely, the sins of the persons thus converted, which shall no more, how many soever they are, be remembered to his condemnation."

Personal Reflection

List three things that you learned or that were reinforced that helped you understand what the Scriptures say about judging, reproving, rebuking and helping fellow Christians who have sinned or have unrepentant sin.

1.

2.

3.

Part Six: Discipleship

We don't want to say that any Christian should wait to disciple someone. However, if you aren't prepared it could be difficult. If you have worked through this book you will have seen many aspects of Christianity that would benefit you if you incorporate the teachings into your daily life and being. Without these Scriptural aids you could easily struggle with your discipling. Our hope is that you will now be ready to step out and disciple someone using your unique method to touch others for Christ. Not everyone Disciples the same. Hopefully this last part of the book will give you some ideas that will help you become the Disciple that Jesus wants you to be.

- Discipleship Made Practical
- Applied Discipleship

Discipleship Made Practical

Chapter Twenty-Seven

We hope that all the information up to now has been informative and in some way may have helped you in your journey as you seek to enhance the Godly man or woman that you are right now. Our intent was to remind everyone what Christianity looks like and what we can do to grow spiritually while handling life's daily issues. Now that we have described a multitude of ways you can enhance your relationship with God and your brothers and sisters in Christ, it is finally time for us to share our take on what it means to be a disciple of Christ.

During our evangelistic trips and in daily life we often asked Christians if they were a disciple of Jesus Christ, many have said, "I don't know!" We want to ask that very question of you, but before you give an answer, we would like to continue our Journey Into Discipleship by giving discipleship a practical definition. The following will be covered in this chapter:

- Discipleship
- New Testament Disciples
- Characteristics of a Mature Disciple

Discipleship

Throughout this book we have attempted to explain what it takes for anyone to become an educated disciple. At this point we want to address what discipleship really is and the requirements that Christ lays upon those who would be His Disciples. So, what is a disciple? The Greek Term μαθητής (mathētēs) usually refers to anyone who is an apprentice, a student or a pupil. It is someone who is truly engaged in learning what the teacher wants him to learn. In Biblical times, a person was considered a disciple when he was studying under and trying to emulate a valued teacher. To modern day Christians, it means a follower of Christ who lives his life following His example and doing what he asked us to do.

"Go therefore and make disciples of all nations, baptizing them in the name of the Father and of the Son and of the Holy Spirit, teaching them to observe all that I have commanded you. And behold, I am with you always, to the end of the age."
Matthew 28:19-20

"Discipleship is a process of not only holding onto your own faith, but growing in it so that you may lead others toward Christ" (Herrick). There are several Scriptures that describe what Jesus expects of his Disciples. They are as follows:

What Jesus says about Disciples	
Matthew 16:24	Then Jesus said to his disciples, "Whoever wants to be my disciple must **deny themselves** and take up their cross and follow me.
Matthew 28:16-20	Then the eleven disciples went to Galilee, to the mountain where Jesus had told them to go. When they saw him, **they worshiped him**; but some doubted. Then Jesus came to them and said, "All authority in heaven and on earth has been given to me. Therefore **go and make disciples** of all nations, baptizing them in the name of the Father and of the Son and of the Holy Spirit, and **teaching them to obey everything I have commanded you**. And surely I am with you always, to the very end of the age."
Luke 14:33	In the same way, **those of you who do not give up everything** you have cannot be my disciples.

Luke 9:23-25	Then he said to them all: "Whoever wants to be my disciple must **deny themselves and take up their cross daily** and follow me. For whoever wants to save their life will lose it, but whoever loses their life for me will save it. What good is it for someone to gain the whole world, and yet lose or forfeit their very self?
Luke 14:26-27	"If anyone comes to me and does not **hate father and mother, wife and children, brothers and sisters—yes, even their own life**—such a person cannot be my disciple. And whoever does not carry their cross and follow me cannot be my disciple.
John 8:31-32	To the Jews who had believed him, Jesus said, "If you **hold to my teaching**, you are really my disciples. Then you will know the truth, and the truth will set you free."
John 13:34-35	"A new command I give you: Love one another. As I have loved you, so you must love one another. **By this everyone will know that you are my disciples, if you love one another**."

New Testament Disciples

Several writers have suggested that there are different types or levels of disciples. Here are three that have been suggested. They are:

- The Casual Disciple
- The Concerned Disciple
- The Committed Disciple

The Casual Disciple

The casual disciple is a Christian who leads a comfortable existence. He has accepted Christ and feels that he is on the way down heavenly road. His prayer life, study of the Word and outreach is sporadic at best. When he compares his Christian life to his prior life as a non-Christian he can see some small changes. This type of disciple usually feels guilty and frustrated. He has yet to figure out what true New Testament Christianity is all about and sometimes is comfortable because he is so lacking in knowledge and the change that should be occurring. After reading the Scriptures on pages 336-337 what do you think Jesus would say to a Casual Disciple?

The Concerned Disciple

This type of disciple wants to be more than a spiritual baby, or child in Christ. He wants to grow. He wants to know what Jesus' will is in his life and attempts to apply it in his daily life. He periodically seeks out Biblical truths in order that he might grow and mature but struggles with knowing what is the right or best thing to do at times. This occurs because of a lack of consistent dedication to studying, learning and participating in training or growth producing activities. After reading the Scriptures pages 334-335 what do you think Jesus would say to a Concerned Disciple?

The Committed Disciple

Have you heard the phrase, 'Let your light shine'? The life of this Christian or disciple is obviously so different that people want to know what makes him that way. He is vibrant, alive, aching to share the good news in his own God given way. Although he has learned much, he is always seeking and wanting to grow spiritually. He has achieved a good working knowledge of the Scriptures, but he still reads and wants to understand it better as time goes on. The Scriptures are not just factual knowledge for him. It is a roadmap that leads to a total change of life because he naturally applies the knowledge. God and the Holy Spirit are truly working in him. He has learned from others who have sought to teach him. This type of disciple has really learned what it means to deny self and follow Christ. It is no longer he who lives, but Christ who lives in him. While in process of learning, this disciple has one or more people that he could speak with and learn from. At least one of them has stayed by his side during his growth process as a friend, fellow Christian and a Discipler. This kind of Disciple is spiritually mature and often

This type of disciple has really learned what it means to deny self and follow Christ. It is no longer he who lives, but Christ who lives in him.

seen as a spiritual leader. After reading the Scriptures on pages 334-335 what do you think Jesus would say to a Committed Disciple? We believe that he would say, 'Well done good and faithful servant.'

Disciples in the New Testament

Now, let's take a look at some of the disciples that are mentioned in the New Testament. What kind of men were they? Did they all excel in their Christianity? Were they special men with special qualities? Were they all totally Committed Disciples who fulfilled Christ's idea of Discipleship? Or did Jesus have Disciples that were at varied stages of Discipleship? Many think that disciples are a special order of Christians who have drawn close to God. Some believe that they are Christians who really have their life in tune with God's will. Read the following Scriptures below and determine what kind of disciples were found in the New Testament.

Disciples of Christ		
Scripture		**Type of Disciple**
Mark 9:33-35	And they came to Capernaum. And when he was in the house he asked them, "What were you discussing on the way?" But they kept silent, for on the way they had argued with one another about who was the greatest. And he sat down and called the twelve. And he said to them, "If anyone would be first, he must be last of all and servant of all."	___Casual ___Concerned ___Committed
John 6:66	After this many of his disciples turned back and no longer walked with him.	___Casual ___Concerned ___Committed
Acts 14:21	When they had preached the gospel to that city and had made many disciples, they returned to Lystra and to Iconium and to Antioch,	___Casual ___Concerned ___Committed

Acts 20:29-30	I know that after my departure fierce wolves will come in among you, not sparing the flock; and from among your own selves will arise men speaking twisted things, to draw away the disciples after them.	___Casual ___Concerned ___Committed

Based on these Scriptures do you believe that there are levels of Discipleship? If so, does that mean all Christians are in some way disciples of Christ? We believe that all Christians are disciples. However, both Christians and Disciples can be at different stages in their spiritual growth. Even the men who walked with Jesus had trouble with faith; they were at various levels of spiritual development. Even so, Jesus considered all those who followed Him as His disciples. As a follower of Christ, you must seek to grow spiritually, so that you too can become a more mature disciple. The overall key to mature discipleship is that you are willing to grow, through the Word, with the help of the Holy Spirit and by applying Biblical principles in your life (See Stages of Spiritual Growth as discussed earlier in this work).

Which type of disciple are you right now? Check where you personally feel you are at this moment in your Christianity. Be honest with yourself. God knows what is in your heart. The purpose of this is to encourage you to grow spiritually.

Casual Disciple - Concerned Disciple - Committed Disciple

1 2 3 4 5 6 7 8 9 10

After considering where you are on this Discipleship continuum, what is one thing you would be willing to work on by yourself or with help from someone else so that you could become a more committed Disciple? Who might you talk to that would help you? Think about it and make a choice to grow if it is needed.

Characteristics of a Mature Disciple

As you grow through study and experience you will become more aware of what you need to look out for in your Christian life. You must daily let God purge you of your sinful ways as you seek to be holy as He is Holy. Always seeking to internalize what He expects of you so that you will grow and mature as His disciple. A mature disciple loves Christ and through service and obedience seeks to become more like him. Such a relationship involves setting aside your goals, ambitions, desires in life and most of all your own will so that you can put Christ first in your life (Luke 9:23).

As you focus on Christ, you must develop the character that will eventually lead you to a maturity, that in turn will assist you in allowing the fruit of the Spirit to be evident in your life. It is through these characteristics, and the fruit of the Spirit that others can see the life of Christ in you. As such, the life you lead and the character you develop are your best tools for sharing Jesus with others.

Remember, mature discipleship does not come all at once. All of us must develop spiritually at our own pace, not anothers. As a result, you shouldn't compare yourself with others, but rather in humility seek to improve yourself through endurance, perseverance (James 1:4), daily examination (2 Corinthians 13:5) and self-discipline (2 Peter 2:4-9?) as you focus on Christ's example. It may or may not be fun, but if you want to challenge yourself to grow, rate yourself using the Character Checklist for New Testament Disciples on the next page.

> *Mature discipleship does not come all at once. All of us must develop spiritually at our own pace, not anothers. As a result, you shouldn't compare yourself with others, but rather in humility seek to improve yourself through endurance, perseverance (James 1:4), daily examination (2 Corinthians 13:5) and self-discipline (2 Peter 2:4-9?) as you focus on Christ's example.*

As we grow close to completing your Journey Into Discipleship, let's look at some specific characteristics that are evident in mature disciples. These characteristics may be found in the following Scriptures: Titus 1:5-9, 1 Timothy 3:1-7, and 1 Peter 5:1-3. You may use the following checklist to better determine if you are in process of developing these important characteristics as God would want you to.

Journey Into Discipleship Character Checklist for New Testament Disciples					
Name: Date:					
Instructions: Rate yourself to see where you may need to grow. 1 = This characteristic is developed as God would have me develop it. 2 = I've almost got this one developed as it should be. 3 = Kind of average. 4 = I'm doing a poor job with this one. 5 = Help! I really need to work on this one.					
Characteristics of a Mature Disciple	**1**	**2**	**3**	**4**	**5**
Have died to self (Galatians 2:20)					
Above reproach					
Hospitable					
Lover of good					
Upright					
Holy					
Disciplined or self-controlled					
Holds firm to the trustworthy word as taught					
Able to teach/give instruction in sound doctrine					
Able to rebuke those who contradict it					
Soberminded					
Respectful					
Gentle					
Manages household well					
Keep children submissive with dignity					
Well thought of by outsiders					
Steadfast					
Loving					
Joyful					
Peaceful					
Patient					
Kind					
Faithful					
Know and Use Your God Given Gift					
Daily examine self to improve on the above					
See handout in the appendices for personal use.					

There are also many qualities or characteristics that are not in any way acceptable for a Christian or Disciple to exhibit or have within them. If they are there, they should not be ignored. They are old sinful, carnal parts of our old self that need to be removed. These can become doorways by which spiritual forces of evil can creep in and disrupt your spiritual life. This too is something that all Christians should be doing in order to spiritually mature. The more you remove sinful, carnal characteristics, the more your life will become a fragrant offering to God the father. One of your greatest aids in accomplishing this is the relationships you have with brothers and sisters. Consider this. If the Holy Spirit is attempting to live through you by exhibiting those Godly traits shown above, how will He accomplish most of those traits if you are not around your brothers and sisters in Christ. Going to the assembly, spending time with brothers and sisters should be safe proving grounds for your growth. This is where you can fully experience the Holy Spirit in your life as you allow yourself to die to self and become more like Jesus Christ and the Holy Spirit.

The more you remove sinful, carnal characteristics, the more your life will become a fragrant offering to God the father. One of your greatest aids in accomplishing this is the relationships you have with brothers and sisters.

We looked at several characteristics that are gifted to us by the Holy Spirit assuming we can get self out of the way. There are also many ungodly characteristics that damage you spiritually, that hurt others and that make it difficult for people to listen to you when you say, "God has changed me and made me a better person." The checklist below lists several of those unwanted characteristics and their spiritual opposites. The spiritual opposite is what you must seek to allow into your life. The Holy Spirit wants to shine through you by exhibiting these wonderful characteristics. You just need to let Him do His work.

Journey Into Discipleship Characteristics not Acceptable for New Testament Disciples		
Name:		Date:
Instructions: Simply put a checkmark next to any characteristic you believe you need to remove.		
Unacceptable Carnal Characteristics	**Which of the below to the left needs to be worked on?**	**Spiritual Opposites**
Pride or Arrogance		Humility
Quick-tempered		Calm
A drunkard		Sober
Violent		Peaceful
Greedy for gain		Generous
Quarrelsome		Amiable
A lover of money		Giving
Domineering over those in your charge		Considerate
Sexual immorality		Morality
Impurity		Purity
Sensuality		Temperance
Idolatry		God
Enmity		Good Will
Strife		Harmony
Jealousy		Admire
Rivalries		Cooperation
Lying		Truthful
Dissensions		Harmonious
Divisions		Unity
Other:		
Other:		
See handout in the appendices for personal use.		

Obviously, the chart above is not a complete list of ungodly, carnal characteristics, nor does it have all of the characteristics that can be found in the life of Jesus or the Holy Spirit. If you identified any unhealthy characteristics as you looked at this list, you should want to rid yourself of that characteristic. Seek to replace the unhealthy characteristics with a Holy, Godly characteristic that will help you mature as a Christian.

You may be thinking, 'How do I get rid of these negative characteristics inside of me?' We are not going to leave you without providing a few possible solutions. First of all, don't think about unwanted characteristics. Block it from your mind. Only focus on what you want to be not what you don't want to be. Next, think about the holy opposite a lot. Think about what it would look like if you let that positive characteristic shine out of you. Think about how it might cause others to be more positively responsive toward you. Meditate on that characteristic for minutes each night before you go to sleep. You could simply repeat the Godly characteristic over and over in your mind before you go to sleep or before you get up if you want. Pray about becoming the holy opposite. Share with a trusted friend or your spouse that you want to be more like that specific holy characteristic. Let them pray with or for you. Ask your brothers and sisters for help. As previously stated, fellowship among believers provides an opportunity to share blessings and burdens with each other. Let others help. If it is a serious problem, seek out your church leadership (elders) and ask for their prayers and aid. Don't just try to fight spiritual forces of darkness by yourself. They are good at what they do.

Now, look back at the Character Checklist for New Testament Disciples (page 340). It shows you other spiritual characteristics that you can enhance or incorporate into your life. No matter how many fours or fives you have on your Character Checklist, the most important thing you must consider is how you can grow, improve or mature. To do this you must take action so that you can become a more spiritually mature Christian. Make a plan. Consistently get into the Word. Get help from your church leadership, or someone else you trust. Life is a journey. Discipleship is a journey. Just remember your destination and keep heading towards it.

Personal Reflection

List three things that you learned or that were reinforced that helped you understand what it means to be a mature New Testament Disciple.

1.

2.

3.

Applied Discipleship

Chapter Twenty-Eight

Discipling is one of the greatest priorities that the church has had since Jesus first spoke to the Disciples who followed him Some of the last words that Jesus spoke was the following. And Jesus came and said to them,

"All authority in heaven and on earth has been given to me.
Go therefore and make disciples of all nations,
baptizing them in the name of the Father and of the Son
and of the Holy Spirit, teaching them to observe
all that I have commanded you.
And behold, I am with you always,
to the end of the age" (Matthew 28:18-20).

Many have the tendency to focus on baptizing people, which is indeed part of the command. Yet, what is the first part of the commandment? He says, "Go therefore and make disciples of all Nations." That should be our focus. The following will be covered in this chapter:

- The Problem with Disciple Making
- Applied Discipleship
- Essential Elements in Applied Discipleship
- The Best Way to Identify Possible Converts
- Spiritual Multiplication
- The Process of Discipleship
- Relational Activities

- The Discipleship Family
- How a Discipleship Family Can Help
- Integration of New Members
- Keeping the Converted...Converted
- Become a Discipler
- Response Ministry

The Problem with Disciple Making

Therein lies the problem that most new Christians face when they begin their spiritual journey. Most churches focus on evangelism, but neglect Discipling. It's almost as if once someone is baptized it's off to the next person that can be saved. Discipling is more than converting someone. It truly is a life journey. It is teaching them more about the milk of the word. It's also gradually teaching them more about the meat of the word so that they can grow spiritually. It's training them in ministry. It's helping them find their place in the body so that they can actively participate. It's teaching them how to teach others and so much more. It takes time with them to help them grow and mature. It's helping them through the hard times. It's taking time to get to know them and help them in the Discipleship journey. It never ends. When a person has finally become a more spiritually mature Christian or Disciple, he then should be discipling others. When he does make spiritual babies, the one that discipled him can see his spiritual family grow and at least to some degree and participate in it. Think about this for a moment. If you are blessed enough to have a child right now, how does it feel to simply look at what God has given you? How does it feel as you watch your child grow and learn and eventually become a Christian? Then your child marries and has a child. Do you ignore that child? Do you rarely or never spend time with him? Do you think, 'That's not my job.' Are you simply not invested in your grandchild's life? Of course not, yet that is often what we do to spiritual children of those we convert. Sometimes we treat those we convert as acquaintances. The teaching stops, the training stops, the relationship is minimized. Afterall, they are saved, now we can go on to the next one. Right? No, that is not what Jesus commanded. He said make disciples, learners, people who are knowledge seekers and who want to be more like Him. That takes time and effort.

We can send them off to be in a group or Bible class, but often those scenarios do not produce quality one-on-one training that many young Christians need. The good thing is that it actually could, if the group was set up properly, but most do not take this issue into consideration (See information on Discipleship Family later in this chapter). What's the bottom line? New Christians need relationship. Relationship building should always be part of the process. Spending time with those you convert is always part of the process. Teaching them from the baby stage to spiritual adulthood is essential. Let's look at how this could be done.

Applied Discipleship

The life of Jesus should reveal to us that the first priority of a church today should be an evangelistic outreach coupled with Discipleship. Spirit filled, spiritually mature Disciples of Jesus Christ should concentrate their efforts on growing disciples until each of them have matured into a position of leadership. This plan of action is revealed in Paul's advice to young Timothy (2 Timothy 2:2).

Paul → Timothy → Faithful men → Others.

In most cases Christ's church has been slow to grasp and apply this principle. As a result, many Christians suffer from spiritual malnourishment. Action must be taken by treating the cause and not merely the symptoms.

Essential Elements in Applied Discipleship

In the section on 'Balance' we spoke of four basic elements that are essential to the discipling process. They are:

- Studying the Word
- Praying to God
- Fellowship
- Outreach

These areas take into consideration the development of the whole man. When properly balanced these areas will produce both internal as well as external fruit. A wise discipler will teach these essential ingredients to each disciple just as Christ did His disciples. Jesus imparted this information to his disciples by:

- Sharing the truths about the New Life (Verbal Teaching).
- Being a consistent example (Modeling).
- Giving assignments to test progress (Training).

- Correcting any misunderstandings (Redirecting).

Every discipler would do well to follow Jesus' plan by developing his own plan unique to his gift and abilities. It also helps when you learn to focus on the unique needs of those you will disciple.

The Best Way to Identify Possible Converts

Dr. Win Arn was a major promoter of church growth for years and had a significant impact on many churches for years. His teachings are still applicable for us today just as they were years ago. His church growth plan can be found in the book titled, The Master's Plan for making Disciples. In his book he reported some statistics that are very eye opening and we suspect that they are still relatively accurate to this day. Based on research, he shared the easiest way to get new people to attend church meetings. He reported that, "Over 14,000 lay people have been asked the question: "What or who was responsible for your coming to Christ and your church?" One of the following eight responses was usually given: (1) some said a special need bought them to Christ and the Church; (2) some responded they just 'walked in'; (3) others listed the 'pastor' [preacher]; (4) some indicated 'visitation'; (5) others mentioned the 'Sunday School'; (6) a few listed 'evangelistic crusade' or 'program' attracted them; (7) others recalled that the church 'program' attracted them; (8) finally, some people responded 'friend; relative' as being the reason they are now in Christ and the church."

What do you think the percentages would be for each of those possibilities? Which one do you think contributed to new members showing up at a church building? Let's look at what Dr. Arn found. Here are the results that come out of his book.

People who Came to Christ/Church	
Category	**Percentages**
Special Need	1-2%
Walk-In	2-3%
Pastor [Preacher]	5-6%
Visitation	1-2%
Sunday School	4-5%
Evangelistic Crusade	½ of 1%
Church Program	2-3%
Friend/Relative	75-90%

If that is still accurate, which we believe it is, then what should be our focus when we are seeking to save the lost. Who should be out 'targets' for discipleship? What would be the best way to connect with them? The obvious 'targets' are family and friends. That does not mean that we cannot reach out to others. It simply means that our success rate will be much higher with family and friends. Jesus often used meals as opportunity to teach. He found ways to meet a need and they often accepted him. Should we do the same? If we focused on people we knew, invited them to dinners or group dinners or if we identified needs they have and helped, might that be the most effective focus? We think so.

Spiritual Multiplication

The goal of disciple-building is to produce the 'Discipleship Effect'. Each Christian should desire to not only share the word, but also his very life to assure that each new convert becomes a disciple maker. A very important question that we need to constantly ask ourselves is, 'How many have been trained up so that they too can become more effective as Disciples? We have already said this, but in our world today one of the easiest ways for people to develop Discipleship as part of a local body is to incorporate it into small groups. However, they must be built in a way that can incorporate the Discipleship concept. It's not difficult, but many churches prefer other methods. There are many churches that have the right idea about using small groups but fail to utilize them in a way that is discipleship producing. They often promote a regurgitation of what the preacher has preached that week or have closed groups that are never intended to grow numerically. We should be identifying ways to promote Discipleship and the multiplication that was intended by Jesus himself and shown by the apostles. It was meant, in our humble opinion, each group should be identifying spiritual needs in that particular group, focusing on individual as well as group growth and developing opportunities for each member to become more discipleship oriented. The Discipleship Family system addresses those and many other issues for a local church.

It has been obvious that spiritual growth is maximized when someone participates in ministry. This is especially true when is it an outgrowth of their gift. A small group should be helping new and seasoned Christians develop ministry, while at the same time they focus on the unchurched and members who are non-active. There is so much that could be done. As each Christian focuses on a few to help them in becoming mature disciple makers, the 'Discipleship effect' becomes obvious as the body multiplies. See the effect of the multiplication concept in Discipleship on the next page.

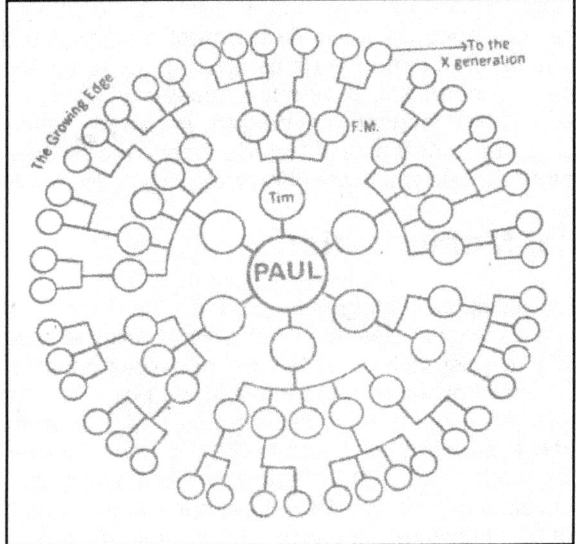

If a church was truly committed to disciple making, they could change their community and possibly the world at an exponential rate far above any other method. Jesus asked his Disciples to do that very thing when he said, "Go therefore and make disciples of all Nations."

The Process of Discipleship

If you are to be successful in discipleship, there are a series of steps you should be considering as you seek to multiply as Paul did in the chart as shown above. However, the greatest practical applications of Discipleship today are found in Jesus' life. If we are to follow His plan, we cannot continue to believe that those who are converted will remain converted unless their conversion is accompanied by disciple building. Jesus intentionally maintained a balance between evangelism and disciple building throughout His ministry. According to Wilson (2009), "Although Jesus did continue to evangelize during all His periods of disciple building, His main emphasis was not on outreach." We like the way Wilson has broken down disciple making in his book. Following Jesus' model for Disciple making can be broken down into eight steps (Wilson, 2009) These have been adapted a bit for our use. Let's look at each step and how it is important in the Discipleship process.

Making Discipleship Practical		
Steps	Action Step	Application
Step One:	Selection	You simply select a few who can in turn do the same (Luke 6:12-16; Mark 3:13-19; John 6:60-71; John 1:29-51).
Step Two:	Association	You associate with those you have selected (Mark 6:30-44).
Step Three:	Consecration	You continue to live the life and attempt to be an example in the faith (Matthew 5:1-12; Luke 6:27-49; Luke 14:25-35; Matthew 7:16-17).
Step Four:	Impartation	You teach what they need to know to become true disciplers of God (John 20:19-23; John 16:33; Matthew 11:28; John 17:6-26; Matthew 16:19).
Step Five:	Demonstration	You demonstrate Discipleship by how you treat them (John 13:15; Philippians 3:17-21; 1 Corinthians 11:2; 2 Timothy 1:6-14).
Step Six:	Delegation	You delegate them to address certain people or group they might be able to touch (Matthew 4:19; John 4:1-2; Mark 6:7-13; Matthew 10; Luke 9:1-6).
Step Seven:	Supervision	You continue to train and aid your Disciple (Mark 9:38; Luke 10:1-24).
Step Eight:	Reproduction	You rejoice in their reproduction and continue to support them (John 15:1-17; Matthew 28:18-20).

We highly recommend the book by Robert Coleman titled, The Master Plan of Discipleship (2020). It is filled with additional information that could be beneficial for anyone wanting to better understand Christ's commission and ultimately become a more powerful force in Discipleship.

The local church and it's building play an important part in disciple making. Win Arn, in his book titled, The Masters Plan for Making Disciples stated, "In effective disciple making the local church is a central part of the process. In fact, disciple-making simply cannot be effective outside the context of the local church. One obvious reason is that the goal is to make disciples; and a disciple is one who is actively involved and incorporated into the life of a local church---namely yours." Dr. Arn was obviously correct. Regardless of how you develop a discipleship plan for your local congregation, it must include how you will incorporate all new disciples into the local church. You must find ways for them to participate in the body in some way and constantly seek to identify ways to help them grow and fulfill their opportunities to become a discipler to others.

Relational Activities

To be spiritually healthy the assembly must be a continuation of each Christian's worship. One of the greatest purposes of the assembly is to fellowship, to uplift one-another and to praise God. The Scriptures below indicate the relational activities that should be a part of our assembling together. Look at the following Scriptures.

Relational Activities	
Colossians 3:16	Let the word of Christ dwell in you richly, **teaching and admonishing one another** in all wisdom, **singing psalms and hymns and spiritual songs**, with thankfulness in your hearts to God.
Ephesians 5:19	Addressing one another in **psalms and hymns and spiritual songs, singing and making melody** to the Lord with your heart,
Acts 2:42	And they devoted themselves to the apostles' **teaching and the fellowship, to the breaking of bread and the prayers.**
Matthew 26:26-29	Now as they were eating, Jesus took bread, and after blessing it broke it and gave it to the disciples, and said, "Take, eat; this is my body." And he took a cup, and when he had given thanks he gave it to them, saying, "Drink of it, all of you, for this is my blood of the covenant, which is poured out for many for the forgiveness of sins. I

	tell you I will not drink again of this fruit of the vine until that day when I drink it new with you in my Father's kingdom." **(The Cup)**
Acts 20:7	On the first day of the week, when we were **gathered together to break bread**, Paul talked with them, intending to depart on the next day, and he prolonged his speech until midnight.

All the above are important, but which one is a natural way to connect with others? In a book titled, The Friendship Factor, McGinnis stated, "It is no accident so many important encounters occurred between Jesus and His friends when they were at the table. There is something almost sacramental about breaking bread with one another." Was it an accident that Jesus often broke bread with others? We think not. And what did he do when he broke bread. He connected with people. He shared life with them. He dealt with their concerns. He taught them lessons they needed to learn. Some listened. Others rejected what He shared. The point is, one of the key times when Jesus shared information or helped people in some way was connected to eating or the sharing of food. Why would that be so? There are several possible reasons. First, if people hunger for food and someone gives it to them, they may be willing to listen to the giver. Their need for food being satiated might cause them to desire to understand why he was doing this for them. It opened up an opportunity for Jesus to share. That applies to you also. Second, when you sit down to eat with others it is usually very easy to begin a conversation. It may simply begin with a thank you and could then lead to answering questions or sharing information. Third, it simply gives opportunity for people to gather together to fulfill a natural need and at the very same time also provides an opportunity for interaction and relational growth.

All of these lead to opportunities that can make it easier for you to speak with people about Jesus and what he means to you and what he can mean to them. As your relationship grows with those you spend relational time with, so do your opportunities to model Christ and to share more about him and what He means to you. We want to urge you to see your neighbors, friends and others as extended family members that need God in their lives. This is also true regarding new baby Christians who are still struggling with understanding what it means to be a Christian. They need your time also. You need to compassionately see all of these people as being in need of God's love and grace and provide opportunities for them to learn more about him and/or grow and mature in Him. It should be evident by now that building relationships is important as you seek to help others come into contact with God. However, we have heard many ask, 'Just how beneficial are relationships when you attempt to save the lost? Are they really that important? Surely there are other ways to help people learn about God.' Yes, there are other ways, but they are often not nearly as effective.

Years ago, a study was reported in Church Growth: American Magazine, that there was a significant importance regarding 'friendship' in helping others become disciples of Christ (Church Growth American January/February, 1981). We are sure that this is true for us today.

Seven hundred and twenty people were identified who were Christians, had been Christians or had been presented with the Gospel message. Here is the interesting data. "Each was asked to classify the person who had presented the gospel into one of three categories: "Friend," "Salesman," or "Teacher." The results were staggering.

- 84% of those who were approached by someone that came on like a teacher simply said, "No thanks!"
- 71% of those who were presented the Gospel by someone that seemed to be a Salesman dropped out of church after a short period of time after being 'converted'.
- 94% of those who were converted by a church member, who shared the message as a friend, were still active in church.

What does this mean for you, us and everyone else who is a Christian? It simply means that relationship or relational evangelism is key to effectively spreading the word about Jesus. What's the key so that we can accomplish this? "Your greatest resource in developing a meaningful and caring friendship is in simply being yourself---natural and unmasked" (Arn, 1982). Caring and spending meaningful time with the unchurched or those who are disconnected is foundational for connecting with others.

The Discipleship Family

Numerous non-Christians have turned away from God, the Bible and the assembly period due to the inconsistency and hypocrisy of many professing Christians. Many people have rejected organized religion because Christ's Spirit is not present in the churches today. The reason for the absence of Christ's Spirit is that there are few churches who are imitating the church we read about in the bible. The church urgently needs to return to the New Testament methods of teaching and training men who will build committed disciples. We need more intimate spiritual time with each other. Disciplers need to spend more time with disciples so that they can learn and apply what they are learning in their lives and ultimately teach others.

One way that this problem can be rectified is by incorporating a small group method into the local church. The early church spent much time in relational activities. Luke reports (Acts 5:34) that Christians met daily from house to house for teaching and fellowship. In our hurry-up world we have little time for quality relational activities and that is a problem.

A Discipleship Family is a group of people who regularly meet in someone's home to encourage, edify, pray and generally assist one another in becoming more like Jesus. Such an environment provides a means by which we, as Christians, can become more involved with one another and at the same time provide a method of natural outreach and in-reach to members who are not active. It was Christ's intention for us to 'make disciples' (Matthew 28:18-20) and later reinforced by His Apostles as expressed in 2 Timothy 2:2 and 1 Thessalonians 2:7-8. We might say that the primary purpose of the Discipleship Family is outreach, but that would not be true. We must not lose sight of the fact that the Biblical concept of outreach/evangelism or discipleship promotes the giving of self to produce mature, multiplying disciples. Obviously, the most intense and probably the most effective method of disciple-making is natural one-on-one relationship. It is for this reason that each Discipleship Family must provide a non-threatening atmosphere so that this type of discipling relationship may be established and hopefully maintained. It is important to have relationship time with non-Christians and with minimally active members. We can do this by spending more enjoyable time with them in-order to show them Christ in how you live day-by-day. Such a relationship can provide you with opportunities to teach non-Christians and help members who are not active.

How a Discipleship Family Can Help

Below is a list of benefits that a small group can provide in a local church. Small groups are designed for the following purposes.

1. Discipleship groups provide churches with a way to get more people involved at a deeper level of relationship.
2. Discipleship groups can provide an opportunity for supportive disciple making by group members.
3. Smaller churches with an inadequate church campus can accommodate a growing ministry of adult groups.
4. Discipleship groups can help each member utilize his gift, ability, skill, etc. in order to build up the church. In other words, each small group becomes a ministry training program. People can lead singing, lead studies, coordinate food or children's activities and more.
5. Discipleship groups can dedicate more time to teaching Biblical facts, Biblical principles and application without being held to a schedule. Each group can go at its own pace depending on the needs of its members.
6. Discipleship groups can accommodate young children and provide additional training or supervision for them. This actually becomes a ministry opportunity.
7. At the same time Discipleship groups can be dedicated to different family situations. Most people need opportunities to spend time with age-appropriate peers. However, that doesn't mean that a group couldn't be a multiage group. Some people prefer such a group.
8. Discipleship groups can and should provide 'kid friendly' options when you have young families. This too can provide opportunities for ministry development. Those who have the gift of teaching or who enjoy teaching or working with younger children could apply their gift in their specific group. One person should not always be the children's minister for the group. It should be shared so that everyone can benefit from the group interaction, learning and relationship building.

Quality spiritual and social time is essential for the unity and growth of Christ's church. This has not, nor will be accomplished through large gatherings, i.e., large assemblies. We recommend that Christian families meet in one another's home for in-reach and out-reach purposes. These meetings could be a weekly event where quality relationships also develop. Obviously, such a meeting should be well balanced to meet the needs of all concerned. Each family group may have specific needs and should be unique. However, certain important teaching should occur in all groups. We urge you to consider this Biblical tried and true method. For specific information as to how you could implement this method into your situation, you should obtain a copy of the Discipleship Family Manual (Crites, 2019). The Discipleship Family can be an option for the local church as an outreach and an in-reach method. It can also provide opportunities for personal ministry for serving each other and for ongoing fellowship.

You would have many options for curriculum in your group. However, this work could be the foundation of what you teach. There are several specific resources that can help you with developing a Discipleship Family. First, you could use the Grace and Salvation book (Crites, 2022) to teach both deeper principles of grace and to help people better understand the salvation process based on biblical teachings. Second, you could use this work, Journey Into Discipleship. It would be a great resource for curriculum. There is also a Journey Into Discipleship Workbook (Crites, 2024) which has many of the teachings from the manual within. Third, another great resource that can be used to teach biblical doctrine is the Comparative Doctrine book. It looks at over fifty doctrinal teachings and shows scriptures for each. It also identifies false teaching that is clearly seen in the world today. Fourth, you could do a study on Spiritual Gifts and Ministry (Crites, 2019). It would help everyone understand what gift of Charismata (Romans 12) they received from God and how they could use it to benefit their brothers and sisters and the Kingdom of God. There are many other works available that would be beneficial depending on need and the specific need of the group should determine what is being taught. If someone is struggling with faith, do a study on faith. If someone is struggling with prayer, do a study on it. The point is that each group may have specific individual needs and should address those needs in a way that benefits all those in the group. The works described above are available online and at bookstores.

Integration of New Members

Let's define integrate so that we can all be on the same page. What does integrate mean? For our purposes it means to help an individual find a meaningful place within the local body and/or their small group in order for them experience a connectedness. Such integration of new members is vital for the individual and for the body of Christ.

With this in mind, how can you help an individual become more integrated? Do you remember us writing about how we all have spiritual gifts? God expects each person to use his or her gift to support the local congregation or body of Christ. It is only a brief step away from saying that if you have small groups, it would be important for that new convert to learn how to utilize their gift in a smaller setting. It would give him or her more opportunities to practice using the Gift that God gave them. Many people are hesitant to take action when they become a member for a multitude of reasons. The real point is that it is not just their job to take action and figure out what their gift or ministry is and then find the person who might be able to help him use it. The responsibility is the disciplers or the church leadership. Leadership should be intentional about finding ways to help each new member or convert become involved or integrated into the body which includes both the local church and the small group. What is their gift? How can that gift be used in the local body or in a small group? If they are not ready to help with ministry or utilize their gift in the local body, then we should encourage them to learn how to use it in the small group. The small group becomes a practice ground for those who need a boost before they take on more responsibility.

Win Arn suggested that you consider five things as you seek to integrate or incorporate new Christians into ministry. The following is an adaptation of what you can find in his book (Arn, 1982).

- Integration for relational purposes into the small group or church should begin before the person becomes a Christian. Relationships could be formed with the possible convert by those who are seeking to teach. The soon to be Christian does not just form a relationship with his or her Discipler, but also others that are involved.
- This integration of the possible new Christian into the small group or local body needs to be a high priority. This should take on the form of relationship building that is centered around Christ. Ultimately, the hope is that the connection and understanding of what it would mean to become a Christian causes the person to convert.
- Integration or incorporation into roles or ministry does not happen automatically. Keep in mind that a new baby, even spiritual ones, do not know what they need. Would you

trust a baby with what they chose to eat? Would you trust a baby to know what was best for him? Obviously the answer is, 'No'. New baby Christians need to be taught, trained and guided into truth and ministry.

- Integration must be orchestrated by church leadership or the small group leader. A baby Christian may not even know what to do or who to ask. Make it easy for him. Guide him through the process of becoming integrated.
- A person, or hopefully the discipler who converted the new Christian, should be an active player in helping the person learn his place in the body.

If the above is not happening, the new convert could easily lose his way and stop participating in congregational activities and/or the small group. The local church and the small group must go out of their way to integrate the person both before and after they become a Christian.

Keeping the Converted....Converted

One of the most important, yet least followed ingredients in the great commission and the discipleship component of Christianity (Matthew 2:18-20) is the concept of teaching new believers to observe the commandments or will of Jesus. This ingredient is one of the most vital elements in the continuation of the individual Christian and his eventual multiplication. When parents are blessed with a new child, certain responsibilities also become theirs. They must train their child to:

- Develop healthy values.
- Develop good habits.
- Base decisions on sound values.
- Develop good self-discipline.
- Seek to internalize, think, speak and act in a morally/spiritually sound way.
- Build healthy relationships (a good village).

All of these elements are taught to ensure a child's life has meaning and value, and far fewer problems. It teaches him to become responsible as he lives according to the values and beliefs taught. However, if the parent does not choose to train his child in a way that is good and spiritual, the child will choose his own direction which is often self-centered, destructive and ultimately self-defeating.

With this in mind, we should be training new converts in the same way. Baby Christians must be taught proper spiritual truths and be given opportunity to learn, grow and spiritually mature. They should learn where their place is in the body and how they can use their God Given gift for the benefit of that body. They should be encouraged to fellowship with believers and build strong relationships. They must be gradually taught the deeper principles of doctrine or Christianity so that they can mature. If those things and more do not happen, they may very well abandon the faith or find a religion that meets their personal wants, needs and desires out of ignorance and because of a lack of personal relationship with a discipler and or a group.

Become a Discipler

The Discipleship methods shown in this chapter are just a few good ways to help make a local body more discipleship oriented. The problem you face is, do you have a way that you can be more Discipleship oriented? Does your local congregation have any discipleship training or methods that they are using? If not, maybe you could offer some options. Regardless, if you want to be a disciple just remember that Discipleship begins with planting the seed. Everyone can easily do that. Simply mention Jesus and that he is important to you. Give a person a card that has a Bible verse on it. Send a card with a religious statement on it when someone you know is sick or when he has something great happen in his life. There are so many possibilities. Use one or more that work for you. Second, you may be the one to water the seed. You may have opportunity to share a Bible concept with someone. You may answer a question that leads them to think more about how Jesus might be the answer in their life. You may help them grow because of a conversation or because of your personal connection with them. If so, that's wonderful. You just watered the seed. Next, you could be the one who actually converts them. Helping a person become a saved individual is a wonderful experience for everyone involved. Usually, when that occurs there is a connection between the two people. That is the opportunity to go to the next step. Last, if you were the lucky one that converted them, you can then Disciple them. They trust you now. Spend time with that person. Teach him. Help him grow spiritually. Help him when he struggles spiritually. Just make sure that he is involved in the church, in a Bible class, in a group. You can be his Discipler. In review there are four distinct and important aspects of helping someone become and grow as a Christian. All four are extremely important, but you may not be the one that does all four for a specific person. However, you should be doing one of these often. They are:

1. Be a seed planter. Mention or tell someone about Jesus.
2. Water the seed. If someone has already heard about Jesus, simply ask if they would like to learn more. Hand them some literature. Give them a Bible if they don't have one. Tell the person you would be willing to try to answer any questions that they may have.
3. Convert the person. Explain the salvation plan in more detail (See the Grace and Salvation (Crites) book for how to do this if needed).
4. Disciple the person. Once they are converted don't stop spending time with them. Continue to teach and grow with them. You could use this book to teach them more about what it means to be a Christian and what it takes to grow spiritually. Help them stay connected to a local congregation, a small group and you can also continue to help the person grow. That's what a disciple would do. You teach others, who in turn will learn how to teach others.

Response Ministry

Having a Discipleship Family or small group that actually reaches out to the lost and non-active members is a powerful way to produce numerical and spiritual growth. The intent was for people to grow together, bring new people into the group, teach them, train them in ministry and then ultimately grow another group, one person at a time as new people were added to the body. The people in each of those groups spent time with each other, prayed for each other, learned with each other and brought new people into their core group. Several of those new people were unchurched. Others were people at the local congregation that were not yet truly connected. As a result, groups grew and split and more people were being discipled one on one or in a small group where they could grow and learn how to utilize their God given gifts in ministry.

Another ministry that can help fuel the Discipleship ministry is called a Response Ministry. When people are baptized or if they placed membership they could be connected with an individual, a family and/or a Discipleship Family group that they could be part of. Preferably they should be placed in a Discipleship Family that has someone they already know and are connected with in it. Everything that could be done to integrate the new member or new convert into the body would be considered. The goal was to get them involved in ministry or with Discipleship Family groups so that they would have a close relationship with several people. As a result, almost all new members could become involved in some way and would grow spiritually. Discipleship Family members should consistently be sending out cards, emails, or make personal calls to invite non-active members to various activities. It would keep everyone involved and some of those who were not involved might gradually start spending time with individuals or families and ultimately became part of one of the groups. Involvement in the body and spiritual growth is the goal for each person.

Regardless of how you seek to integrate new members or Christians it must begin with an attempt at relationship building. The church must also find a way to more consistently teach and help new Christians grow. Not to be redundant but building strong relationships with other more mature Christians is one of the most important elements of helping new Christians grow spiritually. Some methods to accomplish this have been included in this work. However, it behooves all of us to look at the method that the early church used to disciple each other. It was and still is effective. That seems to be God's plan. In following this plan, you fulfill Jesus' greatest command. Go Make Disciples! So Ends Your **Journey Into Discipleship.** Or is it just the beginning?

Personal Reflection

List three things that you learned or that were reinforced that helped you understand how you could apply discipleship in your life or in your congregation.

1.

2.

3.

Appendices

Determining God's Will

Worksheet

Instructions:

1. Write down your question in the space below.
2. Ask yourself the following questions as they pertain to the situation or decision you are trying to make.

Question or decision:

Scriptures	Questions	Response
""All things are lawful for me," but not all things are helpful. 1 Corinthians 6:12a	Will it help you socially, mentally, spiritually or physically.	___Yes ___No
"All things are lawful for me," but I will not be dominated by anything." 1 Corinthians 6:12b	Will this bring me under its power in some way?	___Yes ___No
Therefore, if what I eat causes my brother to fall into sin, I will never eat meat again, so that will not cause him to fall. 1 Corinthians 8:13	Will this hurt others?	___Yes ___No
God created men for His Glory. Isaiah 43:7 1 Corinthians 8:13	Will this Glorify GOD? Could I do this in a way that would bring more glory to GOD? Could I do something different that would Glorify GOD more?	___Yes ___No ___Yes ___No ___Yes ___No

Optional Solution:

Personal Sin and Scripture

Worksheet

Key Scripture: 1 John 1:9

"If we confess our sins, he is faithful and just to forgive us our sins and to cleanse us from all unrighteousness."

Instructions:

1. Identify the sin and place it in the left-hand column.
2. Identify a Scripture you will memorize and place it in the righthand column.
3. Every time you start to struggle or fail to deal with sin, repeat the Scripture to yourself at least five times.
4. If you need help, seek out your brothers and sisters and confess your sins so that they can help you.

Your Identified Sin	Scripture that Counters It

Journey Into Discipleship Revised (Crites and Hill, 2023)

Conversion Examples

These scriptures show you how others have responded to the Gospel.

Scripture	Who	Hear	Faith/Belief	Repentance	Confession	Baptism
Acts 2:37-41	Jews	vs 37		vs 38		vs 38
Acts 8:12	Samaritans		vs 12			vs 12
Acts 8:13	Simon		vs 13			vs 13
Acts 8:26-40	Ethiopian Eunuch	vs 35	vs 37		vs 37	vs 38
Acts 10:34-48	Cornelius	vs 34-44	vs 43			vs 47-48
Acts 16:14-15	Lydia	vs 14				vs 15
Acts 16:25-34	Jailor	vs 30-32				vs 33
Acts 18:8	Corinthians	vs 8	vs 8			vs 8
Acts 19:1-7	Ephesians	vs 5				vs 5
Acts 22:1-16	Paul (Saul)	vs 15				vs 16

STS: The Scriptures shown above may be underlined in Yellow since they address Salvation.

Journey Into Discipleship Character Checklist for New Testament Disciples					
Name: Date:					
Instructions: Rate yourself to see where you may need to grow. 1 = This characteristic is developed as God would have me develop it. 2 = I've almost got this one developed as it should be. 3 = Kind of average. 4 = I'm doing a poor job with this one. 5 = Help! I really need to work on this one.					
Characteristics of a Mature Disciple	**1**	**2**	**3**	**4**	**5**
Have died to self (Galatians 2:20)					
Above reproach					
Hospitable					
Lover of good					
Upright					
Holy					
Disciplined or self-controlled					
Holds firm to the trustworthy word as taught					
Able to teach/give instruction in sound doctrine					
Able to rebuke those who contradict it					
Soberminded					
Respectful					
Gentle					
Manages household well					
Keep children submissive with dignity					
Well thought of by outsiders					
Steadfast					
Loving					
Joyful					
Peaceful					
Patient					
Kind					
Faithful					
Knows and uses God Given Gift					
Daily examine self to improve on the above					
Journey Into Discipleship Revised (Crites and Hill, 2023) *Permission for copying this form is granted for personal use only!*					

Journey Into Discipleship Characteristics not Acceptable for New Testament Disciples		
Name:		Date:
Instructions: Simply put a checkmark next to any characteristic you believe you need to remove.		
Unacceptable Carnal Characteristics	**Which of the below to the left needs to be worked on?**	**Spiritual Opposites**
Pride or Arrogance		Humility
Quick-tempered		Calm
A drunkard		Sober
Violent		Peaceful
Greedy for gain		Generous
Quarrelsome		Amiable
A lover of money		Giving
Domineering over those in your charge		Assertive
Sexual immorality		Morality
Impurity		Purity
Sensuality		Temperance
Idolatry		God
Enmity		Good Will
Strife		Harmony
Jealousy		Admire
Rivalries		Cooperation
Lying		Truthful
Dissensions		Harmonious
Divisions		Unity
Other:		
Other:		
Journey Into Discipleship Revised (Crites and Hill, 2023) *Permission for copying this form is granted for personal use only!*		

Book Series on Christianity

Ultimately there will be several books in this series and supportive works that can help with other issues Christians may face. The first five works take you on a journey towards a deeper understanding of Christianity and your place in the Christian world and ultimately how you can become a more effective disciple. Due to increased requests for how to deal with spiritual warfare a sixth book has been added and should be available soon. The following books are presented in order in which they probably should be read and studied.

Grace and Salvation: This is the first work in the series. It was intended to primarily be read by those who are searching and want to know more about Grace and salvation. It can also be very helpful for any Christian who wants to have a deeper grasp on what Grace really means and the importance of how someone can become a Christian. Learn about all the aspects of grace, and what the Bible says about salvation.

Journey Into Discipleship-Revised: The Journey into Discipleship book covers many aspects of the God-Man Relationship. It is a wonderful reference guide for teaching new converts or those who simply want to know more about God and His plan for us. Some of the areas covered are: Knowing About God, Knowing God, The Holy Spirit, New Life and Sin, Sins Against the Spirit, Brokenness and the Foundation of Spiritual Maturity, Prayer, Knowing God's Word, Outreach and Fellowship and how Discipleship is essential for both the individual and for overall church growth. This is a major rewrite of the original document. It has been significantly updated with new helpful information. This is now available through Amazon or can be ordered through your local bookstore.

Comparative Doctrine: This work will help you learn how to identify Scriptures that address over fifty doctrinal issues. It also shows how several religions have ignored the Bible or have attempted to alter what it says. To help people, or yourself, you must understand what the Bible teaches. This work will help you see specifically what the Bible says about important doctrines. God wants you to internalize His word. Studying it and developing a better understanding of what the Bible teaches will help you grow spiritually and is necessary in helping you identify Biblical doctrine.

It also helps you when you are faced with sharing your Biblical beliefs with someone who wants to know more about the Bible and the Life of Jesus. This is now available through Amazon or can be ordered through your local bookstore.

Spiritual Gifts and Ministry - Leader and Participant Workbooks: These works review the three types of spiritual gifts mentioned in the Bible. Each type has a purpose for the church and each type is distinctively different from the other. There is one specific type of gifts that call for the Christian to use to uplift the body. This work describes what those gifts look like and how they are applied in the body. A test is provided to help all understand what gift or gifts God has given to each of us so that we can fulfill God's will for our lives. This is now available through Amazon or can be ordered through your local bookstore.

Discipleship Family Leader's Manual: This manual helps individuals or churches develop a consistent method for having optional groups for Sunday evenings or weekdays. It has procedures, forms, suggestions for structure of meetings and more. This is now available through Amazon or can be ordered through your local bookstore.

Prayer Journal: Keep track of prayers, who they are for, when God answers them. This is now available through Amazon or can be ordered through your local bookstore.

Sharpening the Sword on Mormonism: Mormon Documents, the Bible and the Truth. This manual is an advanced Sharpening the Sword work that describes the works of Mormonism, how they contradict themselves, how they have changed (additions and deletions in the text), and how their teachings conflict with the Bible. An overall method for working with those believe in Mormonism is included. This is now available through Amazon or can be ordered through your local bookstore.

For more information about the Biblical works please go to www.cpcchristianministry.com.

For other Professional Works by this author please go to Amazon.com/author/russcrites

Suggested Readings and Resources

Arn, W. The Masters Plan for Making Disciples. Pasadena, CA: Church Growth Press, 1982.

Augustine, A. The Works of Aurelioius Augustine, Vol. 15, Anti-Perlagian Works (ed. M. Dods; T and T Clark, 1876)

Barnes, A. Barnes' Notes on the Bible. Omaha, NE; Patristic Publishing 2018 (Reprint from public domain).

Boles, H. Leo The Holy Spirit. Gospel Advocate, 1999.

Bonhoeffer, D. & Metaxas, E. The Cost of Discipleship. New York, NY: Touchstone; 1st edition, 1995.

Coleman, R. The Master Plan of Discipleship, Revel, 2020.

Cottrell, J. The Holy Spirit: A Biblical Study. Joplin, Missouri; College Press, 2006

Cottrell, J. Spirits Holy and Unholy. Mason, OH: The Christian Restoration Association, 2019.

Crites, Jr. F. R; Crites, D. Comparative Doctrine. Dallas, TX: CPC, 2021.

Crites, Jr. F. R. Foundations Workbook. Dallas, TX: CPC, 2016.

Crites, Jr. F. R. Spiritual Gifts and Ministry. Dallas, TX: CPC, 2020.

Crites, Jr. F. R. Guilt and Grace Workbook. Self Published in 1983.

Crites, Jr. F. R. Grace and Salvation: Understanding the Deeper Meaning of Grace. Dallas, TX; CPC, 2022.

Crites, Jr. F. R. Journey Into Discipleship Workbook. Dallas, TX: CPC, 1988.

Crites, Jr. F. R. Prayer Journal: Keeping Track of Answers to Prayer. Dallas, TX: CPC, 2018.

Crites, Jr. F. R. Spiritual Temptation and Testing: Spiritual Growth or Spiritual Death (manuscript).

Davis, J. J. The Perseverance of the Saints: A History of the Doctrine. Journal of the Evangelical Theological Society [JETS] 34/2 (June 1991) p. 213-228

Herrick, G. Understanding The Meaning of the Term "Disciple" bible.org.

Lemmons, A. Dynamic Faith. Franklin Springs, GA: Advocate Press, 1981.

Lewis, C.S. The Screwtape Letters. San Francisco, California: Harper One; Reprint edition, 2015.

McGinnis, A. L. The Friendship Factor. Minneapolis, MN: Augsburg Publishing House, 1979.

Morris III, H. Six Days of Creation. Dallas, TX: Institute for Creation Research, 2013.

Mounce, R. (2006), Mounce's Complete Expository Dictionary of Old and New Testament Words. Grand Rapids, MI: Zondervan, 2006.

Murray, Andrew In his book, With Christ in the School of Prayer, Merchant Books, 2013.

Rogers, R. The Holy Spirit of God. Lubbock, TX: Sunset Institute Press, 2007.

Ortiz, J. Call to Discipleship. Buckingham, 1975.

Pickering, Dr. F. Alan Sharpening the Sword: Probing the Depths of Christianity Through Systematic Theology. Dallas, TX: Ultimate Life, 2021.

Sanders, P. Evangelism Handbook. Montgomery, Alabama: Kachelman Publications, 2017.

Shank, R. Life in the Son. Pismo Beach, CA: Westcott Publishers; Third Printing Edition, 1962.

Torrey, R. A. How to Study the Bible for the Greatest Profit. Fleming H. Revell Company, 1896 (Available on line).

Unger, M. Biblical Demonology. 1952

Vine, W. Vine's Complete Expository Dictionary of Old and New Testament Words. Atlanta, GE: Thomas Nelson Publishers, 1983.

Warden, D. Truth for Today Commentary of 2 Corinthians. Benton, AR: Resource Publications, 2019.

Wilson, C. With Christ in the School of Disciple Building. Nav. Press: 2009.

Yeakley, F. R. Research for the Growing Church, Church Growth: America, January/February, 1981 p. 10.

Research and On-line Resources:

All of the research below supports what God has asked us to become and do in order to maintain a healthy spiritual, physical and psychological well-being.

Aman MM, Jason Yong R, Kaye AD, Urman RD. Evidence-Based Non-Pharmacological Therapies for Fibromyalgia. Curr Pain Headache Rep. 2018 Apr 4;22(5):33. doi: 10.1007/s11916-018-0688-2. PMID: 29619620.

Alberts H, Thewissen R. The effect of a brief mindfulness intervention on memory for positively and negatively valenced stimuli. Mindfulness in press. [PubMed]

Baer RA, Smith GT, Hopkins J, Krietemeyer J, Toney L. Using self-report assessment methods to explore facets of mindfulness. Assessment. 2006;13:27–45.

Basso JC, McHale A, Ende V, Oberlin DJ, Suzuki WA. Brief, daily meditation enhances attention, memory, mood, and emotional regulation in non-experienced meditators. Behav Brain Res. 2019 Jan 1;356:208-220. doi: 10.1016/j.bbr.2018.08.023. Epub 2018 Aug 25. PMID: 30153464.

Biblehub.com

Bränström R, Kvillemo P, Brandberg Y, Moskowitz JT. Self-report mindfulness as a mediator of psychological well-being in a stress reduction intervention for cancer patients: A randomized study. Annals of Behavioral Medicine. 2010;39:151–161.

Bränström R, Kvillemo P, Brandberg Y, Moskowitz JT. Self-report mindfulness as a mediator of psychological well-being in a stress reduction intervention for cancer patients: A randomized study. Annals of Behavioral Medicine. 2010;39:151–161.

Carmody J, Reed G, Kristeller J, Merriam P. Mindfulness, spirituality, and health-related symptoms. Journal of Psychosomatic Research. 2008;64:393–403.

Baer RA, Smith GT, Hopkins J, Krietemeyer J, Toney L. Using self-report assessment methods to explore facets of mindfulness. Assessment. 2006;13:27–45.

Brown KW, Ryan RM. The benefits of being present: Mindfulness and its role in psychological well-being. Journal of Personality and Social Psychology. 2003;84:822–848.

Brown KW, Ryan RM. The benefits of being present: Mindfulness and its role in psychological well-being. Journal of Personality and Social Psychology. 2003;84:822–848.

Carmody J, Baer RA. Relationship between mindfulness practice and levels of mindfulness, medical and psychological symptoms and well-being in a mindfulness-based stress reduction program. Journal of Behavioral Medicine. 2008;31:23–33.

Katherine K. Clifton MD, Cynthia X. Ma MD, PhD, Luigi Fontana MD, PhD, FRACP, Lindsay L. Peterson MD, MSCR Intermittent fasting in the prevention and treatment of cancer. A Cancer Journal for Clinicians, Volume71, Issue 6 November/December 2021 Pages 527-546

Dote-Montero M, Sanchez-Delgado G, Ravussin E. Effects of Intermittent Fasting on Cardiometabolic Health: An Energy Metabolism Perspective. Nutrients. 2022 Jan 23;14(3):489. doi: 10.3390/nu14030489. PMID: 35276847; PMCID: PMC8839160.

Fincham FD, May R. J. Divine Forgiveness and Well-being Among Emerging Adults in the USA Relig Health. 2022 Oct 1. doi: 10.1007/s10943-022-01678-3. Online ahead of print. PMID: 36183033

Gard T, Hölzel BK, Lazar SW. The potential effects of meditation on age-related cognitive decline: a systematic review. Ann N Y Acad Sci. 2014 Jan;1307:89-103. doi: 10.1111/nyas.12348. PMID: 24571182; PMCID: PMC4024457.

Goyal M, Singh S, Sibinga EM, Gould NF, Rowland-Seymour A, Sharma R, Berger Z, Sleicher D, Maron DD, Shihab HM, Ranasinghe PD, Linn S, Saha S, Bass EB, Haythornthwaite JA. Meditation programs for psychological stress and well-being: a systematic review and meta-analysis. JAMA Intern Med. 2014 Mar;174(3):357-68. doi: 10.1001/jamainternmed.2013.13018. PMID: 24395196; PMCID: PMC4142584.

Greeson J, Webber D, Brantley J, Smoski M, Ekblad A, Suarez E, Wolever R. Changes in spirituality partly explain health-related quality of life outcomes after Mindfulness-Based Stress Reduction. Journal of Behavioral Medicine in press.

Hoge EA, Chen MM, Orr E, Metcalf CA, Fischer LE, Pollack MH, De Vivo I, Simon NM. Loving-Kindness Meditation practice associated with longer telomeres in women. Brain Behav Immun. 2013 Aug;32:159-63. doi: 10.1016/j.bbi.2013.04.005. Epub 2013 Apr 19. PMID: 23602876.

Hilton L, Maher AR, Colaiaco B, Apaydin E, Sorbero ME, Booth M, Shanman RM, Hempel S. Meditation for posttraumatic stress: Systematic review and meta-analysis. Psychol Trauma. 2017 Jul;9(4):453-460. doi: 10.1037/tra0000180. Epub 2016 Aug 18. PMID: 27537781.

Hoge EA, Bui E, Marques L, Metcalf CA, Morris LK, Robinaugh DJ, Worthington JJ, Pollack MH, Simon NM. Randomized controlled trial of mindfulness meditation for generalized anxiety disorder: effects on anxiety and stress reactivity. J Clin Psychiatry. 2013 Aug;74(8):786-92. doi: 10.4088/JCP.12m08083. PMID: 23541163; PMCID: PMC3772979.

Kasala ER, Bodduluru LN, Maneti Y, Thipparaboina R. Effect of meditation on neurophysiological changes in stress mediated depression. Complement Ther Clin Pract. 2014 Feb;20(1):74-80.

doi: 10.1016/j.ctcp.2013.10.001. Epub 2013 Oct 18. PMID: 24439650.

Keng SL, Smoski MJ, Robins CJ. Effects of mindfulness on psychological health: a review of empirical studies. Clin Psychol Rev. 2011 Aug;31(6):1041-56. doi: 10.1016/j.cpr.2011.04.006. Epub 2011 May 13. PMID: 21802619; PMCID: PMC3679190.

Keng SL, Smoski MJ, Robins CJ, Ekblad A, Brantley J. Mechanisms of change in MBSR: Self compassion and mindful attention as mediators of intervention outcome; Poster presented at the annual meeting of the Association for Behavioral and Cognitive Therapies; San Francisco, CA. Nov 19, 2010.

Kiken LG, Shook NJ. Does mindfulness attenuate thoughts emphasizing negativity, but not positivity? J Res Pers. 2014 Dec 1;53:22-30. doi: 10.1016/j.jrp.2014.08.002. PMID: 25284906; PMCID: PMC4178287.

Long KNG, Chen Y, Potts M, Hanson J, VanderWeele TJ. Spiritually Motivated Self-Forgiveness and Divine Forgiveness, and Subsequent Health and Well-Being Among Middle-Aged Female Nurses: An Outcome-Wide Longitudinal Approach. Front Psychol. 2020 Jul 9;11:1337. doi: 10.3389/fpsyg.2020.01337. PMID: 32733311; PMCID: PMC7363844.

Longo VD, Di Tano M, Mattson MP, Guidi N. Intermittent and periodic fasting, longevity and disease. Nat Aging. 2021 Jan;1(1):47-59. doi: 10.1038/s43587-020-00013-3. Epub 2021 Jan 14. PMID: 35310455; PMCID: PMC8932957.

Melissa A. Rosenkranz, Richard J. Davidson, Donal G. MacCoon, John F. Sheridan, Ned H. Kalin, Antoine Lutz, A comparison of mindfulness-based stress reduction and an active control in modulation of neurogenic inflammation, Brain, Behavior, and Immunity, Volume 27,2013, Pages 174-184,

Norris CJ, Creem D, Hendler R, Kober H. Brief Mindfulness Meditation Improves Attention in Novices: Evidence From ERPs and Moderation by Neuroticism. Front Hum Neurosci. 2018 Aug 6;12:315. doi: 10.3389/fnhum.2018.00315. Erratum in: Front Hum Neurosci. 2018 Sep 05;12:342. PMID: 30127731; PMCID: PMC6088366.

Orme-Johnson DW, Barnes VA. Effects of the transcendental meditation technique on trait anxiety: a meta-analysis of randomized controlled trials. J Altern Complement Med. 2014 May;20(5):330-41. doi: 10.1089/acm.2013.0204. Epub 2013 Oct 9. PMID: 24107199.

Moro T, Tinsley G, Pacelli FQ, Marcolin G, Bianco A, Paoli A. Twelve Months of Time-restricted Eating and Resistance Training Improves Inflammatory Markers and Cardiometabolic Risk Factors. Med Sci Sports Exerc. 2021 Dec 1;53(12):2577-2585. doi: 10.1249/MSS.0000000000002738. PMID: 34649266; PMCID: PMC10115489.

Nasaruddin ML, Syed Abd Halim SA, Kamaruzzaman MA. Studying the Relationship of Intermittent Fasting and β-Amyloid in Animal Model of Alzheimer's Disease: A Scoping Review. Nutrients. 2020 Oct 21;12(10):3215. doi: 10.3390/nu12103215. PMID: 33096730; PMCID: PMC7590153.

Ojha U, Khanal S, Park PH, Hong JT, Choi DY. Intermittent fasting protects the nigral dopaminergic neurons from MPTP-mediated dopaminergic neuronal injury in mice. J Nutr Biochem. 2023 Feb;112:109212. doi: 10.1016/j.jnutbio.2022.109212. Epub 2022 Nov 10. PMID: 36370926.

Park J, Seo YG, Paek YJ, Song HJ, Park KH, Noh HM. Effect of alternate-day fasting on obesity and cardiometabolic risk: A systematic review and meta-analysis. Metabolism. 2020 Oct;111:154336. doi: 10.1016/j.metabol.2020.154336. Epub 2020 Aug 7. PMID: 32777443.

Raes F, Dewulf D, Van Heeringen C, Williams JMG. Mindfulness and reduced cognitive reactivity to sad mood: Evidence from a correlational study and a non-randomized waiting list controlled study. Behaviour Research and Therapy. 2009;47:623–627.

Robins CJ, Keng SL, Ekblad AG, Brantley JG. Effects of mindfulness-based stress reduction on emotional experience and expression: A randomized controlled trial. Manuscript submitted for publication 2010

Shahar B, Britton WB, Sbarra DA, Figueredo AJ, Bootzin RR. Mechanisms of change of mindfulness-based cognitive therapy for depression: Preliminary evidence from a randomized controlled trial. International Journal of Cognitive Therapy. 2010;3:402–418.

Shapiro SL, Oman D, Thoresen CE, Plante TG, Flinders T. Cultivating mindfulness: Effects on well-being. Journal of Clinical Psychology. 2008;64:840–862.

Shapiro SL, Oman D, Thoresen CE, Plante TG, Flinders T. Cultivating mindfulness: Effects on well-being. Journal of Clinical Psychology.

Shannon M. Cearley, Supriya Immaneni, Padmini Shankar, Irritable Bowel Syndrome: The effect of FODMAPs and meditation on pain management, European Journal of Integrative Medicine, Volume 12, 2017, Pages 117-121,

Simplybible.com

Study on Optimism and Living Longer https://www.science.org › content › article › cheer-optimism.

Upenieks L. Through Him and With Him? A Longitudinal Study of How God-Mediated Control Beliefs Shape the Relationship between Divine Forgiveness and Physical Health in Later Life. J Aging Health. 2021 Aug-Sep;33(7-8):504-517. doi: 10.1177/0898264321996567. Epub 2021 Mar 31. PMID: 33787383.

Toussaint L, Shields GS, Dorn G, Slavich GM. Effects of lifetime stress exposure on mental and physical health in young adulthood: How stress degrades and forgiveness protects health. J Health Psychol. 2016 Jun;21(6):1004-14. doi: 10.1177/1359105314544132. Epub 2014 Aug 19. PMID: 25139892; PMCID: PMC4363296.

Toussaint LL, Shields GS, Slavich GM. Forgiveness, Stress, and Health: a 5-Week Dynamic Parallel Process Study. Ann Behav Med. 2016 Oct;50(5):727-735. doi: 10.1007/s12160-016-9796-6. PMID: 27068160; PMCID: PMC5055412.

Welton S, Minty R, O'Driscoll T, Willms H, Poirier D, Madden S, Kelly L. Intermittent fasting and weight loss: Systematic review. Can Fam Physician. 2020 Feb;66(2):117-125. PMID: 32060194; PMCID: PMC7021351

www.ingramcontent.com/pod-product-compliance
Lightning Source LLC
Chambersburg PA
CBHW071403090426
42737CB00011B/1328
* 9 7 9 8 9 8 6 9 3 7 7 3 1 *